ALABAMA

THE MAKING OF AN AMERICAN STATE

ALABAMA

THE MAKING OF AN AMERICAN STATE

EDWIN C. BRIDGES

THE UNIVERSITY OF ALABAMA PRESS
TUSCALOOSA

PUBLISHED IN COOPERATION WITH THE
ALABAMA BICENTENNIAL COMMISSION

The University of Alabama Press
Tuscaloosa, Alabama 35487-0380
uapress.ua.edu

Typeface: Arno Pro and Myriad Pro

Manufactured in China

Cover images: *(top)* Alabama State Capitol, built 1851, Montgomery; *(bottom)* ruins of
the Bradford Cotton Factory, built c. 1840s, Coosa County. Photographs by Robin McDonald.
Cover and interior design: Robin McDonald

Library of Congress Cataloging-in-Publication Data

Names: Bridges, Edwin C., author.
Title: Alabama : the making of an American state / Edwin C. Bridges.
Description: Tuscaloosa, Alabama : The University of Alabama Press, [2016] | Includes bibliographical
references and index.
Identifiers: LCCN 2016014717| ISBN 9780817319427 (cloth : alk. paper) | ISBN 9780817358761
(pbk. : alk. paper) | ISBN 9780817390846 (e-book)
Subjects: LCSH: Alabama—History.
Classification: LCC F326 .B85 2016 | DDC 976.1—dc23
LC record available at http://lccn.loc.gov/2016014717

Published in cooperation with the Alabama Bicentennial Commission

FOR MARTHA

CONTENTS

ACKNOWLEDGMENTS

T HE PEOPLE WHO PRESERVE, STUDY, and write Alabama history are members of a remarkable and wonderful community. Perhaps there is something self-selecting about a group such as this because people who invest a great deal of time studying the history of a place are bound to care about it and its people. But I think there is even more to be said for our community in Alabama. We work together. We learn from and help each other. And we enjoy each other's company. I feel very lucky that my professional career situated me among such great people.

I want to begin these acknowledgements by thanking these Alabama history colleagues. But I also need to acknowledge to readers that this book is in many ways a community product. It was built from books and articles my colleagues have written, presentations they have made, and personal conversations, some of which have continued for decades. I am deeply grateful for all they have taught me over the years and for their friendships.

Staff of the Alabama Department of Archives and History in the archives room at the State Capitol in Montgomery, Alabama, photographed in 1915: Dr. Thomas M. Owen, director (1); H. S. Halbert, honorary curator (2); J. W. Dubose, historian (3) Gertrude Ryan, librarian (4); Peter A. Brannon, chief clerk (5); Henry Knight, clerk (6); Blendine Higgins Crowell, stenographer (7); Carrol Smith, clerk (8); Josie Shackleford, stenographer (9). The Alabama Department of Archives and History was located in the Capitol until the World War Memorial Building was built in 1940. Before the construction of the Capitol's south wing, the Archives used the House and Senate chambers when the legislature was not in session.

I wish I could thank and acknowledge each colleague at every single point in the text where his or her insights have contributed to what I have written. My purpose in this book, however, has been to write about Alabama history in a way that a nonprofessional would find interesting and readable. To me, that means that the text should not be burdened with the footnotes that would be necessary for full and fair recognition. I hope all of you in the community of Alabama historians who see your work represented here will forgive my omissions of specific credit and will accept instead these general thanks.

There is another group of friends I would like to thank as well—members of the Board of Trustees of the Alabama Department of Archives and History. I started my career in another state where the

archival agency was under the administration of an elected state official. In my work there, the main priority of the people in charge of our agency was virtually always how to get our political leader either re-elected or elected to some higher office.

I came to Alabama in 1982 in part because the Alabama Department of Archives and History is governed by a Board of Trustees. It was one of the best decisions of my life. For my entire career at the Alabama Archives, the basic criterion for every single decision we made was: what is the best course to follow for preserving Alabama's historic records and artifacts and for promoting the understanding of Alabama history? The trustees were my bosses, but we were also colleagues committed to a common cause, and we became friends. I want to express my deepest gratitude to all of them. Also, their kindness in naming me director emeritus after my retirement made it much easier for me to work on this book.

I would also like to thank all the friends who helped review earlier drafts of this book. Leah Atkins has a special place in Alabama history, both as a historian and as an unwavering, energetic friend to us all. She nudged and occasionally pushed me to write this book, and she read large parts of it to help make sure I was on track. Mills Thornton has been a friend since my first months at the Archives, and a teacher. Readers will notice how heavily I have relied on his work, but my obligations to him go well beyond these obvious references. They include years of conversations that have always been both enriching and enjoyable, and he also read an earlier version of the entire manuscript, making important corrections and suggesting additional points to be added.

Other friends read and commented on chapters that relate to their areas of specialization. Following the chronology of the book, they are John Hall, an amazing naturalist now at the University of West Alabama, and Craig Sheldon, who retired from Auburn University at Montgomery but is still an active, generous, and thoughtful colleague. Kathryn Braund at Auburn University picked up the Indian story in the historical period and carried it into the present. She has helped educate me on this important part of Alabama's story.

Richard Bailey, who has retired as a historian from Maxwell Air Force Base, Michael Fitzgerald at St. Olaf College, and Guy Hubbs, recently retired from Birmingham–Southern College, all read and critiqued the Civil War and Reconstruction chapter. Guy actually read an earlier version of the entire draft. All three were insightful reviewers, and they helped me understand more clearly this particularly difficult and complex part of Alabama's story.

David Robb has taught me about several aspects of early Alabama history, and he graciously shared his research findings and insights with me. Frances Robb reviewed, critiqued, and assisted in my photo selections, and she also read an earlier version of the text and provided thoughtful and constructive editorial suggestions.

My colleagues at the Alabama Department of Archives and History have also been extraordinarily helpful. Bob Bradley critiqued the Civil War chapter. John Hardin read the entire manuscript and offered many valuable corrections and suggestions. I consulted many times with John and with Norwood Kerr and Ken Barr on sources. Bob Bradley, Ryan Blocker, and Graham Neeley all helped with artifact images and citations. Graham especially worked with me through the artifact image files and the Archives' source documents on the artifacts. Meredith McDonough, who handles the Department's photo collection, is one of the ablest archivists I have ever known. She provided incredible help with images of photos, documents, maps, and artifacts, and I am deeply in her debt for her ready assistance and useful suggestions.

All these colleagues were part of the team that worked on the *Alabama Voices* gallery at the Archives, as were most of the outside scholars listed above. Steve Murray, now the director of the Archives, was a key member of this museum design team as well, and he has been supportive of my efforts over the last three years as I have continued using the facilities of the Archives in working on this project.

Many other colleagues from outside the Archives also helped with images or research inquiries: Jim Baggett at the Birmingham Public Library Archive; Mike "Mule" Baker at the Army Materiel Command at Huntsville; Robin Brown at the Cobb Memorial Archives in Valley; Farris Cadle, from Garden City, Georgia, an independent researcher in surveying and land title history; Midge Coates from the Auburn University Libraries; Peggy Collins at the Alabama Department of Tourism; Linda Derry from Old Cahaba Historic Site; Boyce Driskell from the University of Tennessee; Jun Ebersole from the McWane Science Center in Birmingham; Carol Ellis at the University of South Alabama; Betsy Irwin at Moundville Archaeological Park; Mary Nicely at the Florence Department of Art and Museums; Betsy Nichols at the Selma Public Library; Greg Speis from Mobile, an expert on historical surveying in Alabama; Beth Spivey at the Selma-Dallas County Museum of History; Bill Tharpe from the Alabama Power Company Archives; Mike Warren and Garland Stansell at Children's Hospital; and Greg Waselkov at the University of South Alabama. Peggy Gallis, one of Georgia's biggest fans of Alabama history, introduced me to several scholars from outside Alabama whose works have been important for this book.

Jay Lamar, director of the Alabama Bicentennial Commission, has been another supporter, and she also edited an early draft of the manuscript. Dave White, formerly of the *Birmingham News* and now a staff member of the governor's policy office, read the manuscript as a nonprofessional historian and a professional writer, and he offered many suggestions that greatly improved the book's readability. Lee Sentell, director of the Alabama Department of Tourism, has been a supporter of this project from the first day I mentioned it to him. I am deeply grateful for his assistance and friendship, for the great leadership he has provided for tourism development in Alabama, and especially for his work in promoting an expanded awareness of Alabama history.

At the University of Alabama Press, my primary contact has been Donna Cox Baker, who has fielded barrages of questions with unfailing grace and also provided very useful editorial comments. Dan Waterman, the Press's editor-in-chief, has been enormously helpful in overall planning and production issues for the book, and he has encouraged me in the project since we first discussed it as a possibility. Robin McDonald, the book's designer, is far more than a gifted graphic artist; his knowledge of Alabama history is wide-ranging, and his own images have added a great deal to improve the balance and quality of the illustrations. I am deeply grateful for all that he has done to make this book so attractive and to produce a design that I think enriches the text.

Finally, I want to thank my long-suffering wife, Martha. To her I owe the most of all, though I will confine my expressions of gratitude here to all that she did relating directly to this book. History is not her first love, or even her second, but she has encouraged and supported me from the start, despite many inconveniences and disruptions to her own plans and interests. She is also a wonderful editor and has read the entire manuscript at each stage of its development. Her delete files contain scores of pages of awkward and unclear sentences, extraneous words, and nonsense. In fact, readers of this book owe her a debt of gratitude as well because her insightful pruning will save them a great deal of time and effort.

Of course, none of these people is responsible for the problems this book has. I did not always accept their recommendations (though I usually did). Also, most of the copy was reworked in varying degrees after they made their comments, and I did not feel I should impose on them for a second reading. In the end, the book simply reflects my best efforts to tell the story of Alabama as I understand it. The writing took much longer than I had expected, but it has been a journey of discovery for me as well. And it has been great fun because the subject is so incredibly interesting.

—Edwin C. Bridges,
Montgomery, Alabama

INTRODUCTION

URING MY YEARS AT THE ALABAMA Department of Archives and History, I have had the privilege of giving tours to many wonderful people. One of our most famous visitors was the scientist Edward O. Wilson, who grew up in Alabama and still has a passion for its history. As we finished, Dr. Wilson paused for a moment and then asked if I thought Alabama's history might actually be as powerful an epic as those of Greece and Rome.

By that time, I had been caught up in the story for many years, and I knew how amazingly interesting Alabama history is. Dr. Wilson's query helped me realize that stories I found so rich might also appeal to people who are not history buffs. We may not have Socrates or Caesar, but as a whole, our story really is a drama of epic proportions.

Alabama history can also serve as window into American history. Almost every great theme in American history can be found in the story of Alabama—from the Stone Age to the Space Age. And on more than a few occasions, events in Alabama helped shape the course of American history.

At this point, I encourage readers who are so inclined to skip the rest of the Introduction and go straight to the story. What follows is a statement of why I thought there was a place for a book such as this and a review of ideas and considerations that guided me in writing it.

Why I have written the book: For more than three decades working at the Alabama Archives, I have been happily situated in a middle ground between academic historians and the general public. I have seen my academic colleagues devote their careers to intensive historical research, and their books and articles have taken Alabama history to new levels of understanding. These colleagues have become my teachers and friends.

Most of their writings, however, are scholarly pieces focused on limited topics, geographic areas, or time periods. Readers interested in a big-picture overview often do not want to start at that level of depth and detail. In fact, many people have asked me to recommend a general history of the state they can read as an introduction. That is what I have attempted to provide with this book.

Founded in 1871, and nicknamed the "Magic City" for the speed of its growth, Birmingham's downtown presents a pleasing combination of modern and historic architecture.

There are other reasons for the book as well. One is that we are approaching Alabama's bicentennial, and a major commemoration is a natural time to pause and reflect on the past. I thought that a book like this might be useful for bicentennial discussion programs. In addition, Alabama is now coming out of a period of major upheaval that began with the civil rights movement and has brought massive changes to the state. As the state changes, we continually need new history books that include the recent past and incorporate new insights we have gained.

The final reason for the book is that I was part of a wonderful team of historians, designers, and staff members at the Alabama Archives who worked for several years on the Museum of Alabama exhibits that opened at the Archives in 2014. I thought a book that explores in more depth issues introduced in the exhibits might supplement what we did and provide visitors a convenient source for further reading. Although the book draws from our design work, it is not intended as a print version of the exhibit. It is, rather, an effort to build on our work and carry it a step further.

Ideas and concerns that guided me in the writing process: As best I could, I have tried to examine what people in the past experienced as they grappled with the challenges of their times. I have tried to take each group seriously and to explore why its members thought and acted as they did. My goal has been to understand, not to assign blame or merit. All people have reasons for what they do that make sense to them. Other people may or may not approve of those reasons, and people may even deceive themselves about what their true reasons are. But a first step toward understanding is trying to see other people's experiences from their perspective.

One concern for me is that readers may feel this book focuses too heavily on our conflicts rather than on our achievements. But I think examining the conflicts is necessary for understanding Alabama history. They are the reason our history is so rich and dramatic. And there is usually more to

be learned from our struggles and difficulties than from our successes.

Another concern is all the interesting and important material I have had to omit. In every area of Alabama history, the deeper one drills, the richer the story becomes. Yet, for this book to function as an overview, it was necessary to enforce a strict discipline of selection, lest it become a tome. Many significant people and incidents receive only passing reference, and some receive none at all. I have had to leave out many of my own favorite stories. The writing process was much like producing a documentary film, in which hours of great footage are left on the cutting room floor as the work is trimmed to a manageable presentation.

The full story of the past is so complex that we cannot begin to know it all. Yet despite the impossibility, we still try our best to make sense of what happened before us. We have to do this, because our understanding of the past serves as the framework that guides us in the decisions we make about the future. A deeper and more accurate knowledge of the past can help us make better-informed and more effective decisions today.

As an overview, this book attempts to trace the broad contours of Alabama history. It is based on the scholarship of Alabama historians of this generation, and I have tried to be as fair and accurate as possible in representing their work. But it is only a sketch of a vastly larger story. I hope readers will find the book both a useful introduction to Alabama's history and a stimulus to explore it further.

FRONT MATTER PHOTOS: Page i: Interior of the dome of the Alabama State Capitol in Montgomery, with murals depicting scenes from Alabama history by Roderick McKenzie; pages ii-iii: Old chamber of the Alabama House of Representatives in the State Capitol; pages iv-v: View from Cheaha Mountain in Cleburne County, the highest point in Alabama at 2,413 feet; pages vi-vii: The McCrary Farm near Huntsville, thought to be the oldest farm in Alabama still in the same family; opposite page: U.S. Geological Survey map of Alabama, created in 1970.

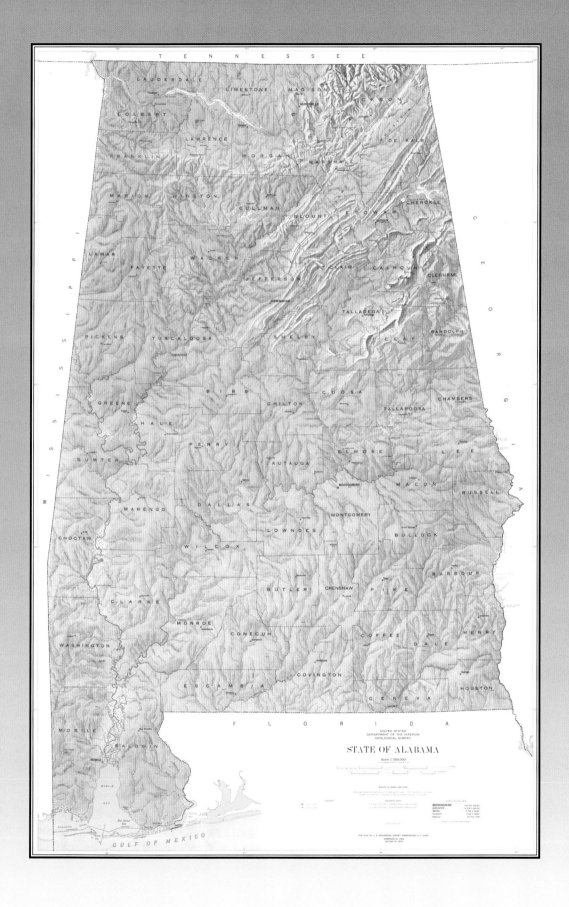

STATE OF ALABAMA

CHAPTER 1

THE FIRST ALABAMIANS

From about 11,000 BC to AD 1700

PEOPLE HAVE LIVED IN WHAT WOULD BECOME ALABAMA *for thousands of years. The first Alabamians arrived during the Ice Age. Their story resembles that of people in other parts of the world where life progressed from a Stone Age culture to an agriculture-based civilization. By AD 1500, Indians in Alabama had built a complex society that included walled towns, skilled crafts, systematic plant cultivation, extensive trade networks, chiefdoms that linked clusters of villages, and a rich community and religious life.*

The arrival of Europeans, with diseases to which the Indians had no immunity, brought a catastrophic loss of life and a collapse of Indian society. The first people of Alabama left no written records to tell their story, but evidence of their lives is still found in the land itself. Some Alabamians today are their descendants.

FIRST ARRIVAL IN ALABAMA

ARCHAEOLOGISTS now generally agree that Asiatic people crossing through Alaska were the first settlers of the Western Hemisphere. During the Ice Age, ocean levels were much lower than they are today because so much water was locked in huge glacial masses. The shallower seas exposed a large land area between Siberia and Alaska that archaeologists call Beringia. People from Asia moved into Beringia and lived there for thousands of years, and some of them migrated from there into the Americas.

Mural of a funeral procession at Moundville about AD 1400. Located in present-day Hale County, Moundville was one of the most important centers of Mississippian culture in North America. Its walls enclosed twenty-six mounds. (Murals shown in this chapter were prepared for *The First Alabamians* gallery at the Alabama Department of Archives and History by Karen Carr Studios.)

Below: Paleo-era projectile points. These beautifully crafted points are shown at three-quarters of their actual size. They were big and sharp enough to pierce thick hides of the many large animals that lived in North America, most of which were hunted to extinction by the Paleo Indians.

Ongoing archaeological research is helping to map the settlers' dispersion across the Western Hemisphere. Findings at Monte Verde, Chile, show that humans reached the southern tip of South America before 12,000 BC. Remains found in the Meadowcroft Rockshelter in southwestern Pennsylvania appear to be even older.

New genetics research supports the findings of the archaeologists. One recent DNA study concluded that the great majority of Indians in the Western Hemisphere descend from a relatively small founder group that lived in Beringia about 21,000 to 18,000 years ago. Interestingly, the human DNA studies are supported by genetics research on Indian dogs. A study published in 2013 traces their origin to East Asia as well, noting several breeds today that are their descendants.

We do not know exactly when people first reached Alabama. The oldest evidence of habitation verified by radiocarbon testing dates from about 11,000 BC. Many tools and projectile points found in Alabama are similar to those from other sites where Indian presence before 11,000 BC has been scientifically confirmed. The early Alabama objects, however, have been loose finds, not embedded with organic material that can be tested for its age. Given the number of these objects and the proven reach of early Indian migrations, it seems almost certain that people arrived in Alabama even before 11,000 BC. We just do not have hard evidence yet.

THE PALEO PERIOD (11,000 BC TO 8,000 BC)

Archaeologists refer to earliest settlers as Paleo (from the Greek word *old*) Indians. They were Stone Age people, living very much as their counterparts across the world did then and very much as their ancestors had for thousands of years before.

Paleo Indians organized themselves in small bands, ranging in size from twenty to fifty or more people and composed mostly of extended family members. Bands often met together for trade, ceremonial occasions, hunting, and finding mates. They would also fight each other to defend or acquire territory.

As foragers and hunters, Paleo Indians probably moved seasonally to take advantage of food sources. They may have kept a base area they regarded as home, but they would abandon it as food sources were depleted or new opportunities appeared. Their numbers in Alabama would probably have been counted in the thousands rather than tens of thousands.

Many projectile points that survive from this era are large, beautifully worked pieces, sharp enough to have pierced the thick hides of

Opposite page: Mural of Paleo Indian life. The first Indians arrived in Alabama at the end of the last Ice Age expansion more than 13,000 years ago.

Right: Jun Ebersole, curator of collections at the McWane Science Center in Birmingham, showing the hand of a ground sloth, a *Megalonyx jeffersonii*. Found in a cave in northwest Alabama, these remains date from about 35,000 years ago and are the most complete specimen set for the species ever found. Below: Mastodon tooth found by Robert G. McLean in 2004 in a creek in Butler County. Mastodons were among the large Ice Age animals in Alabama that the first settlers hunted.

mammoths. North America was then home to many different kinds of large animals, including mammoths, mastodons, giant bison, ground sloths, saber-toothed cats, camels, and wild horses. Because these animals had never been exposed to human beings, they lacked an instinctive fear of people.

In the course of 2,000 years or so, the Paleo Indians hunted to extinction thirty-four of the forty-seven *genera* of large mammals known to have inhabited North America. It was the second large mass extinction in history caused by human beings, following one in Australia, where a similar process had played out thousands of years earlier.

The many projectile points and scrapers found across the Tennessee River Valley indicate that it was one of the most densely settled parts of North America. The oldest known site of habitation in Alabama, with intact deposits and organic remains, is Dust Cave, near Florence. Archaeologists working the site literally scraped off hundred-year slices of accumulated debris as they dug down to the original cave floor, which dates to around 11,000 BC.

Because most materials used by the Paleo Indians have decomposed, we have only limited remains from their lives to study. Anthropological research on remote societies where

Excavation trench cut by archaeologists into the floor of Dust Cave in Lauderdale County, the oldest known site of human habitation in Alabama. The residue of daily life built up on the cave floor to a depth of almost fifteen feet over the course of thousands of years.

Stone Age practices continued into recent times has aided in the study of Paleo Indians, and new technologies such as genetics keep opening new avenues of investigation. The amazing discoveries of the last half-century give hope of much more information and a deeper understanding still to come.

THE ARCHAIC PERIOD (8,000 BC TO 1,000 BC)

GLACIERS did not reach Alabama during the last expansion epochs of the Ice Age, but the climate was much colder then and resembled a wet version of today's Minnesota. By about 8,000 BC, however, temperatures warmed, and the climate changed to something like what it is now. New plant and animal life emerged that fit this new environment. Melting icepacks caused a rise in sea level that covered Beringia and also moved the Alabama coast to its present location from a hundred miles farther out in the Gulf. The climate changes brought changes in the lives of Alabama Indians, as they adapted to the warmer environment. Archaeologists use these changes to mark the end of the Paleo period and the beginning of the Archaic period.

In setting these large historical periods, archaeologists readily acknowledge that the time boundaries are not hard and fast. Life for early Indians continued from generation to generation with little noticeable change. Yet there were changes, and even small changes over the course of hundreds of years eventually produced clear differences.

In the Archaic period, the great animals of the Ice Age were gone, but the new climate supported many species of smaller animals. Meat sources included deer, bears, rabbits, turkeys, squirrels, raccoons, ducks, and turtles. Streams and rivers yielded fish and mussels. Ancient layers of discarded mussel shells found along many Alabama riverbanks are a reminder today of people who ate there thousands of years ago. Along the Gulf Coast, Indians could add oysters, crabs, and other marine life to their diet.

Paleo Indians also relied on a variety of plant food that they gathered—including nuts, acorns, seeds, berries, roots, and greens. Learning to nurture some plants to increase their production was another major development. By the late part of the period, Paleo Indians were planting or tending plots of gourds, squash, sunflowers, and even some grains—adding new reliability to their food supply.

Paleo Indians also developed new and better vessels for cooking food. They learned to quarry large chunks of soapstone, using harder rocks as tools. By scraping out the centers of these pieces, they created pots. Cooking meat and vegetables in pots meant that more of the nutrients were captured in stews rather than lost as drippings into

Archaic-era points. Points of this period are generally smaller than those of the Paleo period, since the animals the Indians hunted were generally smaller. The points shown here would have been used for knives or spears, since the bow and arrow was not yet in use.

Mural depicting life for Archaic Indians after the end of the last Ice Age expansion. The older man is demonstrating a spear thrower, called an atlatl.

a fire. Increasing the nutritional yield of their food could mean the difference between life and death for people struggling at the margin of survival.

With the changes in climate and food sources also came new weapons and tools. The large, carefully worked projectile points required for piercing a mammoth's hide were no longer needed and were replaced by smaller and more varied points. A throwing device, called an atlatl, added range and power to the thrust of Indian spears. Other tools fashioned from stone, bone, hide, and wood aided the Indians in gathering, preparing, and cooking food, as well as in making clothing, building shelters, and supplying a few modest comforts.

Learning to make pottery from clay was an advancement of the late Archaic period. Clay was far easier to work than stone, and clay pots

were lighter. They could be used to gather, store, and transport food, as well as to cook it. Because fire-hardened clay is relatively durable, the pot fragments that have survived from this time period have become an important tool for archaeologists studying the lives of the early Indians.

As Archaic Indians learned more ways to enhance their food supply, they were able to remain longer in the same place. The cultivation of plants, in fact, required some degree of sustained care, at least through the growing season. Long periods of occupancy in Dust Cave and in Jackson County's Russell Cave reflect an increasing tendency toward a more settled lifestyle.

As Archaic Indians gained greater mastery over their environment, their numbers slowly increased, and their lives became a little more

Top: Soapstone bowl. The sides still show the scrape marks of the harder rocks its maker used in carving it. Above: Russell Cave in Jackson County. Now a National Historical Monument operated by the National Park Service, Russell Cave provided shelter for people in Alabama from about 10,000 BC to AD 1650.

Mural depicting Woodland-era life. Pottery making, the cultivation of plants, use of the bow and arrow, and a more settled life help mark this period of early Indian history.

comfortable. Tools became more sophisticated, and more objects of personal adornment appeared. Materials brought from many miles away—copper, sea shells, and certain rocks, for example—show that a system of trade connected Alabama Indians to people in other parts of eastern North America.

The Archaic Indians also began building earthen mounds for both ceremonial and burial purposes. The burials show that some individuals were singled out for special honors, indicating the emergence of more complex social systems. The burials also show evidence of belief in some form of afterlife.

THE WOODLAND PERIOD (1,000 BC TO AD 1000)

ABOUT 1,000 BC, Indian culture in Alabama (as in other parts of North America) reached a new level of complexity. There were more people, more tools, more systematic agriculture, and a more settled community life. Archaeologists use these changes to mark the beginning of a new period they call Woodland.

By the Woodland period, pottery making was a standard part of Indian life. The different kinds of vessels, ornamentation styles, and types of clay the Indians used help archaeologists today trace cultural

Top: Woodland-era stone gorget. As people settled in the same place for longer periods, they made and accumulated more material goods, such as objects of body ornamentation. Above: Woodland-era pot. This pot was found more than a century ago by an amateur archaeologist at a gravel pit in central Alabama.

changes and regional distinctions in the period. The variety of decorative motifs and an increased beauty of design also show an expanded aesthetic consciousness.

Woodland people kept regular gardens, and they cultivated more plants, such as beans and grains, than their ancestors had. Their growing reliance on plants for food increased both their need and their ability to stay longer in the same place. And a more settled lifestyle allowed them to build larger and more long-lasting structures for home and community life.

Two other significant Woodland innovations were cloth and the bow and arrow. Handmade fabrics contributed both comfort and convenience to daily life. Woodland women learned to dry, work, and then hand-spin vegetable fibers into thread. They did not use looms but looped and tied the cross-threads to produce workable fabrics. The bow and arrow increased the ability of hunters to kill game, further improving the variety and reliability of the food supply.

As Woodland Indians became more settled, they formed communities that were linked together into tribal groupings, providing greater security and an enriched social life. Their expanded social networks, along with increased ceremonial activities, brought more occasions for sharing the stone and clay pipes that came to be widely used in ritual smoking.

The size, number, and obvious importance of the earthen mounds also help mark this period. Most early mounds appear to have been burial sites for leaders. Funerary material in the burial sites show the continuing growth of a social hierarchy. Some mounds also had structures on top for ceremonial use, suggesting an expansion of ritual activity. Woodland-era mounds have been found and studied across Alabama, though, sadly, many have also been lost over time to erosion, agriculture, and construction.

Top: Woodland-era projectile points. The variety of points increased during this period. Very small points for arrowheads mark the emerging use of the bow and arrow. Above: Woodland-era stone pipe. A cane stem would have been inserted from the side for smoking. Right: Woodland-era earthen mound. This forty-three-foot-tall mound in Florence is thought to have been built between 100 BC and AD 400.

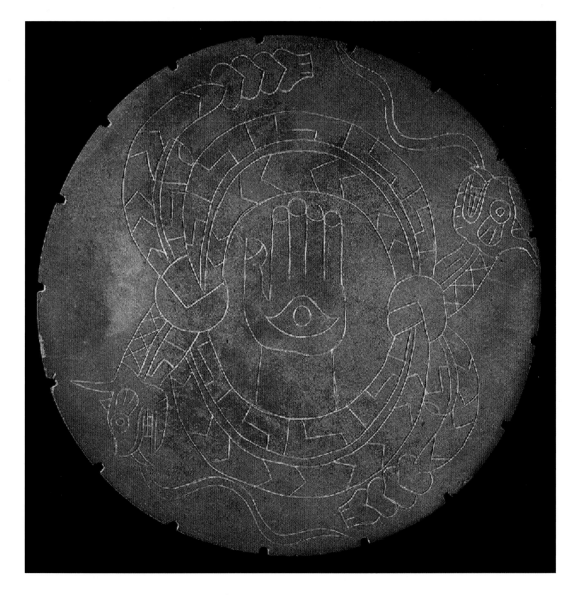

THE MISSISSIPPIAN PERIOD (AD 1000 TO AD 1550)

THE Mississippian period was the high-water mark in Alabama's Indian history. People of this period built on the achievements of their Woodland ancestors, creating a substantial and relatively prosperous society.

Major increases in corn production appear to have made this success possible. Whether the cause was a more productive variety of corn, better cultivation techniques, or both is not certain. But the ability to produce and accumulate surpluses of food that could be stored and used whenever needed was a great boon.

The Mississippians' production of corn and other food through systematic planting paralleled similar developments in other cultures

Rattlesnake Disk. This stone disk showing entwined serpents with a hand and eye in the center has become Moundville's iconic image. The disk is just over twelve inches in diameter and half an inch thick.

Left: Serpent-Bird Bowl, sometimes called the Duck Bowl. Indian art reached its apogee during the Mississippian era. This bowl, excavated at Moundville in 1906 by Clarence Bloomfield Moore, is widely regarded as a masterpiece of Mississippian art. Opposite page, above: Mural depicting Mississippian agriculture. Since Indians did not have beasts of burden, they did not use plows. Women and girls worked garden plots with hoes and planting sticks. Below: Mural depicting a chunky game. Men competed to throw their spears closest to that point where a rolling disk would stop.

around the world that historians refer to as the Agricultural Revolution. It was a major turning point in the story of human development. Increased production of plant food through agriculture made possible increases in population, leading to the growth of the first towns and cities, and to a whole new cultural system.

As the Mississippian Indians expanded their agricultural production, they lacked the beasts of burden that most agrarian cultures in other parts of the world had been able to domesticate. All the species of these large animals in North America had been hunted to extinction ten thousand years earlier. But with rich forests and rivers nearby, the Mississippians also continued to supplement what they grew with animals they hunted, fish they caught, and nuts, berries, and greens they gathered.

As their food supply improved and their population increased, more people were freed from the burden of full-time food gathering and production. And with more time to hone their skills and a growing demand for their products, Mississippian artisans crafted beautiful pots, tools, ceremonial objects, and items of ornamentation that are still admired and prized today.

Mounds that were substantially larger than those of earlier periods were a distinctive feature of Mississippian culture. While some were still used for burials, many appear to have been built to provide elevated lodges for clan or town leaders and high platforms for ceremonial events. Moundville, along the Black Warrior River in present-day Hale County, features twenty-six mounds surrounding a large central plaza. The population living inside the walls has been estimated at about one

Top: Moundville Archaeological Park. One of Alabama's most historic sites, Moundville was preserved in the 1930s through the extraordinary personal efforts of Walter B. Jones, then Alabama's state geologist. It has been subsequently maintained and protected as a part of the University of Alabama Museums. Above: Clay figure from a pot fragment. Mississippians often depicted human faces and fanciful creatures on their pottery.

thousand, and another ten thousand or so people lived nearby. At its peak, Moundville was one of the largest Mississippian towns in North America.

Other Mississippian centers in Alabama were at what is now Bessemer, at Bottle Creek in the Mobile-Tensaw Delta, and at Florence and Hobbs Island in the Tennessee Valley. These towns appear to have been regional chiefdoms to which smaller nearby towns were attached. All were located along streams or in river valleys where rich alluvial soil supported the easy cultivation of corn. Some of the towns were surrounded by protective log walls.

The Mississippians appear to have lived mostly in small, one-room houses. House walls were made by anchoring vertical wooden posts in the ground, weaving cane or branches through them, and then covering the resulting lattice with a clay plaster. Open hearths in the earthen floors were vented through the roof, without a chimney. Roofs appear to have been made of grass thatch, sheets of bark, or, in southern Alabama, palmetto branches.

One of the mysteries of the Mississippian culture is its apparent decline in the latter part of the period. Archaeologists speculate on possible causes, such as climate change, some kind of failure in the corn harvests, or warfare and political breakdown. Burial sites show that warfare was a destructive part of life in the last half of the Mississippian period. But for whatever reason, Moundville was largely abandoned as a place of residence by about AD 1400, though it continued to be used as a necropolis where nearby people brought their dead for burial.

ALTHOUGH the Mississippian culture suffered internal stresses before the 1500s, those problems paled beside the death and desolation that Europeans brought. Historian Alfred Crosby coined the term *Columbian Exchange* to describe the aftermath of 1492, when people from two hemispheres, separated for thousands of years, came into contact. What followed was an exchange of people, animals, plants, microbes, technologies, and ideas that altered life in both worlds.

What this exchange first brought to Alabama Indians was wave after wave of epidemics, and death on a horrific scale. Many contagious

Mural scene depicting the first contact between a small Mississippian Indian community and a band of soldiers from de Soto's expedition.

diseases originate in animals and then mutate genetically to attack people. Because Indians had no cattle, sheep, horses, or pigs, they had not been exposed to a number of common European illnesses, such as measles, scarlet fever, typhoid, typhus, whooping cough, cholera, diphtheria, smallpox, chickenpox, and many respiratory infections caused by viruses. Traditional medical practices, such as purging and sweating, actually increased the Indians' death rates.

Each Spanish landing, even those as distant as Florida, brought the potential for new waves of epidemics. Juan Ponce de León "discovered" Florida in 1513, but less well documented were landings by private ships that swept the Florida coast, seizing Indians to work as slaves in new Caribbean settlements. The first Spanish explorers to touch what is now Alabama were probably members of an expedition led by Alonso Álvarez de Pineda, who mapped the Gulf Coast in 1519. Nine years later, Pánfilo de Narváez and Álvar Núñez Cabeza de Vaca followed with more extensive exploration.

De Soto meets Chief Tuscaloosa. This engraving from *Histoire de la conquête de la Floride par Ferdinand de Soto* (1731) imagines the first encounter at Atahachi between de Soto and Chief Tuscaloosa, who is seated left under the sunshade.

Indians in Alabama had probably suffered effects of European diseases passed on through other groups even before 1540, when Hernando de Soto and his expedition arrived in the area. Under de Soto's command, more than six hundred Spanish soldiers plundered and pillaged their way through Alabama, leaving a trail of death and destruction in their wake. With their protective armor, powerful horses, metal weapons, and ferocious war dogs, they were almost impossible for the Indians to defeat.

In earlier expeditions through Central and South America, the Spanish had developed tactics for seizing local leaders and holding them hostage. By threatening their hostages' lives, the Spanish forced Indian communities to provide laborers, food, and women. De Soto used these same tactics in Alabama.

Archaeologists agree about some sites marking de Soto's route, but others are disputed. The locations of two camp sites in Florida have been confirmed by archaeological research, but de Soto's exact route across Alabama is less certain. Most researchers agree that he entered Alabama from the northeast corner of the state and travelled southward along the east side of the Coosa River. Four narratives written later by members of the expedition describe general features that fit this route. These de Soto chronicles are the first written records we have that describe what is now Alabama. They tell of substantial Indian chiefdoms along the way, with towns lining the river valleys.

In the early part of October 1540, de Soto reached the town of Atahachi, home of Chief Tuscaloosa (which means *Black Warrior* in English). Archaeologists believe they have located the site of Atahachi a few miles west of Montgomery. The de Soto chronicles describe Chief Tuscaloosa as a very large, well-built, and dignified man, but de Soto took him hostage and made the usual demands for food, baggage bearers, and women. Tuscaloosa replied that these things would be waiting at the town of Mabila, several days' travel away.

When de Soto arrived at Mabila on October 18, he found a site protected by many warriors and a stout log wall more than fifteen feet tall—probably a trap the Indians had prepared in advance. After de Soto refused Tuscaloosa's order to leave, a fight broke out that grew into a full battle. According to the Spanish accounts, de Soto's troops killed thousands of Indians. Only twenty-two Spanish were killed, but almost a hundred and fifty more were wounded, and they lost horses and supplies as well.

After taking time to regroup, the Spanish continued west beyond the Mississippi River and then returned back to it, where de Soto died. The site of the town of Mabila and the great battle is still a mystery for Alabama archaeologists. Finding it has become something of a modern version of the Grail Quest for many of them.

Above: The Battle of Mabila. This engraving, also from *Histoire de la conquête de la Floride par Ferdinand de Soto*, imagines the Battle of Mabila. Below: Brass Spanish capstan candlestick. Candlesticks of this type were made during the mid-to late-1500s. This one was found in the mid-1990s at an old Mississippian site in Dallas County.

Through the mid-1500s, the destruction wrought by de Soto and the even greater losses caused by European diseases led to a population and cultural collapse among Alabama Indians. The next Spanish expedition to enter Alabama was led by Tristán de Luna in 1559, just nineteen years after de Soto. De Luna sent scouting parties into the interior to trade with the Indians, but one party traveled for three weeks and found only a single village. The death rate among Alabama Indians may have been as high as ninety percent. The population loss was so great that by the 1600s, bison from the West were migrating into the region, grazing on old fields that Indian women had once tended.

REBUILDING (AD 1561 TO AD 1700)

De Luna's expedition was the last Spanish incursion into Alabama for more than a century. None of the expeditions had found gold or silver. All had been costly. Some had been disasters. So after the mid-1500s, the Spanish lost interest in the interior southeastern part of North America.

As the conquistadors turned their attention elsewhere, surviving Indians in Alabama began rebuilding. At the same time, other Europeans, especially the British, began establishing settlements along the Atlantic coast, where occasional fighting between Indians and European colonizers continued. Some Indians from these areas fled and sought safety among Alabama Indians.

Spanish lug-eyed hoe. This hoe, dating from the late 1600s, was found by an amateur archaeologist at an old Indian site in central Alabama in the early 1900s.

In the Alabama interior, Indians were partially insulated, but not totally cut off from European influences. European-made objects, such as metal hoes, cloth, jewelry, and glass beads, found their way into Alabama, traded by Indians who lived closer to European settlements.

When a new generation of Europeans ventured into Alabama again more than a century after the Spanish had left, they found the Indians living in small villages called *talwas*, usually built alongside creeks or rivers. The "three sisters" of agriculture—corn, beans, and squash—still provided their basic food supply, supplemented by game they hunted or trapped and whatever they gathered from the forests, meadows, and streams around them. Each talwa was a self-governing community, but most were linked to other towns in larger groupings based on cultural, kinship, linguistic, and political ties.

Alabama Indians of the late 1600s no longer built mounds, and their art was not of such exquisite beauty as in the peak years of the Mississippian culture. Their numbers were also tragically reduced from what they had been two centuries earlier. Not more than about twenty thousand people lived in all of what is now Alabama, the remains

A MAP OF LOUISIANA AND OF THE RIVER MISSISSIPI By Iohn Senex

of a population that had probably exceeded one hundred thousand people just two centuries earlier.

In this second wave of contacts, Europeans no longer expected to find cities of gold. This time they came to trade. But they were also players in a new competition among European powers for imperial dominance over North America.

British settlements along the mid-Atlantic coast already reached down to Charles Town in South Carolina. The French were expanding from their base in Canada into the Mississippi River Valley. In 1682, Robert de La Salle explored the Mississippi River to the Gulf of Mexico, naming the territory through which he passed *La Louisiane* and claiming it for France. Two years later, he returned to establish a colony on the Gulf of Mexico, but he died in the unsuccessful attempt.

As the 1600s ended, what would become the state of Alabama was still clearly Indian land. They set the terms under which outsiders were admitted. Yet the number of outsiders was increasing, and their growing power presaged many new struggles and hardships to come for the Indians in Alabama.

Map of Louisiana and the Mississippi River by John Senex (1721). Spanish Florida, French Louisiana, and British colonies along the Atlantic Coast were European footholds around the Indians of Alabama. The dotted line from Florida up through what is now Georgia, the Carolinas, and Alabama shows the supposed route of de Soto.

CHAPTER 2

THE LAND OF THE INDIANS

1700 to 1814

IN THE EARLY 1700S, *Spain, France, and Great Britain all claimed parts of the land that would become Alabama. That land was actually occupied by about twenty thousand Indians, most of whom were members of a tribal grouping known by the British as Creeks. For almost a century, the Creeks prospered in their dealings with the Europeans. They used European weapons to attack other tribes and sold their captives to the Europeans as slaves. Deerskins soon replaced Indian slaves as the major trade commodity, and the deerskin trade grew into a major enterprise that continued for several generations.*

After the American Revolution, however, a new power threatened the Creeks' independence, as settlers from the recently formed United States began pushing into Creek land. The Creeks struggled to hold the settlers back, but their resistance efforts were finally crushed in what Americans called the Creek War (1813 to 1814). The treaty ending that war forced the Creeks to cede a large part of their land to the United States and left them locked in a diminished reserve, encircled by the state of Georgia and the new Mississippi Territory.

"Me-na-wa, A Creek Warrior," (detail), 1836, from *History of the Indian Tribes of North America* by Thomas McKenney and James Hall. Menawa, which means "Great Warrior," was a leader of the Red Stick Creeks and was in command at the Battle of Horseshoe Bend, where he was severely wounded. He continued as a Creek leader in the years after the battle. This lithograph is based on a portrait by Charles Bird King that was painted while Menawa was in Washington protesting an improper cession of Creek land. In 1836, at the age of seventy, Menawa was forced to leave his land and move west to what would become Oklahoma.

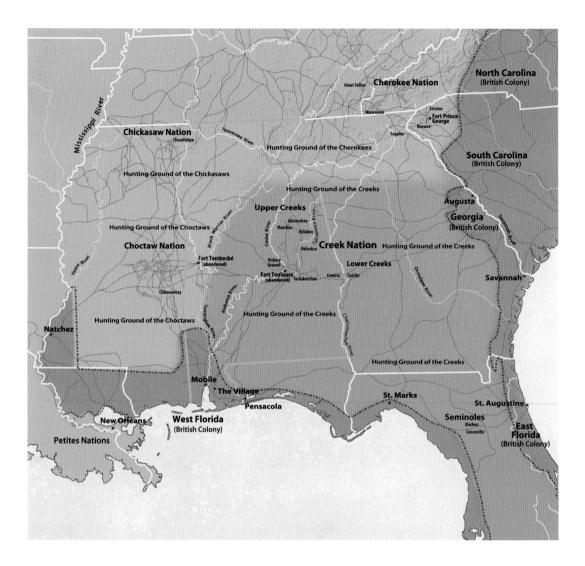

Map showing the principal Indian towns and trading paths in the Southeast just before the American Revolution (with modern state boundary lines superimposed). The medium green, covering most of present-day Alabama and Georgia, denotes Creek land. The darkest green depicts areas under European control. The lightest green denotes neighboring Indian lands.

THE SETTLEMENT OF MOBILE

IN 1698, Louis XIV tried again to plant a French settlement on the Gulf Coast. La Salle had died in the effort eleven years earlier, but Louis still hoped to secure the land that bore his name, *La Louisiane*. Pierre Le Moyne d'Iberville, a Canadian-born French officer, led the new expedition. His fleet set sail from France in late 1698 and arrived at Pensacola Bay in early 1699, just months after Spanish settlers had landed there.

Iberville sailed farther west along the Gulf Coast and built a temporary fort at Biloxi Bay. In 1702, he moved the colony to a new site at Twenty-Seven Mile Bluff, upriver from present-day Mobile. That site, Fort Louis de la Louisiane, was the first European settlement in Alabama. Access to river systems reaching far into the interior gave the French at Mobile a strategic advantage over the Spanish in Pensacola.

Iberville left Fort Louis after a few months, turning over command of the colony to his capable, twenty-two-year-old younger brother, Jean-Baptiste Le Moyne de Bienville. Bienville negotiated with local Indians and the Spanish to secure supplies and keep the colony alive. In 1711, after a disastrous flood, he abandoned Fort Louis and moved the settlement downriver to the present site of Mobile. Fort Louis and then Mobile served for fifteen years as the capital of French Louisiana until 1717, when the capital was moved and eventually established at New Orleans.

To help in the hard labor of clearing land and farming, the French began using enslaved Indians, a standard practice for early European colonizers. The Europeans provided weapons to Indians with whom they were friendly and sent them on raids against other tribes. The Indian allies then sold their captives to the Europeans and used the proceeds to pay their debts and buy trade goods and more weapons. Thousands of enslaved Indians were also shipped to plantations in the Caribbean.

Enslavement and the warfare that went with it brought still more misery and death to Indian people. Entire communities literally disappeared from history. Just ten years after the French first settled at Mobile, the Indian population in the area fell by more than half, to around two thousand people.

Archaeological excavation of a 1706 barracks at Fort Louis. A team from the University of South Alabama, led by Greg Waselkov, has worked for years on the site of Old Mobile.

The first shipment of enslaved people of African origin arrived in Mobile from the West Indies in 1721. Both the Spanish and British were already using slaves from Africa in their Caribbean plantations, and black slavery soon replaced Indian slavery at Mobile. Though enslavement under the French was harsh, conditions were governed by the *Code Noir,* which provided a number of legal protections for slaves.

The *Code Noir* was originally issued by Louis XIV and then recompiled for French Louisiana by Bienville in 1724. It stipulated, for example, that husbands, wives, and young children owned by the same master could not be separated by sale. It also allowed enslaved people to buy their freedom. Once freed, they were to enjoy "all the rights and privileges inherent to our subjects born in our kingdom." Some former slaves eventually became slaveholders themselves. Slavery in early Mobile was considerably more flexible and humane than it became later during the cotton era of the 1800s.

Bottle and porringer taken from archaeological excavations at Fort Toulouse. The site of the fort, located near Wetumpka, is now a property operated by the Alabama Historical Commission.

THE CREEKS AND THE DEERSKIN TRADE

MOST of the Indians who lived in the future state of Alabama were members of a tribe that the British called Creeks. The Lower Creeks lived in the Chattahoochee River Valley, with some of their towns in what is now Georgia. The Upper Creeks lived in the Coosa and Tallapoosa river valleys. Creek towns were closely related by language and tradition, but their territory also included unrelated Indians who had moved into the area seeking refuge from warfare elsewhere. Most new arrivals gradually became part of what later became the Creek Nation.

The Choctaws, Chickasaws, and Cherokees also claimed land in Alabama, but their claims were mostly to hunting lands, part of their extended territories. Their principal towns were all outside Alabama.

British traders began making regular trips into Creek country by the 1680s. They usually offered the best trade goods of the three European rivals, and they became the Creeks' primary trading partners. The alliance was interrupted in the spring of 1715 when some Creeks joined the Yamasees of South Carolina against the British. Angered by cheating traders and the effects of the Indian slave trade, the Yamasees, Creeks, and other tribes launched fierce attacks against the South Carolina settlements.

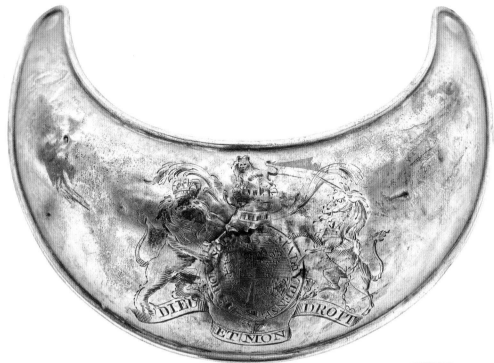

The South Carolinians were able to repel the attacks, but the conflict caused the Creeks to adopt a more neutral position in dealing with Europeans. They invited the French to build a fort in their territory just above the confluence of the Coosa and Tallapoosa rivers to counterbalance growing British power. Fort Toulouse, established in 1717, became the easternmost point of French control in the southern part of North America. Still more Indian towns from the east moved into Creek territory after the Yamasee War, but the Indian slave trade faded away, replaced by the deerskin trade.

For nearly a century, the Creeks generally prospered from the deerskin trade. Europeans prized deerskins highly for gloves, book covers, hats, saddles, and clothing. Before the Industrial Revolution, good cloth was still relatively expensive, but deerskin breeches were durable and comfortable to wear. Historian Kathryn Braund has described them as "the eighteenth-century equivalent of modern denim jeans."

By the mid-1700s, the Creeks were supplying tens of thousands of skins every year to British traders. Pack horses loaded with metal implements, cloth, ornaments, rum, and muskets left Charleston, Savannah, or Augusta traveling into Creek country. They returned loaded with deerskins, as well as bear oil, hickory-nut oil, medicinal barks, and beeswax.

Alabama's first historian, Albert Pickett, actually knew and talked with some of the traders who were still alive in the early 1800s. They described pack trains of small sturdy horses bred for the trade, loaded

Top: Silver gorget. This ornamental piece would have been worn on the chest from a string hung around the neck. It bears the royal coat of arms of the United Kingdom and the maker's mark of Hester Bateman, London, 1781. Above: Rhenish salt-glazed stoneware mug, found in archaeological excavations in Macon County. It bears the excise mark of Queen Anne of England (1702–1714).

with sixty-pound bundles on each side and another on top. Traders drove the ponies in groups of ten, wrote Pickett, and "used no lines, but urged them on with big hickories and terrible oaths." Bottles of rum, slung across the drivers' saddles and regularly consulted, made the long, hard miles more bearable.

To secure ever more deerskins, Creek hunters ranged from the Tennessee Valley in the north to the Tombigbee Valley in the west and to Florida in the south. Deer hunting was based on old traditions, but commercial-scale hunting and the increased contact with outsiders brought changes to Creek life.

Some European traders began settling in Creek country, operating trading houses and often taking Creek wives. Because Creek society was matrilineal, the children of these unions were regarded as Creek. Most of them were also bilingual, and they often enjoyed special favors and benefits from their fathers. They tended to be among the more successful Creeks in negotiating this new, blended world.

The process of encounter and adjustment between Creeks and Europeans—a continuation of the "Columbian Exchange" —lasted for generations, from the late 1600s into the early 1800s and beyond. The Creeks remained committed to their own traditions and way of life, choosing new materials and practices that fit their tastes and preferences. But trade goods, intermarriages, and even some of the ideas of the outsiders began to alter Creek culture.

Top: Traders often carried rum in glass bottles, both for their own use and to trade with the Creeks. Above: French cannon abandoned at Fort Toulouse in 1763. Later, the Creek Indians took possession of the cannon, and after their defeat, the Americans carried it to Montgomery. In March 1825, the breech blew off as the cannon was fired in celebration of the inauguration of President John Quincy Adams.

A BRITISH COLONY

THE first major threat to Creek preeminence was the Seven Years' War (1756–1763), known in America as the French and Indian War. No major fighting took place in Alabama, but the victorious British forced the French to give up their North American territories. After more than sixty years of French rule, Mobile became a British town. Fort Toulouse was abandoned. Also as part of the peace treaty, the Spanish, who had been allies of the French, had to cede Florida to the British though they received Louisiana from the French in compensation.

British officials tried to be fair in dealing with the Indians. They worked to keep settlers from encroaching illegally onto Creek land

and to ban deceitful and unethical traders. Nevertheless, with the defeat and departure of the French and Spanish, the Creeks lost the ability to play the European powers against each other.

The British divided their new Gulf acquisitions into two colonies. All of Florida from the Apalachicola River eastward to the Atlantic Coast became East Florida. The remainder of Spanish Florida west of the Apalachicola River, combined with French Gulf Coast territory extending west to the Mississippi River, became West Florida (see map on pages 32–33).

When the British took possession of Mobile at the end of the war, they found a town that had grown only modestly under French rule. A Catholic parish had been formed in 1703, shortly after the first settlement, so the Church was solidly established, and new plantations had spread around Mobile Bay. But Mobile's economy had remained largely stagnant.

Economic conditions improved somewhat during the years of British rule. Deerskins were the major export, along with lumber, tar, and turpentine. Local plantations increased their production of rice, indigo, and tobacco. The British strengthened the old French Fort Conde and changed its name to Fort Charlotte. For a short time, Mobile was the capital of British West Florida, but British officials soon transferred the seat of government to Pensacola.

THE CREEKS AND THE AMERICAN REVOLUTION

IRONICALLY, Britain's success against the French in the Seven Years' War led to conflict with its North American colonies, and in 1776, thirteen of those colonies rose up in rebellion. Only Canada, the Caribbean Islands, and the two youngest colonies, East and West Florida, remained loyal. As the fighting began, some loyalists from the rebellious colonies sought refuge in Mobile. Others fled to Indian land and to the new settlements along the Tensaw and Tombigbee rivers just north of Mobile.

British agents tried to enlist the Creeks against the Americans, and a few Creek war parties did join them in occasional raids. Overall, the Creeks seemed to prefer the British, but a few long-time traders from Georgia worked energetically to discourage Creek involvement in the war. At its end, the Creeks had been active enough to arouse American fear and resentment, but not enough to affect the outcome.

Top: Miniature of Robert Farmar, an American-born British officer who took possession of Mobile from the French in 1763. Above: Ring and case of Robert Farmar. After leaving the British army, Farmar built a large plantation at present-day Stockton and became one of the wealthiest and most successful men in the Mobile Bay area.

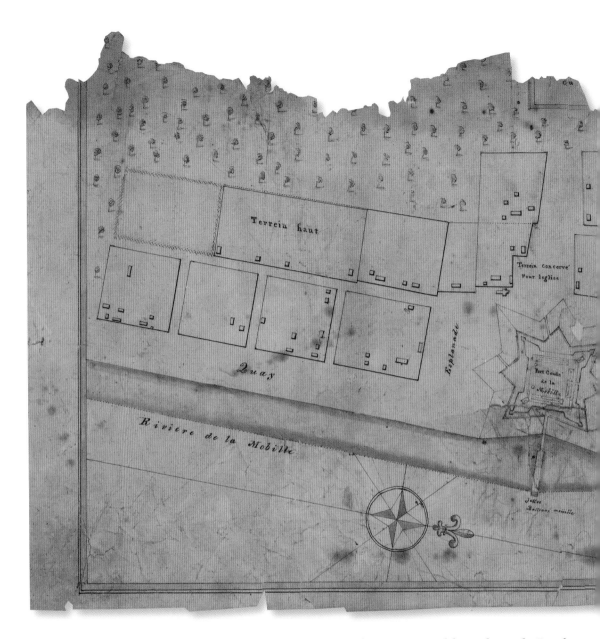

Terrein haut

Terrein Conserve Pour leglise

Esplanade

Quay

Fort Conde de la Mobille

Riviere de la Mobille

Jolies Batteries mobille

Spanish map of Mobile, prepared just after their forces seized the town from the British during the American Revolution.

The most important military action in Alabama during the Revolution was the Spanish seizure of Mobile. In 1779, acting as an ally of France, Spain declared war on Great Britain. Bernardo de Gálvez, the vigorous governor of Spanish Louisiana, captured Mobile in March 1780 and then Pensacola in 1781, restoring to Spain part of its old colony of Florida.

After seventeen years of British rule, from 1763 to 1780, Mobile, the Bay area, and the Tombigbee settlements all fell under Spanish control. But Spain's hold on its recovered colony of West Florida was relatively weak. At the end of the Revolution, the new United States succeeded Great Britain as the dominant power in North America, a change that portended disaster for the Creeks. The Americans cared

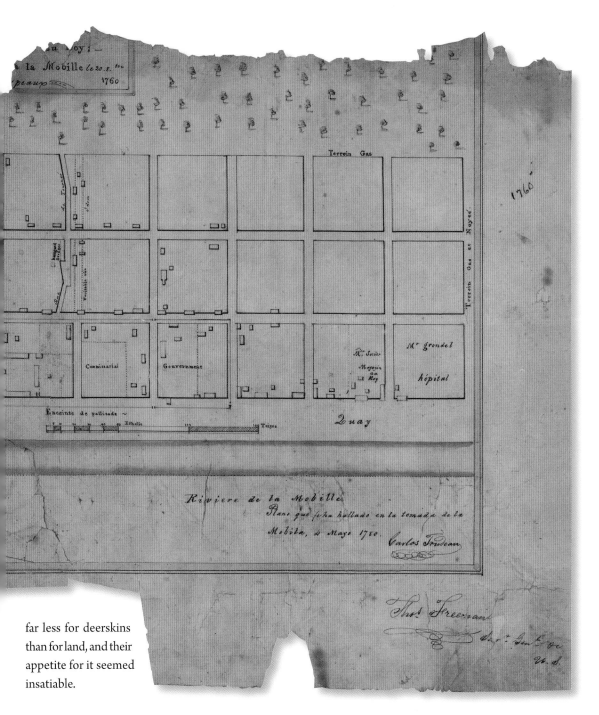

far less for deerskins than for land, and their appetite for it seemed insatiable.

THE CREEKS AND THE TREATY OF NEW YORK

In the aftermath of the American Revolution, Spain, Georgia, and the United States all claimed parts of the future state of Alabama. Spain claimed most of the southern half of the territory (up to 32° 28' latitude) as part of Florida. Georgia declared that its boundaries extended all the way west to the Mississippi River. The United States

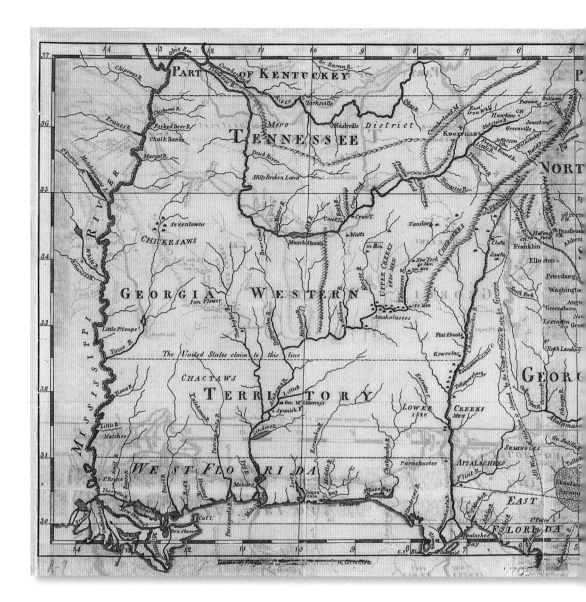

maintained that the U.S. boundary with Spanish Florida was the 31st parallel and that the western land claimed by Georgia belonged to the nation as a whole.

During the Revolution, a key agreement reached by the states had been that the vast, unsettled territory west of the Appalachian Mountains would become the shared property of the nation. At the time of the agreement, most of Georgia was occupied by British troops, so Georgia was the one state that had not formally accepted its terms. After the Revolution, Georgians insisted that the western land was still theirs.

The land these claimants disputed, however, had belonged to Indians since before recorded time, and it was still occupied by them. The settled part of Georgia at the time consisted only of a narrow strip along the Savannah River and the Atlantic Coast. Everything to the

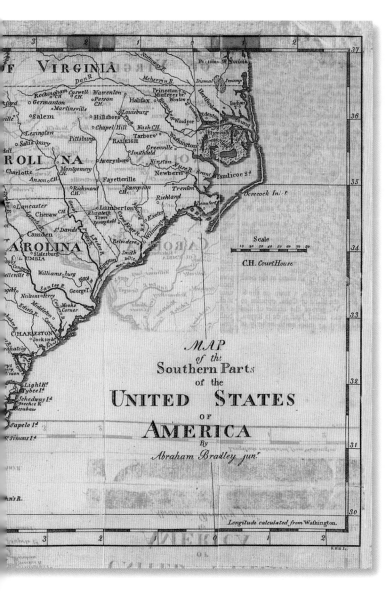

MAP
of the
Southern Parts
of the
UNITED STATES
OF
AMERICA
By
Abraham Bradley jun.

Scale

C.H. *Court House*

Longitude calculated from Washington.

Abraham Bradley map of 1796, showing present-day Alabama and Mississippi as part of Georgia's western territory, and also East and West Florida. The horizontal line running from the confluence of the Yazoo and Mississippi rivers to the Chattahoochee River was the northern boundary line Spain claimed as part of Florida. The 31st parallel is the line from the Mississippi to the Chattahoochee showing the northern boundary of West Florida as claimed by the United States. Today, this line serves as the boundary between Florida and Alabama from the Perdido River eastward.

west was still Indian land, based on old prewar treaties that were still in effect. Within months of the end of the Revolution, Georgia concluded new treaties with the Cherokees and a few Creek leaders for additional land cessions reaching to the Oconee River in what is now the east-central part of Georgia. Most Creeks, however, rejected the treaty as a sham, because the signatories were only marginal leaders who had no authority to speak for the Creek people.

When Georgia settlers began crossing into these Oconee lands, Creek warriors raided their farms to drive them out. When the Georgians retaliated, the Creeks responded with still more attacks. Through the mid- and late-1780s, the border area between Georgia and the Creeks flared in sporadic violence as the Creeks fought to protect their land from encroachment. During the skirmishing, a new leader emerged among the Creeks who gave voice to their cause and plan to their actions.

Alexander McGillivray was the son of a Scottish trader and a Creek mother, who was herself the daughter of a Creek woman and a French officer (from Fort Toulouse). McGillivray spent part of his childhood in Charleston, but when the American Revolution erupted, he and his father remained loyal to Great Britain. His father returned home to Scotland, but McGillivray fled to his mother's homeland among the Creeks. The revolutionaries of South Carolina and Georgia quickly confiscated the family's considerable properties. With his mother's lineage from a prominent Creek clan and his own impressive organizational skills, McGillivray emerged as the Creek's leader during the post–Revolutionary War period.

A letter to General Andrew Pickens in September 1785 illustrates McGillivray's forcefulness as a Creek advocate. Pickens was one of the commissioners delegated that year by Congress to negotiate with the Creeks. By this time, McGillivray had already cultivated relations with the Spanish to secure their help. Replying to a letter from Pickens, he declared:

We want nothing from you but justice. We want our hunting-grounds preserved from encroachments. They have been ours from the beginning of time, and I trust that, with the assistance of our friends, we shall be able to maintain them against every attempt to take them from us.

The conflict between Georgians and the Creeks was one of many problems George Washington inherited when he took the oath as the first president of the United States on April 30, 1789. After a special commission to the Creeks failed, Washington dispatched a secret representative, Marinus Willett, to meet with McGillivray. Fearing that Georgians would try to sabotage his efforts, Willett traveled through western South Carolina and then south to McGillivray's home, a few miles north of present-day Wetumpka, in central Alabama.

Willett invited McGillivray and other Creek leaders to New York City, the temporary seat of the federal government, where they would meet President Washington and discuss a treaty of friendship with Secretary of War Henry Knox. After extensive deliberations, a party of approximately thirty Creek warriors and chiefs left Alabama with Willett in July 1790.

They rode in three wagons and on horseback through South and North Carolina to Richmond and then Philadelphia. Some towns along the way received them with great fanfare. When they arrived in New York on a sloop from Elizabethtown, New Jersey, members of the Tammany Society, wearing Indian look-alike costumes, met them at

Presidential medal presented to a Creek chief at the conclusion of the Treaty of New York. This is the only known surviving medal of six that were crafted on short notice for Secretary of War Henry Knox by New York silversmith Van Voorhis.

Plate 21.   Page 165

Daggett, Hinman & Co. Sc.

The two groups must have created a spectacle as they paraded up Wall Street to President Washington's house, where the Creek visitors were presented with great pomp and ceremony.

The Creek visit to New York is an entertaining story, but the treaty itself, signed on August 7, 1790, was a significant event in American history. Known as the Treaty of New York, it was the first treaty entered into by President Washington. After appearing in person before

Hopothle Mico, or the Talassee King of the Creeks. The Creek delegation arrived in New York just after John Trumbull had finished a portrait of George Washington. The Creeks would not sit for him, but, using "stealth," he completed sketches of five leaders.

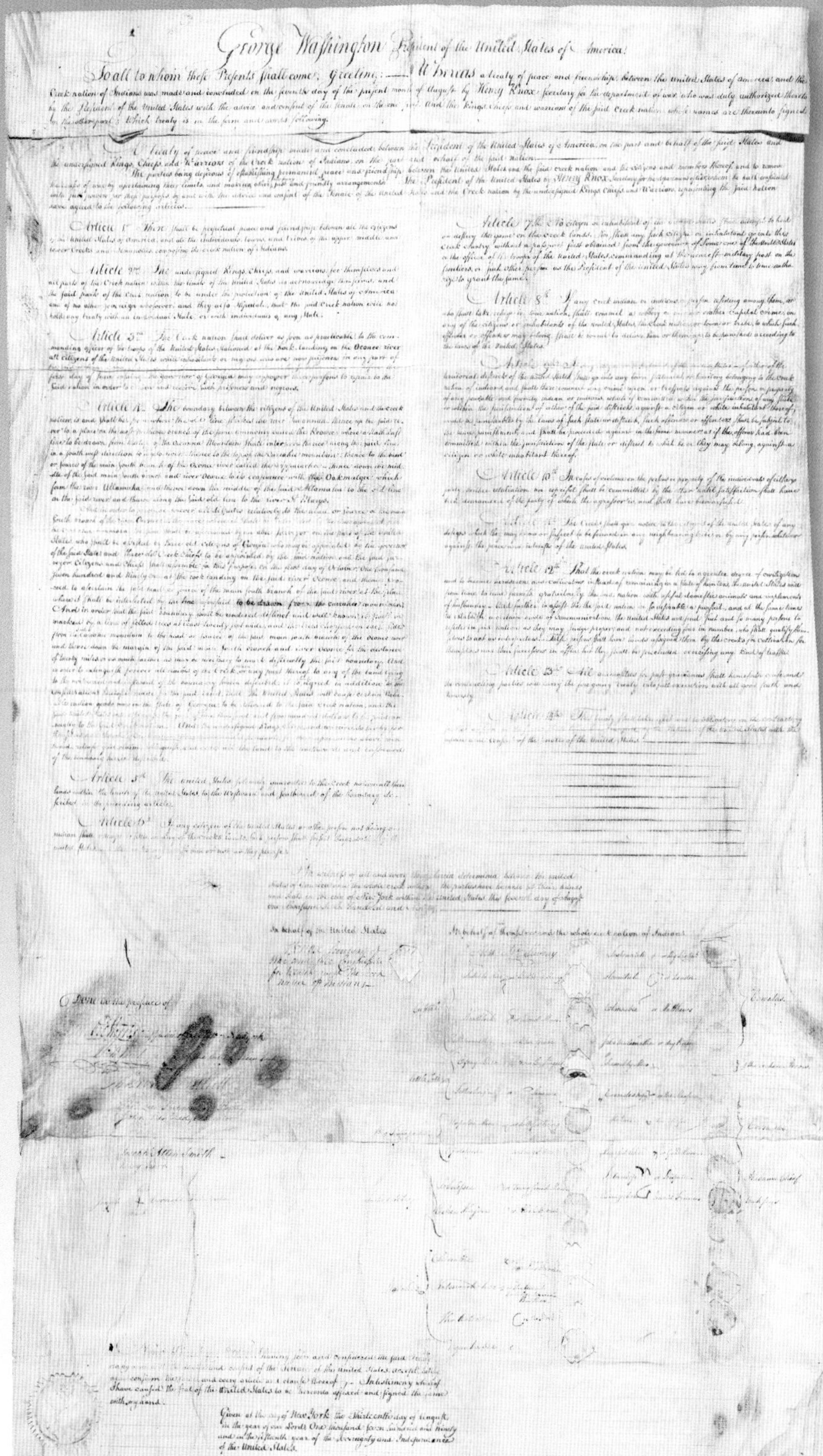

the Senate and being questioned aggressively over treaty details, the exasperated Washington decided thereafter to send rather than carry treaties for ratification. His decision set a precedent that continues today, generally minimizing the "advice" part of the "advice and consent" authority over treaties stipulated for the Senate in the Constitution.

In the treaty, the Creeks ceded a tract of their land east of the Oconee River, which had been the subject of so much fighting during the previous seven years. In return, the United States agreed to "solemnly guarantee to the Creeks, all their [remaining] land within the limits of the United States."

The treaty also revealed President Washington's larger vision for relations with the Indians. With the deerskin trade in decline, both from over-hunting and a decrease in demand, Washington initiated a program to help the Creeks learn new ways to support themselves. The federal government would assist the Creeks in a process of transition, teaching them American practices of farming and herding. Theoretically, the Creeks would then settle into a new agrarian lifestyle and live peaceably side by side with the Americans. An additional benefit of this change would be to free more Indian land for American settlement, since great tracts would no longer be needed for hunting deer. Article 12 of the treaty specified:

That the Creek nation may be led to a greater degree of civilization, and to become herdsmen and cultivators, instead of remaining in a state of hunters, the United States will from time to time furnish gratuitously the said nation with useful domestic animals and implements of husbandry.

For the citizens of Georgia, who expected to push the Creeks off what they regarded as their state's land, the treaty was a galling federal intrusion into their internal affairs. Just two and a half years earlier, Georgians had enthusiastically ratified the U.S. Constitution, in large part because they thought a strong central government would help protect them from the Indians. Now the government they had supported seemed bent on protecting the Indians instead. In denouncing the Treaty of New York, Georgians used, for the first time in American political history, the claim of "state rights."

McGillivray and the Creeks were soon as unhappy about the treaty as the Georgians. Settlers continued crossing into Indian land, openly defying the federal government. They even intimidated federal officials sent to implement the treaty's provisions, and President Washington

Opposite page: The Treaty of New York, 1790. The original treaty has faded, but it bears the signatures of George Washington, Henry Knox, and Alexander McGillivray. Other Creek chiefs made their marks.
Above: Letter from Secretary of War Henry Knox to the commander of the U.S. fort on the St. Mary's River. This letter informed the commander of the Treaty of New York and of the special treatment to be accorded to McGillivray.

seemed incapable of restraining the fractious Georgians. Then in 1793, McGillivray died at age forty-two, leaving the Creeks to continue their struggle without a leader of his ability.

ALABAMA BECOMES PART OF THE
MISSISSIPPI TERRITORY

IN a strange and little-known international incident, a band of disgruntled Georgians who were sympathetic with the French Revolution organized an attack against Spanish Florida in the spring of 1794. Spain was then an ally of Great Britain and an enemy of France. The Georgians wanted to help the French, but the raid might also allow them to seize Spanish land for themselves as personal booty.

The new French ambassador to the United States at the time was Edmond-Charles Genêt, generally known as Citizen Genêt. When President Washington learned that Genêt was providing financial aid and even military assistance for the attack against Florida and for another by Kentuckians against New Orleans, he vigorously denounced this flagrant violation of American sovereignty. The French government eventually acceded to Washington's demand, recalling Genêt and withdrawing naval support for the invasion.

The Georgia insurgents, however, had prepared themselves for action, so they redirected their attack from Florida westward toward Creek land. They crossed the Oconee River, then the boundary between Georgia and the Creeks, and began building forts and forming their own government on the west side of the river. They claimed they were out of reach of Georgia officials since the Treaty of New York denied Georgia control over land held by the Creeks.

Angered yet again by the lawless Georgians, President Washington threatened to send federal forces if Georgia's governor did not suppress the illegal settlements. In late summer 1794, the governor finally called out the state militia and, after some defiant posturing, the adventurers eventually abandoned their forts. But Georgia's growing frustration over its challenged western claims set the stage for yet another scheme, often regarded as the greatest fraud in American history.

In late 1794, four companies of land speculators proposed to purchase a large part of Georgia's western land claims. The companies'

Map from Farris Cadle's *Georgia Land Surveying History and Law*, showing tracts of Georgia's claimed western land that the state sold in 1795 to four land companies. The sale became infamous as the Yazoo Land Fraud.

shareholders included prominent state and national officials, among them two U.S. senators and a Supreme Court justice, as well as leading American financiers. A bill authorizing the sale was presented in the Georgia legislature as an act to provide funds for paying the militia, which had just been called up to clear the illegal settlements. To secure the bill's passage, company agents bribed legislators with money, slaves, and shares of stock. After Georgia's governor signed the bill into law in January 1795, the state promptly sold approximately forty million acres of its western land claims to the four companies for about one-and-a-half cents per acre. The sale included substantial portions of what is now Mississippi and Alabama.

The Yazoo Land Fraud, as the sale came to be known, triggered furious and conflicting reactions. Georgia residents were outraged over the bribery and the cheap sale of what they saw as the state's greatest treasure. Officials in Washington were angered at the violation of the old western land claims agreement and of the Treaty of New York.

After years of controversy, a state-federal commission finally negotiated a settlement in 1802. Georgia agreed to surrender most of its western land claims, keeping only land north and west of the Chattahoochee River—what is now northwest Georgia. The agreement thus set what would become Alabama's eastern boundary. All the disputed land west of the new Georgia boundary became part of the Mississippi Territory.

The 1802 agreement also marked a major shift in federal policy toward the Indians. Rather than continuing to help the Indians remain on their land, President Thomas Jefferson's administration agreed to Georgia's demands that the federal government should work toward removing all the Indians who remained inside the state's boundaries.

The north face of the Ellicott Stone. Just a few years after being set as part of the 31st parallel survey, the stone would become the benchmark for surveying the southern half of Alabama. It is one of the smallest, oldest, and most important landmarks in Alabama.

Meanwhile, the United States and Spain had resolved their dispute over the northern boundary of Florida. Ten months after Georgia's passage of the Yazoo sale act, in the 1795 Treaty of San Lorenzo (Pinckney's Treaty), the Spanish accepted America's claim of the 31st parallel, today's boundary between Alabama and the Florida panhandle. Since Mobile Bay was south of the 31st parallel, Mobile and the Bay area remained part of Spanish Florida.

The Treaty of San Lorenzo provided for a survey commission with representatives of both nations to mark the new boundary. To lead the American team, President Washington appointed Andrew Ellicott, who at the time was completing the survey of the new town of

Washington, D.C. In April 1798, Ellicott began surveying the 31st parallel, starting at the Mississippi River and working his way eastward.

The astronomical instruments Ellicott needed were so bulky and cumbersome that he secured a schooner to carry them along the coast and sail up rivers to meet the survey crews at crossing points. Ellicott would unload the instruments and at night track stars and planets, taking repeated sightings to fix the location of the 31st parallel as closely as possible. The survey team would then set an eastward line based on his astronomical observations, cut trees to mark the boundary, and build fire mounds at intervals to try to help keep the line straight. A boundary stone planted by Ellicott still stands north of Mobile just off Highway 43, inscribed in Spanish on one side and English on the other.

In 1798, as Ellicott began his survey, Congress created the Mississippi Territory to provide a system of government administration for the land Spain had ceded. In 1804, the land surrendered by Georgia was added to the Spanish cession, and the new territory grew to include most of the present-day states of Alabama and Mississippi. Natchez, then the largest town in the Mississippi Territory, became the territorial capital.

SETTLING THE MISSISSIPPI TERRITORY

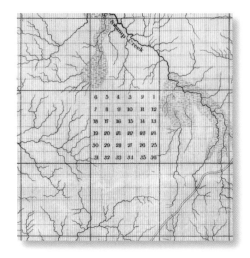

Detail from an 1818 map of the southern Mississippi Territory by John Gardiner. This detail shows nine townships created by the land survey, each six miles by six miles, located along the Alabama River, southeast of Cahawba. The center square shows the further division of a township into thirty-six sections of six hundred forty acres each.

THE only part of Alabama then occupied by American settlers was a small area north of Mobile above the 31st parallel, known as the Tombigbee settlements. All the rest was still Indian land. In 1800, the governor of the Mississippi Territory established Washington County to provide a local government for the area, though the new county, which ran from the Pearl River in present-day Mississippi eastward to the Chattahoochee River, was larger than some states and included a substantial area still under Indian control. Eventually, sixteen counties in Mississippi and twenty-nine in Alabama would be formed from Washington County.

In the early 1790s, the Spanish had built Fort San Esteban on the Tombigbee River to strengthen their presence in the area. After Ellicott determined that the fort was north of the 31st parallel, the Spanish surrendered it to the Americans in 1799. Fort San Esteban became the American Fort St. Stephens, and in 1803, the U.S. government set up a trading house for the Choctaw Indians at the site. St. Stephens soon became the most important town in the southeast part of the Mississippi Territory.

The sale of federal land in a new territory followed procedures established by the U.S. Land Ordinance of 1785. After an Indian cession,

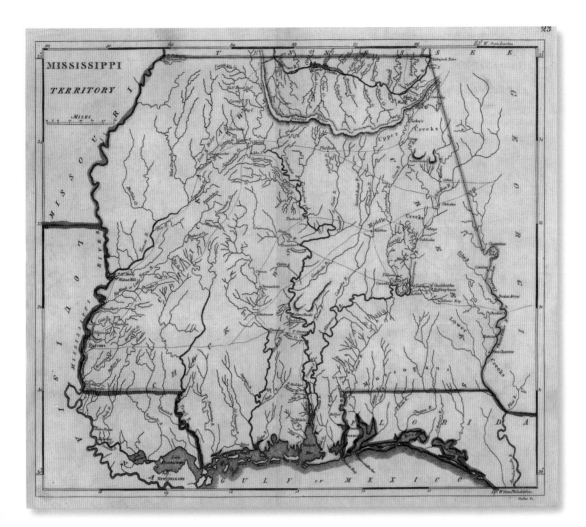

preexisting claims were resolved first, and then the land was surveyed. The surveys divided the land into squares of six miles on each side, called *townships*, which were further divided into thirty-six *sections* of one square mile, or six hundred forty acres, each.

By the time Alabama land was opened for sale, Congress had reduced the minimum purchase size from a full section to a quarter section, one hundred sixty acres. Land sales for a newly opened tract began with an auction so that buyers would have to compete for the best land. After the auction, all remaining parcels could be purchased by the first person to pay the set price of $2 an acre, later reduced to $1.25, to be paid over four years.

The practice of opening land sales with an auction meant that wealthy people and speculators usually got in first, buying the best parcels at prices sometimes far above the minimum. But the Mississippi Territory was so vast there was plenty of land for less wealthy settlers as well. They could find a place they liked and build a cabin without paying anything, living off the public domain by hunting, fishing,

Mathew Carey map of Mississippi Territory. By the time this map was prepared in 1814, the United States had seized the Gulf Coast west of the Perdido River from Spain. The map shows St. Stephens, the future territorial capital, as F. Stevens. Note also the accentuation of the ridgeline separating the Tennessee River watershed from the southern three quarters of Alabama.

and growing vegetables. Their hogs and cattle could range freely and feed on the forest mast. These "squatters" were subject to losing their farms if someone bought the land they lived on, but there was much more untaken land to which they could move. A federal policy called "preemption" allowed squatters, if they could afford it, to buy the plot they had settled on before it was sold to another purchaser.

The effects of federal land-sale policies helped shape Alabama history in an important way. Wealthy planters usually purchased the best river-bottom land, and later, land in the Black Belt, where the soil was excellent for growing cotton. Poorer people usually settled in places no one wanted to buy, such as the hill country, the sandy Wiregrass, or areas that were hard to reach. From the first days of Alabama's territorial life, geographic differences also entailed social and cultural differences.

In the Tombigbee settlements, the resolution of prior claims was among the most complex anywhere in the United States. Without access to many of the original records, territorial officials had to reconcile claims based on Indian sales and cessions, and on old English and Spanish land grants.

One of the federal land commissioners was Ephraim Kirby, a Revolutionary War veteran and a distinguished judge from Connecticut. For Kirby, the chaos and disorder of the area—and many of the people in it—were an abomination. Settlers there had come from a wide variety of places and backgrounds and had lived for years without the civilizing influences of any meaningful legal, religious, or social institutions. In an 1804 letter to President Jefferson, Kirby complained bitterly about the horrible people he dealt with:

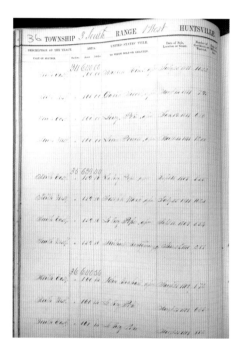

Page from the tract book recording the first land sales in north Alabama. This page shows Leroy Pope purchasing six of the twelve quarter sections stretching across what would become the new town of Huntsville.

The present inhabitants (with few exceptions) are illiterate, wild and savage, of depraved morals, unworthy of public confidence or private esteem; litigious, disunited, and knowing each other, universally distrustful of each other.

Because claims in the Tombigbee settlements took so long to resolve, land sales there proceeded slowly, and a new tract of land north of the Tennessee River began attracting greater interest. Both Cherokees and Chickasaws claimed large portions of North Alabama as hunting ground, but neither tribe had substantial settlements there. In 1805 and 1806, the two tribes ceded a tract between and on the outer limits of their claims to the United States.

Even before the treaties of cession were signed, squatters from Tennessee had begun moving onto the land. By 1805, for instance, John Hunt had built a cabin at the Big Spring in what is now Huntsville. His experience illustrates how federal land policies worked. When the newly surveyed lots were finally offered for sale in 1809, Leroy Pope, a wealthy planter from Georgia, bought the land Hunt had settled on, plus other lots around it. Hunt was compelled to move on and leave his cabin behind.

Pope and Hunt were not alone in finding the area attractive. By December 1808, even before land sales began, approximately five thousand people had moved into the newly ceded tract. The numbers were large enough to warrant the creation of Alabama's second county, called Madison in honor of the man just elected president but not yet inaugurated, James Madison.

THE FEDERAL ROAD AND MORE INCURSIONS

In 1803, the United States bought the colony of Louisiana from the French, who had recovered it from Spain in a treaty three years earlier. The Louisiana Purchase encompassed a massive expanse of land west of the Mississippi River, from the Gulf of Mexico to the Rocky Mountains. It also included the city of New Orleans, and gave the United States full control of the Mississippi River. Unrestricted American access to the Gulf of Mexico greatly increased settlement interest and land prices in the Mississippi River Valley.

With New Orleans now an American city, President Jefferson wanted to build a postal road connecting it to Washington. The most direct route ran southwest from Washington parallel to the Atlantic Coast, and then turned west in Georgia across Creek land. According to one proponent in 1805, this route was hundreds of miles shorter than the alternative Natchez Trace.

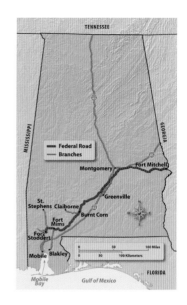

In 1805, President Jefferson invited a group of Creek chiefs to Washington for treaty discussions. Jefferson's administration had begun a policy of encouraging Indian debt, which it expected to leverage into land cessions as repayment. With the deerskin trade continuing to decline, the Creeks, as planned, fell deeply into debt. In the Washington Treaty of 1805, they ceded additional land in Georgia in return for money to help them repay their debts and purchase more trade goods.

The Creeks also agreed in the treaty to Jefferson's request for the postal path across their land. In late 1806, contractors for the U.S. Postal Department began to cut a four-foot-wide horse path, basically following old Indian trails. The path crossed so many streams, rivers, and bogs, however, that it was often difficult to use, and important mail continued for years to be sent by the Natchez Trace.

Top: Map of the Federal Road. This modern map of the Federal Road shows its path laid over Interstate Highways 85 and 65. **Above:** Remnant of the Federal Road in Lee County. A few unaltered sections of the Federal Road still exist, often characterized by steep banks rising above a roadbed pounded down by the passage of thousands of wheels, hoofs, and human feet.

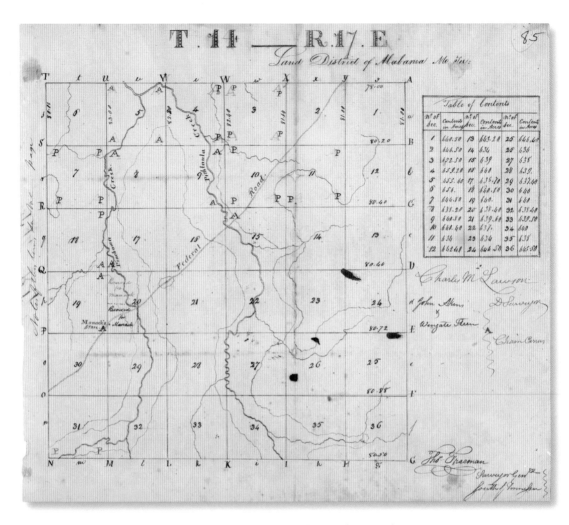

Survey of Township 14, Range 17E of the Land District of Alabama in the Mississippi Territory. This survey of land near present-day Pintlala, in western Montgomery County, shows the Federal Road, as well as details of the thirty-six sections. Also noted in sections 19 and 20 are the reserves and store of Sam Monac (or Monack), a Creek who operated a store and inn on the Federal Road.

In 1811, as the threat of war with Great Britain grew, Congress authorized widening the path to sixteen feet so it could be used by military wagons. Since army engineers, rather than postal contractors, managed this construction, the result was a more usable road, though one that was still difficult, especially during times of high water.

With its widening, the postal path became the Federal Road, and hundreds, then thousands, of settlers began using it each year. Travelers first had to secure passports signed by the governor of Georgia granting them permission to pass through Creek lands. The Creeks were allowed to build inns and taverns along the road as a new source of revenue.

The 1805 Treaty was a divisive issue among the Creeks, and many Upper Creek towns opposed it. When Americans widened the path in 1811 without Creek approval, most Creeks resented the action. As more Americans crossed though their territory, Creek anger increased. An influential Lower Creek chief, William McIntosh, enriched himself personally by assisting the Americans, which added to the friction inside the Creek nation.

Left: William McIntosh, painted from life by Joseph and Nathan Negus in 1821. McIntosh, a prominent Lower Creek leader, worked with the Americans in securing permission for the Federal Road and later fought against the Red Sticks in the Creek War. Above: Benjamin Hawkins, appointed in 1796 to be Principal Temporary Agent for Indian Affairs South of the Ohio River. Born in North Carolina, Hawkins studied at what became Princeton University and joined George Washington's staff as a translator during the American Revolution. He was a member of the U.S. Senate from North Carolina during the early 1790s, taking a special interest in Indian affairs.

During these years, Benjamin Hawkins was the U.S. agent to the Creeks. Hawkins had been appointed by President Washington to help implement the policies of the Treaty of New York intended to bring the Creeks "to a greater degree of civilization." He pursued this mission with vigor for twenty years, encouraging Creeks and other southeastern Indians to take up American-style farming, herding, and domestic practices.

Hawkins was also a key figure in negotiating and implementing Indian treaties and in the construction of the Federal Road. He lived among the Creeks, spoke their language, and traveled frequently through the Creek Nation, as it came to be called. He encouraged the development of the Creek National Council as the governing body for the Creeks—trying to establish a structure of national governance for a people whose traditional center of authority had always been their town, their talwa.

Creek Indian, by Lukas Vischer, 1824. Vischer, an artist and collector from Basil, Switzerland, painted this and several other watercolors from life during part of his travels in the southeast United States.

CREEK CULTURE IN CRISIS

EUROPEAN traders lived among the Creeks for more than a hundred years, as did other outsiders, such as fugitive slaves who escaped from owners in the United States or Florida. During these years, many Creeks adopted tools, practices, and even the lifestyle of the Americans. Some Creeks even established plantations and used enslaved workers. Over the course of many decades, intermarriage between Indians, whites, and blacks created a more complex and fluid culture than had existed earlier for the Creeks, or than existed at the time in the United States.

The story of Robert Grierson and his family illustrates some of the changes that were taking place in Creek culture. Grierson was a Scottish trader who had been a loyalist during the American Revolution, and he took refuge among the Creeks. He established a trading house and built a home at the Creek town of Hillabee near the present-day Clay/Tallapoosa county line. There, he took as his wife a woman named Sinnugee, who was of Indian, Spanish, and possibly African ancestry.

Grierson and Sinnugee had eight children, who variously took spouses of white, black, and mixed Indian ancestries. Grierson lived on his own farm outside the town, raising cattle and later using slaves to grow cotton—becoming one of the wealthiest men in the area. When President Washington's representative Marinus Willett came to Alabama in 1790, he first met the Creek leader Alexander McGillivray at Grierson's house.

These kinds of lifestyle changes brought new divisions to the Creek world and accentuated old ones. Children of European and American parents, like those of Grierson, tended to follow naturally the way of life Benjamin Hawkins sought to promote. A number of prominent Creeks moved to unoccupied land in southwestern Alabama to establish plantations away from their talwas. They lived very much like their American neighbors in the Tombigbee settlements.

These new ways, however, clashed fundamentally with many core traditions of Creek society. In the Creek talwa, the welfare of the community and clan were dominant concerns, not the interests of private individuals. The people of the talwa owned the land in common. And the mother's family, not the father's, controlled the children and the resources.

American ways also clashed with traditional Creek roles for men and women. In Creek culture, men hunted and provided security. Women ran the household and cooked the food, and they also planted and tended the gardens. Life following a plow seemed humiliating and degrading to most Creek warriors because cultivating plants had always been women's work. Creek men derided plows as "horse traps," demeaning to the noble horse.

By the early 1800s, the Creeks were in economic, social, and spiritual turmoil. They still wanted the goods to which they had become accustomed, but traders wanted money in exchange, not deerskins. Creek debts continued to mount, along with settlement pressure on their borders. Excessive alcohol consumption, often encouraged by unscrupulous traders, made problems worse. The Creeks' homeland and their way of life both seemed to be under assault.

"Tens-kwau-ta-waw, The Prophet," from *History of the Indian Tribes of North America* by Thomas McKenney and James Hall, 1836. Beginning in 1805, Tenskwatawa experienced a series of visions that led him to reject encroaching white settlers as "children of the Evil Spirit."

Amid the despair and resentment, a new spiritual movement emerged, spreading southward into Creek country from tribes to the north. Its leaders were two Shawnees, Tecumseh and his brother, The Prophet. Their parents appear to have lived for a while in Alabama, and their mother may have been part Creek. In 1811, Tecumseh traveled to Alabama to try to win the Creeks to his views, and he found a ready audience.

The two men spoke of cleansing, purification, and a return to traditional Indian ways. The movement they led resembled those of people in other places colonized by Europeans, from Africa across the Middle East to the Far East. In all these lands, native groups eventually rose up in resistance, and one form of resistance was always a kind of fundamentalism, an aggressive reassertion of ancient traditions.

Tecumseh and The Prophet rejected the poverty and humiliation that Indians endured. They urged fellow Indians to cast off the trappings of European and American culture and to cast out the people who had brought those evils to the Indian world. Their supporters among the Creeks came to be called Red Sticks, referring to traditional Creek war clubs.

As Creek discontent grew, some of the more aggressive Red Stick warriors began to attack white settlements and travelers on the Federal Road. In response, Benjamin Hawkins pressured the Creek National Council to discipline the renegades. When the Council sent warriors to execute members of a Red Stick band who had killed white settlers, Red Stick supporters were angered by the Council's cooperation with the Americans. The Council's actions also violated the traditional rights of the talwas to discipline their own members. As tensions mounted inside the Creek Nation, Red Stick bands began attacking supporters of the National Council.

The conflict escalated into a Creek civil war, dividing neighbors and families. As cycles of reprisal grew more violent, some National Council supporters fled to Georgia, while others sought refuge in the new plantations in southwestern Alabama. In broad terms, the Red Sticks were strongest among the Upper Creeks, while the Lower Creeks tended to support the National Council. But the divisions were not clean and precise, and supporters of both sides lived in both areas.

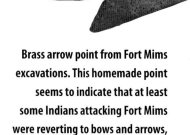

Brass arrow point from Fort Mims excavations. This homemade point seems to indicate that at least some Indians attacking Fort Mims were reverting to bows and arrows, though Creeks had used muskets by then for over a century.

THE CREEK WAR

THE simultaneous outbreak of civil war among the Creeks and the War of 1812 between the United States and Great Britain was not a coincidence. Widening the Federal Road had been an American defensive precaution for supporting New Orleans in the event of war with Britain. The widened road brought new encroachments into Creek land, which increased Creek resentment. At the same time, the prospect of possible help from Britain emboldened the Red Sticks.

Some Americans remembered British efforts to use Indians against them in the American Revolution and feared renewed Indian violence. Other Americans welcomed the prospect of a war with the Creeks as an opportunity to seize still more of their land.

This volatile mix exploded in the summer of 1813. A Red Stick trading party traveled to Pensacola to buy arms and supplies from the Spanish, who were then allies of the British. As the Red Sticks returned home, a unit of the Mississippi territorial militia attacked them on Indian land at Burnt Corn Creek, in southwestern Alabama. Neither side won the skirmish, but the Red Sticks drove off the militia and were heartened by their success.

Settlers in the area, including Creeks who were aligned with the National Council, feared that worse violence would follow. They began gathering for mutual protection in forts that were hastily being built or reinforced. One was on the farm of Samuel Mims, near the Alabama River, in what is now northern Baldwin County.

Around noon on August 30, 1813, about seven hundred Red Stick warriors attacked Fort Mims, led by William Weatherford, a nephew of Alexander McGillivray. Weatherford himself had adapted successfully to American ways and owned a plantation in south Alabama, but he also resented American abuses and intrusions onto Indian land.

The commanding officer of the militia at Fort Mims had been negligent in his duties. He had not sent out scouting patrols, set up an effective watch, or secured the fort's entrances. Inside were about four hundred people—members of the militia, families from the area, Creek supporters of the National Council, and enslaved workers from local plantations.

The fighting at Mims was vicious and lasted for hours, but at its end, the Red Sticks had killed about two hundred fifty men, women, and children and taken others captive. In the rage of battle, they mutilated the bodies of many victims. They suffered heavy losses as well, before leaving the fort aflame. Archaeologist and historian Greg Waselkov, in his excellent book about Fort Mims, notes that the Red Stick victory was "one of the greatest in the history of Native American warfare."

Above: Part of a gate hinge from Fort Mims. One failure attributed to the commanding officer at Fort Mims was not properly securing the gates. Below: Diagram of the Fort Mims site, drawn by the burial party for reporting back to Mississippi territorial officials on what they found at the remains of the fort.

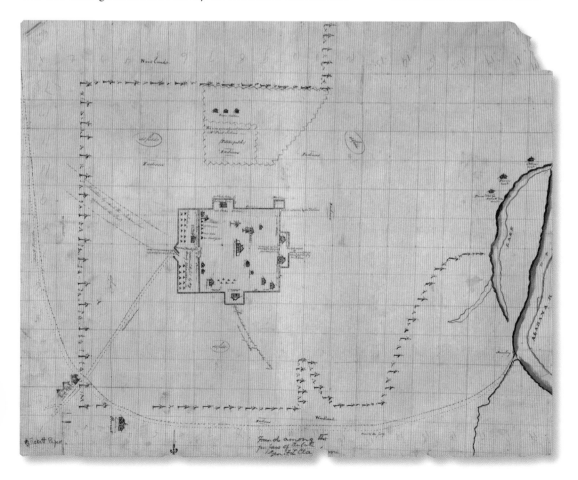

DAVID CROCKETT

I am happy to acknowledge This to be this only correct likeness that has been Taken of me. David Crockett

Top: David Crockett. The famed frontiersman served with the Tennessee Militia in the Creek War and later described his experiences in his autobiography. Above: Major Benjamin Smoot of the Mississippi Territorial Militia. At Holy Ground his unit fought in tandem with the Choctaw allies of the Americans led by Pushmataha.

In the days after the battle, Red Stick parties also attacked other forts and settlements in the area. Four decades later, William Weatherford would be romanticized and given the name Red Eagle in a popular poem by a noted Alabama writer, Alexander Meek.

News of the Fort Mims Massacre, as it was immediately called, raced across the United States as fast as personal communication could carry it. Governors in surrounding states promptly called out militia units to crush the uprising, and their troops descended almost simultaneously on the Red Sticks.

From the east, General John Floyd led the Georgia militia against Autossee, a Red Stick stronghold near present-day Shorter in Macon County. Approximately four hundred National Council Creeks fought alongside Floyd's troops. On November 29, 1813, they destroyed the town, though many of its occupants escaped. Floyd himself was wounded and withdrew his poorly supplied troops to Fort Mitchell, on the Chattahoochee River.

The Mississippi territorial militia, led by General Ferdinand Claiborne, attacked from the west. His troops were joined by Choctaws, who had long been enemies of the Creeks. On December 23, they attacked the Red Stick stronghold of Holy Ground, between present-day Montgomery and Selma. Like Floyd's forces, they also routed the Red Sticks, looted and destroyed the town, and withdrew. Alexander Meek's poem about William Weatherford describes Red Eagle riding his horse off a high bluff into the Alabama River to escape, a story that became a staple in state school textbooks for generations.

The most tenacious invaders were the Tennessee militia, in rival commands led by generals John Cocke and Andrew Jackson. Jackson's troops were accompanied by a number of Cherokees, also longtime enemies of the Creeks. On November 3, after ranging across the upper Coosa River Valley, one of Jackson's units attacked the Creek town of Tallushatchee, a site near present-day Ohatchee in Calhoun County.

David Crockett, the future congressmen and celebrity frontiersman, was part of the attacking force. His description of the battle in his autobiography conveys a sense of the war's strange viciousness. As the militia closed in on Tallushatchee, many of the Red Sticks surrendered, but Crockett saw a number of them retreating into a house. The soldiers turned toward the house, and:

We saw a squaw sitting by the door, and she placed her feet against the bow she had in her hand, and then took an arrow, and, raising her feet, she drew with all her might, and let fly at us, and she killed a man, whose name, I believe was Moore.... [H]is death so enraged us all, that she was fired on, and had at least twenty balls blown through her.... We now shot them like dogs; and then set the house on fire, and burned it up with forty-six warriors in it. I recollect seeing a boy who was shot down near the house. His arm and thigh was broken, and he was so near the burning house that the grease was stewing out of him. In this situation he was still trying to crawl along; but not a murmur escaped him, though he was only about twelve years old. So sullen is the Indian, when his dander is up, that he had sooner die than make a noise, or ask for quarter.

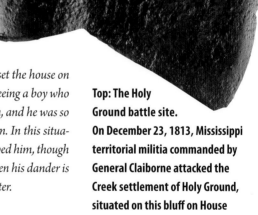

Top: The Holy Ground battle site. On December 23, 1813, Mississippi territorial militia commanded by General Claiborne attacked the Creek settlement of Holy Ground, situated on this bluff on House Creek. Above: Axe head discovered during an archaeological survey of Holy Ground. It could have been used both as a tool and a weapon.

Residents of the Creek town of Hillabee, the home of Robert Grierson, sent word to Jackson of their wish to surrender. General Cocke, whose movements were not coordinated with Jackson's, attacked the town, killing about seventy warriors and capturing many others. Conflicts between Jackson and Cocke, supply problems, and expiring militia terms hamstrung the Tennesseans' efforts through late 1813, but Jackson renewed the attack in mid-January.

By that time, a remnant of about one thousand Red Stick Warriors had gathered inside a great loop of the Tallapoosa River, known by the

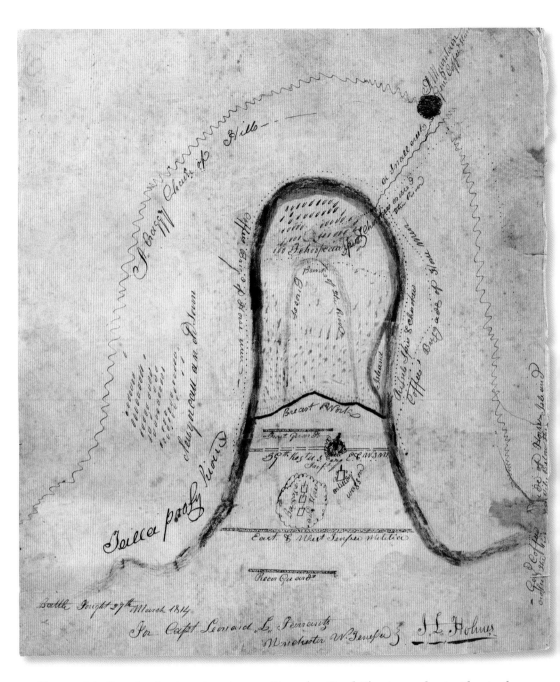

Diagram of the Horseshoe Bend battleground, drawn by J. L. Holmes. The village of Neuyorcau is noted on the left of the bend.

Americans as Horseshoe Bend. The river and a stout barricade across the neck of the peninsula served as the Red Sticks' defensive works. Jackson moved against the Red Sticks with a force of more than three thousand three hundred U.S. Army soldiers, Tennessee militia, and Indian allies.

Earlier raiders had burned the nearby Creek village of Neuyorcau, which had been named for the now meaningless treaty signed at New York twenty-four years earlier. On March 27, 1814, part of Jackson's forces charged the barricade, while General John Coffee led other troops and Indian allies across the river at the tip of the bend. Attacked on two fronts, heavily out-armed and outnumbered, the Creeks were overwhelmed and massacred. The next day, Jackson wrote to his wife that not more than twenty escaped. Among these, however, was the remarkable warrior Menawa, who suffered multiple wounds, but survived and continued to serve in the years afterward as a major Creek leader.

Alabama's early leaders clearly recognized Horseshoe Bend and the Creek War as a turning point in the state's history. Two years after the battle, the Mississippi territorial legislature would name Montgomery County in honor of Lemuel Montgomery, one of the first American soldiers killed in the attack at Horseshoe Bend. In 1819, the new state of Alabama named Jackson County for Andrew Jackson. And in 1841, the state legislature named Coffee County for John Coffee.

The slaughter at Horseshoe Bend did not end the violence. Jackson's troops swept down the Tallapoosa River Valley, destroying other Creek towns, farms, and buildings—leaving behind a path of ruin and desolation. Many Creek survivors, having lost their homes and food supplies, wandered starving in the forests.

Above: General John Coffee. Coffee was a commander under General Jackson at Horseshoe Bend, and his troops, which included Indian allies, crossed the Tallapoosa River to attack the Red Sticks. He later moved to Alabama and became a prominent resident of Florence. **Left: General Andrew Jackson,** painted by Ralph Earle in 1825. A print based on this portrait was widely circulated in the 1828 campaign and was the image of Jackson many Americans had in their minds when they voted for president that year.

In early August 1814, Jackson summoned surviving Creek leaders to a treaty conference at a new fort he had built on the site of old Fort Toulouse. The Creek leaders who gathered at Fort Jackson were mostly friends of the United States, members and supporters of the National Council. Some had just fought alongside Jackson against their own people. Most Red Stick leaders were either dead, under arrest, or on the run. Some who refused to surrender fled south and joined the Seminoles in Florida to continue the fight.

With the Creeks' military power broken, their leaders at Fort Jackson had virtually no leverage for bargaining. In the treaty Jackson forced them to sign, they ceded more than half of their land to the United States. What remained to the Creeks afterward was a reduced tract straddling the Chattahoochee River, inside the state of Georgia and the Mississippi Territory.

The Creek War was in many ways a part of the War of 1812. In action elsewhere, American troops seized Mobile and Mobile Bay from the Spanish in 1813, arguing that it was rightfully theirs as part of the Louisiana Purchase. The U.S. government added the area to the Mississippi Territory. To help defend the new acquisition, American troops hastily erected Fort Bowyer to guard the eastern side of the entrance to Mobile Bay (now the site of Fort Morgan).

Map of the entrance to Mobile Bay (detail). This coastal survey was ordered by General James Wilkinson after the United States took control from the Spanish. Completed in April, 1813, the map, by Joseph Kennedy, shows the location of Fort Bowyer on Mobile Point, on the eastern side of the entrance to the bay.

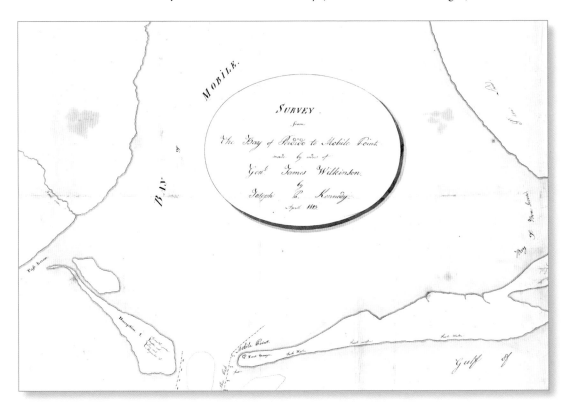

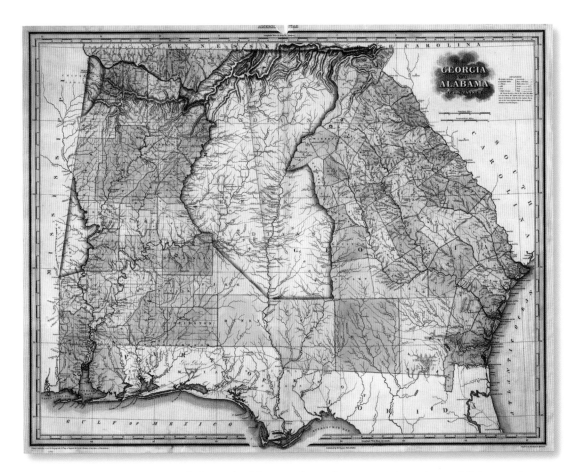

In September 1814, the British dispatched four naval vessels to attack Fort Bowyer. Their plan was to take Mobile and then march overland to attack New Orleans, but the Americans' gritty defense cost the British one ship and caused them to withdraw. Rather than renew the attack, the British decided instead to assault New Orleans directly.

Andrew Jackson, fresh from his conquest of the Red Sticks, hurried to New Orleans to defend the city. His stunning, lopsided defeat of seasoned British forces there followed on the heels of his stunning, lopsided defeat of the Red Sticks in Alabama, and Jackson instantly became an American hero. The two victories set him on route to the presidency, and to a new kind of politics that would change the character of American government.

The land ceded by the Creeks in 1814 totaled more than twenty million acres. Most of the Creeks who lived on that land were driven, often impoverished and dispirited, into the remaining Creek reserve. The Creek cession, combined with smaller tracts ceded in 1816 by the Cherokees, Chickasaws, and Choctaws, would soon be surveyed and opened for new settlement as part of the Mississippi Territory. And within just a few years, this former land of Indians would make up a substantial part of the new state of Alabama.

An 1823 map of Alabama and Georgia, published by H. S. Tanner in 1823. This map shows the remaining Creek-Cherokee land inside Alabama and Georgia nine years after the Treaty of Fort Jackson. A notable feature of the Creek cession in 1814 was the large strip running the full length of the Florida boundary, designed to cut the Creeks off from further Spanish assistance.

CHAPTER 3

COTTON STATE

1814 to 1861

HE LAND CEDED BY ALABAMA INDIANS *was opened for settlement just as textile mills of the Industrial Revolution called for ever more cotton. Supplying cotton would make Alabama one of the wealthiest areas in the United States. In just over two generations, the state grew from a rough frontier into a society of almost a million people, with towns, colleges, churches, mills, riverboats, and railroads.*

This prosperity, however, was based on slavery, which became an integral part of Alabama's way of life. Most white Alabamians were not slaveholders, but they generally accepted slavery and its benefits. They did not, however, readily accept the political leadership of slave owners. Clashes between yeoman farmers and planters marked Alabama politics from the dawn of statehood to secession.

ALABAMA FEVER

MANY scholars believe the Industrial Revolution was the most important historical development since the Agricultural Revolution, when civilizations based on farming first emerged. With the new machines of the Industrial Revolution, one person might produce more than a hundred people could by hand. In 1810, the U.S. Census Office estimated the productivity increase of the cotton gin at a thousand to one. The Industrial Revolution and the creation of machines that multiplied human productivity laid the foundations of our world today.

The dominant industry of the early Industrial Revolution was textiles. By the late 1700s, British inventors were building machines that could rapidly spin cotton fiber into thread, which was wound onto racks of whirling spindles. New power looms wove the thread into cloth that merchant companies sold in markets around the world.

Scene of loading cotton on the Alabama River, from *Ballou's Pictorial Drawing-Room Companion,* **November 28, 1857.**

As the 1800s began, both Great Britain and New England had the skills, systems, factories, and finances for a burgeoning textile industry that would ultimately employ hundreds of thousands of workers. But first, they had to have the cotton. Following the defeat of Napoleon in June 1815, the price of cotton was particularly high, as British manufacturers strained to satisfy pent-up demand that had been deferred during the long years of warfare.

For American planters, the recently ceded Indian tracts of the Mississippi Territory offered fertile new land for growing cotton. In states along the Atlantic Coast, much of the soil was "farmed out," depleted by years of production without renewal. As new land in Alabama was opened for settlement, planters from the older states looked southwestward to start anew, and to make their fortunes.

The hunger for this new land was so great that it became known as "Alabama fever." In 1817, a North Carolina planter, James Graham, complained to a friend about how many people were leaving his state: "The Alabama Feaver [*sic*] rages here with great violence and has carried off vast numbers of our citizens. . . ." John Campbell, one of the new settlers, wrote to a relative that same year about the Huntsville area:

The farmers here in the course of 3 or 4 years acquired immense estates by raising cotton. Three or four years ago lands could be purchased here for $4 or $5 an acre that are now selling for $25 and $30. . . . The town is full of gentlemen from Virginia, Kentucky and the Carolinas who like ourselves have been exploring the country [Tennessee Valley]. . . . It is an elegant cotton country.

Planters brought their enslaved workers with them, as well as all their personal treasures they could carry. In addition, traders purchased other enslaved people away from their families, friends, and homes in older states like Maryland and Virginia. The slaves were marched in coffles for hundreds of miles, the men usually chained together, and sold again to clear fields and grow cotton in Alabama. The opening of Alabama for settlement at a time of high cotton prices launched a major extension of slavery into the new states of the interior.

But numerous though the planters and slaves were, they were not the majority of the immigrants to Alabama. Most settlers were what historians call *yeoman farmers*, people who lived primarily by the work of their own hands. They hunted, herded, made, grew, and traded for almost everything they had. Especially in Alabama's early years, few yeoman farmers owned slaves.

Bold spirits from the mid-Atlantic and New England states also joined the migration, often as merchants, professional people, and land speculators. The non-Indian population of what would become Alabama increased by more than 1,300 percent between 1810 and

Above: A squatter or "cracker," as drawn by Captain Basil Hall during an 1828 trip through Georgia and Alabama. Hall wrote that squatters are "men who set themselves down on any piece of vacant land that suits their fancy, till warned off by the legal proprietor. The man sketched here lived, I was assured, almost entirely by hunting and shooting." Opposite page: A digitally restored copy of the 1818 John Melish map of Alabama. This rare map was prepared after Alabama became a territory, but before statehood—and before the adjustment of the southern part of the western border to give Mississippi all of Pascagoula Bay. The rectilinear grid spreading across the territory shows the progress of land surveys, then still underway.

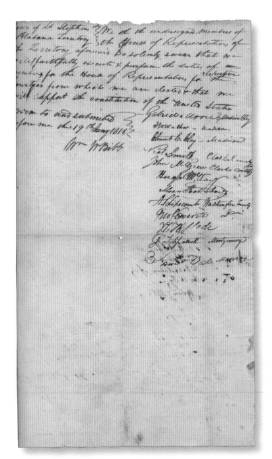

1820, from 9,046 to 127,901 people. Albert Pickett, who arrived from North Carolina during that time, later described the migrant rush:

The flood-gates of Virginia, the two Carolinas, Tennessee, Kentucky and Georgia were now hoisted and mighty streams of immigration poured through them, spreading over the whole territory of Alabama. The axe resounded from side to side, and from corner to corner. The stately and magnificent forests fell. Log cabins sprang, as if by magic, into sight. Never before or since, has a country been so rapidly peopled.

THE ALABAMA TERRITORY

As its population grew and the Mississippi Territory advanced toward statehood, Congress had to decide whether and how the territory might be divided. Because southern members of the U.S. Senate wanted to keep a balance between slave and free states, they insisted on a division of the territory. Two new slave states from the Mississippi Territory would balance the new free states of Indiana and Illinois, then in the process of admission. After complex maneuvering, Congress divided the territory into eastern and western portions.

Signatures confirming oaths taken by Alabama's first legislators at St. Stephens. Among the distinguished signers are Sam Dale, a hero of the Creek War, and John Williams Walker, who would chair Alabama's constitutional convention in 1819.

On March 1, 1817, President James Madison signed an act sponsored by Senator Charles Tait of Georgia, launching the statehood process for Mississippi, the older and more heavily settled half of the territory. Two days later, on his last full day in office, Madison signed an act to create the Alabama Territory from what remained after Mississippi's separation. The act designated St. Stephens as the new territory's capital.

On September 25, 1817, President Madison's successor, James Monroe, appointed Charles Tait's former colleague in the U.S. Senate, William Wyatt Bibb, to be the Alabama Territory's governor. In 1816, Bibb had conceded his seat as one of Georgia's U.S. senators because of public resentment at home over his vote in favor of a large congressional pay increase. Bibb then moved to what would become Autauga County, Alabama, built a plantation, and started a new career as territorial governor in this more congenial political climate.

The establishment of Alabama Territory was to take effect when Mississippi had "formed a constitution and state government." It remains unclear today whether the territory's official beginning date was August 15, when the Mississippi convention formally adopted its new constitution; or September 25, when President Monroe acted on that information to appoint Bibb as governor for Alabama; or October 6, when the new government elected under the Mississippi constitution formally convened; or even December 10, when Congress officially recognized Mississippi's statehood. Governor Bibb did not call the Alabama territorial legislature into session until after Mississippi's formal admission into the Union in December.

Alabama's first legislature that gathered at St. Stephens in January 1818 was composed of the representatives from Alabama who had served in the old Mississippi territorial legislature. In a remarkably productive session, they passed bills to create more counties; provide for roads, bridges, and ferries; expand the militia; charter corporations and schools; and authorize a census to document the population required for statehood.

THE BIRTH OF A STATE

THE second session of the territorial legislature met at St. Stephens in November 1818. Since the census returns showed that Alabama's population was large enough for statehood, legislators formally petitioned Congress for admission to the Union. They also fixed districts for delegate elections to a constitutional convention.

The location of the state's future capital was one of the assembly's most divisive issues. Governor Bibb proposed a new town at the junction of the Cahawba and Alabama rivers, which he felt was a central location. Tennessee Valley delegates joined their west Alabama colleagues in urging Tuscaloosa. An early road from Tuscaloosa to Huntsville made the former far more accessible than Cahawba for people from north Alabama.

Bibb won the battle, and the capital was located at Cahawba. The assembly designated Huntsville as the temporary capital until the new Cahawba state house was ready for use. In 1826, however, a renewed campaign for relocation—along with a flood and a yellow fever outbreak at Cahawba—would eventually persuade legislators to move the capital to Tuscaloosa.

Alabama's friend in Congress, Senator Charles Tait, sponsored the bill allowing the Alabama Territory to proceed to statehood, and President Monroe signed it into law on March 2, 1819. The act called for an election in May of forty-four delegates who would meet in Huntsville in July to draw up a state constitution.

Gravesite of Caroline Brown and her infant daughter. Caroline was the daughter of Judge William and Temperance Fitts Crawford. Little is left at St. Stephens today except for the archaeological remains of old buildings and graves. This stone reads in part: "All who knew thee loved thee—and the tears of the stranger fell on thy grave."

The document those delegates drafted was the most liberal state constitution in the Union at the time. It provided for universal white adult male suffrage without any property or tax qualifications. It gave the greatest power to the legislature, thought to be the most democratic arm of government. And it required annual elections for members of the state House of Representatives to ensure they would be truly responsive to the people. It also included extensive guarantees of personal freedom, such as freedom of religion and speech, the right of due process, and protection from imprisonment for debt.

In addition, the constitution included provisions specifically protecting rights of slaveholders, though it allowed the general assembly to enact laws "to oblige the owners of slaves to treat them with humanity." The constitution's Declaration of Rights section rephrased the words written forty-three years earlier in the nation's Declaration of Independence about "all men" being "created equal." It declared instead "that all freemen, when they form a social compact, are equal in rights." A new social order was being established in Alabama consciously incorporating racial slavery on land that less than a

Above: Cahawba Capitol cupola. The only surviving part of Alabama's first Capitol is the cupola, now on the Lowndesboro CME church. Below: Key to the Capitol at Cahawba. The structure was later used as the courthouse for Dallas County, but it fell into disuse after the county seat was moved to Selma in 1866. Right: Map of the four sections where Governor Bibb located the new state capital at Cahawba. The small arch along the Alabama River shows the remains of old Indian walls and mounds, near which Alabama's first Capitol was built.

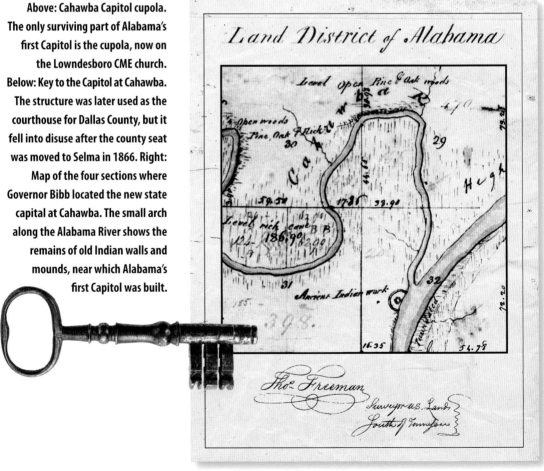

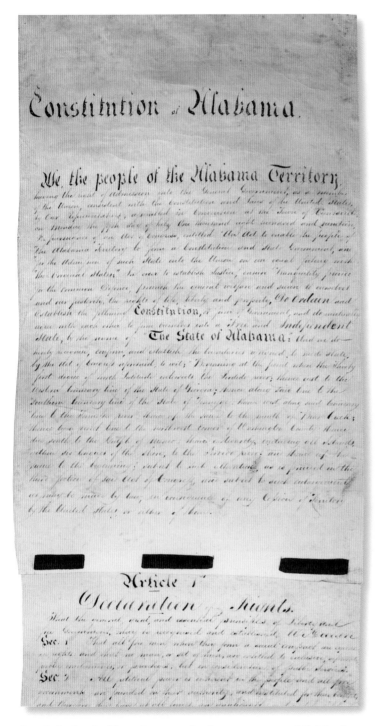

decade before had been home to the far more open and fluid culture of the Indians.

The Huntsville delegates completed their work in less than four weeks. On August 2, they signed the constitution and sent it to Washington for review by Congress. They also set September 20 and 21 for the first state elections. In those elections, Alabama voters rewarded

William Wyatt Bibb's achievements as territorial governor by electing him the first state governor.

Less than three months after the elections, Congress passed a resolution accepting Alabama's constitution. The resolution declared it to be "republican, and in conformity to the principles of the articles of compact between the original states and the people." When President Monroe signed the resolution on December 14, 1819, Alabama became the twenty-second state admitted to the Union.

POLITICS IN A NEW DEMOCRACY

Two prominent Georgians, Charles Tait and William Wyatt Bibb, smoothed the path to Alabama's statehood. After statehood was secured, Tait followed Bibb in moving to Alabama, where he was appointed the state's first federal judge. Both men were part of an informal network of former Georgia planters who moved to Alabama in these early years and whose connections, education, and wealth made them the new state's natural leaders.

Leroy Pope, who had purchased much of the land that would become Huntsville, was a member of this group. So was Pope's son-in-law, John Williams Walker, who chaired the 1819 constitutional convention and became the state's first U.S. senator. Thomas Bibb, the first president of the state senate and Alabama's second governor, was also a former Georgia planter.

All these men had lived in the valley of Georgia's Broad River, a tributary of the Savannah northwest of Augusta. Just after the American Revolution, a close-knit group of Virginia families had settled there, intending to grow tobacco and replicate life in Virginia. In the mid-1790s, they began switching from tobacco to cotton, and they thrived. By the 1810s, however, after years of farming had depleted their soil's fertility, many of these Georgians caught Alabama fever. In early land sales, Broad River planters acquired some of the best tracts available.

They also became early business leaders. Alabama's first bank, the Planters and Merchants Bank of Huntsville, was established by Leroy Pope and John Williams Walker. Its banknotes served as a principal

Top: Constitution Hall Park. Alabama's first constitutional convention met at this site. With both original and reconstructed buildings, the park today offers insight into the story of the convention and life in early Huntsville. Above: Brass measuring vessels for a half-bushel, a gallon, a quart, and a pint. The federal government provided these vessels to the new State of Alabama to ensure that Alabama conformed to national standards for measures of volume.

form of cash in the Tennessee Valley during the last part of the 1810s, before the days of a standard federal currency. In effect, the notes were promises by the bank that it would redeem them upon request for the equivalent value in gold or silver. As prices for cotton and land soared during the late 1810s, the Planters and Merchants Bank flourished.

At its first session in 1818, the Alabama territorial legislature eliminated the eight percent interest rate cap that had been in effect for loans in the Mississippi Territory as a way to attract investment and promote growth. Alabama's higher interest rates also meant that the owners of the Planters and Merchants Bank enjoyed even greater profits. In late 1819, however, as the territory completed its final steps toward statehood, the United States suffered one of those great financial crashes that periodically sweep across global markets. Prices for cotton and land plummeted. Many people who had borrowed money at high interest rates to buy land and slaves at inflated prices suddenly could not repay their loans.

When the Planters and Merchants Bank suspended the redemption of its banknotes, people who held them were stuck with worthless, or at least severely depreciated, currency. The legislature aided the bank by accepting its notes as payment for taxes, but that concession meant that the state's treasury was quickly filled with paper currency worth far less than the face value.

As the Alabama economy plummeted, public resentment against the bank surged. Because the bank owners and the politicians who had authorized and assisted the bank were members of the Broad River group, opponents denounced them as the villains of the financial debacle. Men who had been the state's early leaders were now seen as self-serving manipulators.

Resentment of the "Georgia Aristocracy," as opponents began calling the group, was not entirely new. After Leroy Pope had purchased the land where John Hunt squatted, he proposed naming the new town he founded at the site Twickenham, after a fashionable London suburb. But Madison County's representatives to the Mississippi territorial legislature reflected the views of their yeoman-farmer constituents. They prevailed upon the legislature to name the town Huntsville in honor of the area's first settler—and the man whom Pope had forced off the site of the town.

In the early 1820s, political opposition to the Georgians coalesced behind Israel Pickens. A former North Carolina congressman who also had contracted Alabama fever, Pickens proposed setting up a new bank that would be owned by the state. Its profits would benefit everyone, not just a small clique of influential private owners. Fueled by resentment against the Georgia aristocracy, Pickens's campaign swelled into a cause that stirred the passions of his supporters, and he won election as governor in 1821.

Wooden leg of Judge Charles Tait. As a young man in Georgia, Tait lost his leg in an injury while hauling tobacco to market. He relied on a wooden leg for the rest of his life— from his years in the U.S. Senate to his service as Alabama's first federal district judge.

Top: Banknote of the Planters and Merchants Bank of Huntsville. This note for one dollar was signed by Leroy Pope and printed in 1824, after the bank resumed issuing banknotes. Above: Stamp with the seal of the Planters and Merchants Bank. The objects on the seal illustrate the economic development interests of the time—from the plow at the bottom to the wagon and flatboat for transporting cotton to market.

The banking fight opened the door to a new, more strident style of politics in Alabama. William B. Long, editor of the Huntsville *Democrat,* angrily denounced the Broad River planters as the "royal party" and fought to head off any sign of its political revival. One of his major causes was an effort to impeach Alabama Supreme Court judges because of a ruling that had been unfavorable to debtors.

Historian J. Mills Thornton has described the special political dynamics that emerged in Alabama in these years. According to Thornton, sharply differing worldviews held by yeoman farmers and planters created a political divide that shaped Alabama life for the entire antebellum period and beyond.

Both groups happily embraced America's role as a new republic of liberty, but their visions for the republic differed fundamentally. For the yeoman farmers, the driving concern was maintaining their personal independence, remaining free from control by anyone else. Virtually every other country in the world at the time was ruled by some form of monarchy, and the new Americans were keenly conscious of their country as an innovation. The ancestors of most Alabama yeoman farmers had lived under some form of aristocratic control from time immemorial. The fear that some new group might gain too much power and establish an aristocracy in America was very real to them.

Although Alabama's yeoman farmers were not subordinate to anyone, they were also not entirely independent. Most were members of small communities in which people depended on each other for swapping goods, collaborating on big projects, and even ensuring their common security. But exchanges inside these communities were voluntary actions between equals, based on a system of mutuality. Any special privileges enjoyed by an elite few threatened the fine balance of equality by which these communities functioned.

In retrospect, the planters' lifestyle and aspirations seem almost designed to provoke the yeoman farmers' fears. Not only were the planters wealthier and better educated, they also did not depend on the labor of their own hands. While yeoman farmers bartered with their neighbors, planters were part of a complex international market system. They borrowed money to leverage production and tracked the prices of cotton in Liverpool. The Planters and Merchants Bank, with its small group of wealthy owners and close ties to government, was yet another reminder to yeoman farmers that the rich and powerful were always to be suspected.

For planters, the independence offered by America meant the freedom to improve themselves—financially, intellectually, socially, and morally. Though planters acknowledged the equality of all white men before the law, they viewed society itself as a natural hierarchy of wealth and distinction. They hoped to ascend in that hierarchy.

Thus, the two groups also differed radically over the role of government. For yeoman farmers, a primary function of government was to

Engraving of Pleasant Hill in 1838 based on a sketch by Philip Henry Gosse. Later a famous British naturalist, Gosse taught school for eight months at Pleasant Hill, southeast of Selma. His letters about life in Alabama were published in 1859 and included this engraving depicting crude conditions at the time in what would become a prosperous planter community.

protect the people against threats to their personal liberty—by Indians, foreign powers, or prospective aristocrats at home. Planters, on the other hand, saw the government as an agent for building a better society. They regarded schools, banks, roads, canals, and, later, railroads as improvements that benefitted everyone. To yeoman farmers, each of these planter interests could be seen as yet another effort by the wealthy to enrich themselves and to extend their power.

These fundamentally differing views made early Alabama politics volatile and often strident. Yeoman sensibilities meant hair-trigger hostility toward any threats to the finely balanced system of equality they cherished. Politicians learned to rouse yeoman farmers to action by warning of some new peril, real or imagined, that might threaten their freedom or well-being. Andrew Jackson is usually portrayed as winning the presidency in 1828 through his appeal to "common man," but that political style had already found a home in Alabama several years earlier.

For the entire antebellum period, Alabama politics usually revolved around the struggle between these two sets of antagonists. Planters seemed always to be proposing new projects, and yeoman farmers seemed continually to see the projects as new threats to their liberty. The two groups clashed not only over banks, but also over debtor laws, regulation of the professions, congressional apportionment, school funding, taxes, social reform proposals, railroads, and an

Below: Poplar Grove, the first brick house in Huntsville. Built by Leroy Pope in 1814, the house came to symbolize the gap between the wealthy "Georgia aristocracy" and ordinary Alabamians. It still stands as one of the beautiful old residences in the Twickenham neighborhood. The front portico was added by a new owner in the late antebellum period. Opposite page: Temperance Fitts Crawford. This portrait by Thomas Sully depicts the wife of William Crawford, president of the Tombigbee Bank and Charles Tait's successor as federal district judge in Alabama. She was also the mother of Caroline Brown, whose gravestone at St. Stephens is shown on page 61.

array of other issues. The battle lines were not always clear and hard, and some people from each group supported ideas of the other. But for Alabama political life as a whole, the differences between the two groups created a basic fault line that continued for generations.

Ambrotype of the steamboat *Wave*, probably taken in the 1850s. Cotton bales are stacked around the deck to a height of more than fifteen feet.

BUILDING THE COTTON STATE

ONLY two generations separated Alabama statehood in December 1819 from the Secession Convention of January 1861. Some of the leaders at Huntsville in 1819 were still politically active at the beginning of the Civil War. But during that interval, they witnessed an era of remarkable growth and change. The population increased from fewer than 130,000 to almost a million people, and soaring cotton production brought Alabama unprecedented wealth.

Changes in transportation were an indicator of the larger transformation. In the 1810s, planters had floated their cotton bales downriver to market on flatboats. Without power to return upstream, rivermen broke up their boats and sold the wood along with the cotton when they reached port. Less than two years after statehood, on October 22, 1821, the first steamboat pulled up to the riverbank at Montgomery, having powered itself all the way up the Alabama River from Mobile. Within just a few years, steamboats ran regular routes on Alabama rivers, stopping at landings along the way to pick up bales of cotton and deliver goods and passengers.

Steamboats revolutionized transportation in Alabama. When the Marquis de Lafayette traveled through the state in 1825 as part of his great tour of the United States, his ride on the Federal Road through Georgia to Montgomery was bone jarring. After reaching Montgomery, however, he continued in comfort by steamboat to Mobile, New Orleans, and up the Mississippi River (though he did almost drown in a steamboat accident on the Ohio).

Improved transportation made it easier to sell more cotton, and ever-increasing cotton production drove the development of almost everything in early Alabama. Basil Hall, a British naval officer who traveled through the state in 1828, described a people obsessed by cotton. Following the same route Lafayette had taken three years earlier, he reported on his riverboat trip from Montgomery to Mobile:

Cotton was the sole topic. . . . At every deck or wharf, we encountered it in huge piles or pyramids of bales, and our decks were soon choked with it. All days, and almost all night long, the captain, pilot, crew, and passengers, were talking of nothing else. . . . [At every stop] "What's cotton at?" was the first inquiry.

Cotton production also tied Alabama to world financial markets. In fact, international economic cycles helped shape Alabama's antebellum history. The Panic of 1819 led to a period of lower cotton prices and recession that continued into the mid-1820s. A gradual recovery in the second half of the 1820s led to the famous "flush times" prosperity of the early 1830s. Another worldwide panic in 1837 brought another decade of recession, lasting until the late 1840s, when a new period of expansion began that continued until the Civil War.

Planters who could ride out the down cycles generally flourished in the up cycles, but the recessions were often brutal. Many overextended or unlucky planters lost everything they had. Several railroad projects begun in the prosperous mid-1830s had to be put on hold after 1837 and were not resumed until the 1850s.

Top: Portrait of the Marquis de Lafayette, showing him at the time of his visit to Alabama in April 1825. Above: Iron pot from the *Henderson*, one of three steamboats that carried Lafayette's party and state dignitaries from Montgomery to Mobile in April 1825. The *Henderson* sank just weeks after Lafayette's visit, and this pot was found in its wreckage by an amateur diver in the 1980s.

Throughout these market fluctuations, Alabamians produced more and more cotton. Mobile became the Cotton City, its economy dominated by the cotton trade. By 1860, Mobile's population of 29,258 made it the state's largest city, far exceeding Montgomery (8,843), Tuscaloosa (3,989), and Huntsville (3,634).

The great portion of the cotton that provided Alabama's wealth was produced by enslaved people, but through the 1840s and 1850s, many yeoman farmers began trying their hands at cotton. Growing cotton was a way to secure extra cash and some of the conveniences it could buy. Some of these yeoman farmers were also able to purchase an enslaved worker or two to help them farm.

FROM FRONTIER TO ANTEBELLUM SOCIETY

A CHARACTERISTIC feature of antebellum Alabama was an awkward blending of frontier roughness and civilized refinement. The wealthy planters who moved to Huntsville from Georgia brought with them china and silver, books, refined manners, and the desire to create a cultured society. The elegance and sophistication they brought to a place that, just a few years before, had been Indian land often surprised early Huntsville visitors.

Yet most of Alabama remained a rough frontier even into the 1850s. Marion Sims, a doctor from South Carolina who settled in central Alabama in the mid-1830s, wrote to his fiancée about the small town he chose: "Mount Meigs . . . is nothing but a pile of gin-houses [for cotton gins], stables, blacksmith shops, grog-shops, taverns and stores, thrown together in one promiscuous huddle."

In another letter, Sims described Mount Meigs as "unquestionably one of the most dissipated little places I ever saw. At this moment there are about a dozen or twenty men, of the most profane cast, drunk and fighting, in the street below my window, with a negro playing a banjo (I believe it is so called) in their midst." But Sims looked past this crude frontier stage to envision the "very desirable" place and "excellent" society he expected "in the course of the next twelve to fifteen months."

Many Alabama towns like Mount Meigs actually achieved the transformation Sims anticipated. With their growth came churches, schools, literary societies, fraternal organizations, and even reform associations. As the number of churches grew, alcohol consumption and public drunkenness declined. Beginning in the 1830s, colleges sprang up across Alabama, most of them connected with religious denominations. Mansions with white columns became a symbol of antebellum

Above: Section of Mobile water pipe. Mobile's first water system was built about 1840. The centers of logs were drilled out with an auger, and metal joints connected the log sections. This piece was recovered during the construction of the Bankhead Tunnel a century later. Opposite page, above: Statue carved in wood of Minerva, the Roman goddess of wisdom. In the 1850s, this statue stood over the entrance to the Eufaula Female Academy. Opposite page, below: Thornhill in Forkland. James Innes Thornton was a young Virginian who moved to Huntsville, where he began practicing law in 1820. He then moved to Greene County and became a successful planter, building this house in 1833.

opulence, though most of them were built during the prosperity of the 1850s.

The booster spirit of the planters and their allies in the towns helped drive the growth of new social institutions. Perhaps nothing shows their confidence and enthusiasm better than a speech given by John Tyler Morgan in 1858 at the opening of a railroad leading into Cahawba. Referring to ancient Indians whose mounds and earthworks had been a conspicuous feature of the young town, Morgan described how the "high mounds" had given way before "the appropriating energy of this generation":

We have gathered their labors and heaped them together in the embankment for the Railroad, where their curious pottery, their crude implements of warfare, and their bones mingle in a singular tribute to the superiority of their successors in the dominion of this soil.

Religion was another transforming force in Alabama society. A nationwide religious revival movement known as the Second Great Awakening had begun in the early 1800s, and by the late 1820s, its camp meetings, revivals, and evangelical preaching were taking hold in Alabama. Spiritual fervor seemed to spread in waves and had numerous local variations, depending on the preachers and their congregations, but its overall effects were profound.

Page one from a record book of the Pisgah Presbyterian Church in Dallas County dated March 10, 1834. The second paragraph is a summary of the people who met to form the church, sixty-eight white and fourteen "colored" members. Their names are listed on the following pages.

Reports from Tuscaloosa in the early 1820s described conditions resembling those of Mount Meigs—shabby buildings, public drunkenness and profanity, open gambling, pigs in the streets, violence, and the lack of "enough of a religious or moral Principle in the Body politic to cause the Laws to be put in execution." Within a generation, however, came churches, revivals, Sunday schools, and Bible and tract societies—along with campaigns to reduce liquor consumption, initiatives to prevent gambling and violations of the Sabbath, and benevolent associations to help the needy.

Following a revival in 1845, the Tuscaloosa *Monitor* reported: "This is not a temporary excitement. Religion is the theme of almost every tongue. It has taken hold upon the young men. A large number of them have made an open profession, and cast the world behind. Gay and fashionable young ladies have embraced religion."

The Second Great Awakening had two related thrusts: to save souls by spreading the Gospel and to create a better, more moral society. Some churches and some people focused more on one concern than the other, but the practical result for Alabama was an increase in social order and in the percentage of people who regarded themselves as Christian.

At statehood in 1819, according to historian Wayne Flynt, there were not more than fifty Baptist churches in Alabama, "most of them very small." A large percentage of the population did not belong to any church. By 1860, there were 805 Baptist churches in the state, with a membership of 237,000. Although black members were included in the Baptist totals, the numbers were still very high for a state with a white population of only 526,271. Methodist numbers were nearly as large.

The workings of this social transformation were very uneven, however, and were still in process as the antebellum period ended. Despite progress, especially in the towns, large parts of rural Alabama still resembled a frontier. When journalist (and future landscape architect) Frederick Law Olmsted traveled through Alabama in 1853, one of the major points he stressed in articles for his New York

newspaper readers was how un-developed much of the state still was: "A large part of Alabama has yet a strikingly frontier char-acter. Even from the State-house [dome], in the fine and promis-ing town of Montgomery, the eye falls in every direction upon a dense forest, boundless as the sea, and producing in the mind the same solemn sensation."

Another of Olmsted's obser-vations was even more telling: "Much of the larger proportion of the State live in log-houses, some of them very neat and comfortable, but frequently rude in construction, not chinked, with windows unglazed, and wanting in many of the commonest conveniences possessed by the poorest class of northern farmers." And there were still vast expanses of forests. In Covington County as late as 1854, almost ninety-five percent of the land remained in the public domain, though some of it was occupied by squatters who were still unable or unwilling to pay for the land on which they lived.

Top: Jefferson Baptist Church, built in 1860, in Marengo County. Above: This cabin was built by Clarke County settler Josiah Allen Mathews in 1830. It was moved to the Clarke County Historical Museum and restored in 2005. On the right is a corncrib.

Despite all the public land that was available for settlement, many Alabamians looked hungrily at the territory in east Alabama still occupied by Indians. In 1826, federal negotiators, yielding to growing pressure by Georgia, forced the Creeks to cede all their remaining land in that state. Over the next few years, most Creeks left Georgia in a series of removals to the west, to present-day Oklahoma, or they moved across the Chattahoochee to the remaining Creek reserve in Alabama.

At the same time, the Alabama legislature began to pass "extension" laws that imposed state civil and criminal laws over Indian land. These laws undercut traditional Indian self-government and nullified Indian laws that were in conflict with state laws. Some extension laws limited hunting and fishing by Indians and ultimately prohibited tribal council meetings.

In May 1830, Congress passed the Indian Removal Act, which had been proposed by President Andrew Jackson. Ironically, the new commitment to Indian removal spurred even more encroachments onto their land. Alabama settlers rushed in to grab the best parcels before anyone else could, despite protections for the Indians that were part of the federal law.

In desperation, Creek leaders signed another treaty in 1832, attempting a new approach to the conflict between Alabamians and the Indians. The federal government agreed to cover the costs for Creeks willing to move to the West, but for those who chose to remain in Alabama, the terms of land possession would be changed. Instead of maintaining a large reserve under tribal control, individual parcels of land would be given to each Creek man—a section (640 acres) for chiefs and a half-section (320 acres) for all others. The remaining unallocated land would then be sold to settlers.

Before the surveys could be completed, however, still more settlers pushed into the Creek reserve. Packs of swindlers, using a variety of schemes and tricks, defrauded individual Creeks of their allotments. Violations of the treaty terms and of federal laws were so egregious that President Jackson sent federal troops to Alabama to protect Creek landowners. But these troops had to confront people who had been Jackson's political supporters and were following his lead in pressing for Indian removal. After seeing that his efforts were failing, Jackson essentially capitulated and left the Creeks to fend for themselves in a very uneven struggle.

In the spring of 1836, a few bands of discontented Creeks rose in another effort at armed resistance, which was quickly put down by state militia and federal troops. After this Second Creek War, troops began rounding up and forcibly removing the Alabama Creeks who remained. That summer, thousands were transported west under armed guard. Treaties with the Choctaws and Chickasaws forced the cession of their Alabama lands as well, and also committed them to removal to the West.

Although Alabama was not the historic home of the Cherokees, some had moved into what would become the state in the early 1800s. Northeastern Alabama became a refuge for Cherokees who were fleeing from the Carolinas, Georgia, and Tennessee. In 1838, state militia and regular army troops gathered Alabama's Cherokees into collection centers and began driving them westward, too.

The Trail of Tears was not a single action or route, but a series of forced removals that played out through the mid-1830s. The removal process brought enormous suffering for the Indians. Thousands died from diseases in the collection camps, the hardships of travel, the effects of weather, and the failure of private contractors to provide the promised transportation, food, and supplies. When the survivors finally reached their new homeland in present-day Oklahoma, they suffered attacks by other Indians, more diseases, and more failures by officials and contractors to furnish necessary (and promised) assistance.

Some Indians did stay in Alabama. Small numbers remained on land they had been allotted. Others hid in remote areas. Many people of mixed Indian and white ancestry lived on as American citizens, usually minimizing their Indian heritage. Black people who shared Indian ancestry were generally classified as blacks and kept enslaved.

William Weatherford, who had led the Red Sticks in the Fort Mims Massacre, lived out his days as a plantation owner in South Alabama. His many descendants in Alabama today are indistinguishable from

Above: William Weatherford's gravesite. The space around the Weatherford monument had become overgrown when this photo was taken in 1940 as part of the Federal Writers' Project. Opposite page, below: Osceola. After the Battle of Horseshoe Bend, Osceola's family fled to Florida, where he joined the Seminoles in resisting the Americans, until his capture by deceit under a flag of truce in 1837. Opposite page, above: Osceola's earrings. Osceola was wearing these earrings when artist George Catlin painted the portrait from which the adjacent print was made. He was then in captivity at Fort Moultrie in Charleston, and he died shortly after the portrait was completed.

their friends and neighbors. In 1984, the U.S. Bureau of Indian Affairs formally recognized the Poarch Band of Creek Indians near Atmore because the tribe was able to document its continuous history as a distinct community. It is the only federally recognized tribal group in Alabama.

SLAVERY

RACIAL attitudes were an important factor in Indian removal. Many white Alabamians, like their counterparts in other states, considered Indians an inferior race, incapable of assimilation into white society. They justified removal as a humane option that would allow the tribes to continue their traditional ways in the open spaces of the West.

Similar attitudes framed most white Alabamians' views on slavery. They accepted slavery as a fact of life or as a necessary evil for which there was no feasible alternative. But some whites in the early days of statehood did challenge the acceptance of slavery. James G. Birney, for example, was a member of the first state legislature and later mayor of Huntsville. In the late 1820s, as his religious convictions grew stronger, Birney began asking increasingly critical questions about slavery's morality.

Birney's initial interest was the American Colonization Society, which promoted the transportation of freed slaves to new homes in Liberia. In many ways, the idea of colonization resembled that of Indian removal. After a few years, however, Birney began to reject colonization as both inhumane and impractical. As his questions grew more searching, the resistance and hostility of his neighbors increased, and Birney began to feel more out of place in Alabama. He left the state in 1832, moved north, and became a nationally prominent abolitionist. In 1840 and 1844, he was nominated to be the Liberty Party's candidate for president of the United States.

The resistance Birney encountered reflected a hardening of proslavery views across the South in the early 1830s. In August 1831, Nat Turner led a slave uprising in Southampton County, Virginia, in which approximately sixty white people were killed. Stories about the uprising raised the level of fear among white southerners and prompted discussions about preventing future insurrections. While Birney and a few allies favored some form of emancipation, most white Alabamians chose a course of tighter controls and strengthened internal security.

Through the 1830s, the Alabama legislature passed one law after another to tighten restrictions on black people in the state, both enslaved and free. State law made it a crime to teach an enslaved person to read

James G. Birney, by Asa Park. Birney was an early Alabama legislator and mayor of Huntsville who became an abolitionist. He left the state and ran as the nominee of the Liberty Party for president of the United States in 1840 and 1844.

or write. Slaves could not keep a gun, sell goods for their own profit, travel without permission, or own a dog. Every newly freed slave had to leave the state within a year, and new laws made freeing slaves more difficult. The state's militia, which had originally protected citizens against Indian attacks, now turned to defending against possible slave uprisings.

The increasingly strident voices of abolitionists in the North intensified southern defensiveness. In the early 1800s, few Americans justified slavery as anything more than a necessary evil. From the mid-1830s on, however, as southern attitudes hardened, many whites began asserting that slavery was a positive good. They argued that it exposed black people to the benefits of a superior civilization and to the opportunity for moral and social improvement. They also attacked the system of wage labor in the North, decrying its meanness and impersonal harshness.

Top: Magazine print of a slave auction in Montgomery, publication date unknown. The auction site appears to be at the fountain at Court Square. Above: Slave bill of sale. John A. Stringer sold Pinkney, a boy "of about eight years old," to Presley Davis for the sum of $300.

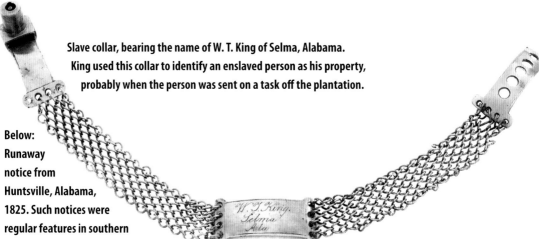

Slave collar, bearing the name of W. T. King of Selma, Alabama. King used this collar to identify an enslaved person as his property, probably when the person was sent on a task off the plantation.

Below: Runaway notice from Huntsville, Alabama, 1825. Such notices were regular features in southern newspapers, and each tells a brief and often haunting story that provides a small window of insight into the institution of slavery.

50 DOLLARS REWARD.

RANAWAY from the Subscriber, living four miles west of Huntsville, on the night of the 24th instant, the following Negro Fellows, viz:

JERRY, a bright mulatto fellow, between twenty five and thirty years of age, nearly six feet high, spare made and very active; he had on when he left me a blue broad cloth coat and blue cassinet pantaloons.

MINOR, a very stout built fellow, about twenty-two years of age, has a down look spoken to, his back considerably marked with the lash, and has rather a sulky disposition; he wore off a common homespun dress.

JIM, a stout built fellow, about 20 years of age, five feet eight inches high, keeps one of his eyes about half shut, has rather a down look and speaks slow when spoken to,—he wore off a blue broad cloth coat.

WIGGIN, a stout built fellow, about twenty-two years of age, five feet eight inches high, has a down look when spoken to, one of his fore teeth out, and wore off a blue broad cloth coat.

The subscriber thinks it probable that some white person has been instrumental in inducing those negroes to run away.

The above reward will be given for the apprehension and delivery of said slaves to me, or secure them in any jail so I get them again, or so much in proportion for either of them. I am disposed to think they are aiming for some of the free states

WILLIAM E. PHILIPS.

July 25, 1825. 12

☞ The Editors of the Nashville Whig, Knoxville Register, Columbian, Columbia, Tenn. and Hopkinsville (Ky.) papers, will insert the above 4t and forward their bills to this office.

While forms of involuntary servitude had existed in Europe, Asia, Africa, and the Americas since before recorded history, slavery in the cotton South took on a unique and particularly harsh character. It was based exclusively on race and was backed up by a theory of racial superiority. It was fixed and perpetual. And it was businesslike and profit-driven. As owners pushed for more productivity, overseers developed systems for measuring the output of enslaved workers and for pushing them to work at ever-accelerating rates of speed. It may sound melodramatic today to talk about owners using whips, but the regular and ruthless use of whips was at the core of extraordinary production increases that are documented in plantation records over the course of the antebellum period. At the basic level, slavery depended on physical violence for its continuance.

Southern defenders of slavery generally ignored clear evidence around them of the system's brutality and inhumanity. While some owners did try to keep enslaved families together, tens of thousands were broken up—husbands, wives, or children sold away from each other with no recourse. Some owners were considerate, but many were hard driving and a few were even sadistically brutal. Sexual contact between white men and enslaved women may sometimes have been consensual—if any acts between a master and his property can ever be called that—but there is no doubt that coercion and force were also used. The many different laws enacted by the Alabama legislature to make slavery more secure were themselves clear evidence of its demeaning and dehumanizing character.

Despite these conditions, enslaved people were often able to carve out niches in which they could find some degree of personal space and

Opposite page: Waldwick plantation production record. This journal entry from a plantation near Gallion in the Black Belt records the amount of cotton picked each day by men and boys for the 1858 crop. Careful record keeping was part of the discipline for coercing ever-increasing rates of production.

Cotton picked   Men & Boys.

Date	Preston	Phill	Wash	Tom	Clair	Peter	Riley	Glass	Alfred	Hewit	Somers	Scott	Bob
Aug 17	131	140	131	at.	116	115	110		114		106	106	104
18	157	143	140	at	142	at	108		114		at.	111	123
19	122	120	113	at	95	at	75		65		at	71	91
20	280	277	85	at.	203	at	99		210		at.	202	216
21	219	208	245	at	178	at	138		130		at	132	150
23	245	258	260	at.	211	at	166	175	185		at.	175	190
24	251	255	262	at.	193	at	167	180	169		at.	151	192
25	225	235	232	at	195	at	145	160	157		at.	159	185
26	260	253	243	at.	200	at	152	178	171		at.	162	190
Aug 27 at home	195	211	196	at.	162	at	142	141	148		at.	148	153
28	207	195	187	160	157	at.	125	142	138		at.	130	138
30	212	219	205	11	166	75	60	60	126		at.	133	137
31	225	299	205	86	186	155	130	144	139		at.	134	141
Sept 1	245	298	227	200	184	214	152	165	154		at.	153	176
2	325	304	293	280	226	265	170	196	216		at.	237	235
3	214	217	187	177	185	205	153	161	170		at.	162	180
4	296	271	255	240	195	246	192	201	199		at	189	202
6	249	236	227	96	197	218	at.	90	169		at	153	171
7	326	299	291	285	227	250	211	228	200		180	211	216
8	380	345	326	294	275	263	202	226	227		198	232	232
9	at	280	275	261	218	230	180	213	95		180	190	207
10	at	295	300	247	211	255	185	210	188		175	205	210
13	327	295	288	97	200	246	75	84			66	191	215
14	301	282	261	259	210	258	182	187	168		179	207	214
15	324	295	272	256	220	240	204	214	220		189	201	225
16	276	256	253	241	180	221	160	180	170		162	160	200
17	387	321	350	298	177	298	147	182	168		149	169	165
at home 18	at.	260	246	231	190	211	165	192	185		170	194	192
20	285	270	265	108	206	240	80	91	193		81	184	195
21	302	273	268	230	194	244	180	196	197	140	164	195	205

Top: Slave cabin, Faunsdale Plantation in Marengo County. Surviving slave cabins are now rare. This one was built by enslaved carpenters Joe Glasgow and Peter Lee. Above: Stairwell of the State Capitol. Horace King, a black carpenter, built these stairs, as well as a number of covered bridges in Alabama.

meaning. Within the tight limitations of slavery, the routines of daily life usually allowed some opportunities for enslaved people to attend to personal interests. Many found comfort and even joy in family life, their communities, religion, music, and other expressions of art. Some enslaved people became skilled workers, craftsmen, and artisans, winning respect and even admiration for their work. Perhaps the best known in Alabama was Horace King, who built covered bridges in Georgia, Alabama, and Mississippi, and constructed parts of the state's Capitol. King was emancipated by a special act of the Alabama legislature in 1846 and continued to work as a business partner of his former master.

Many southern whites deceived themselves about what they saw in communities of enslaved people and claimed that most slaves were content. There was a clear contradiction, however, between these claims and the considerable exertions of the state to prevent possible slave uprisings. The question of what enslaved people themselves wanted was answered unequivocally at the end of the Civil War. When the opportunity for freedom came, virtually all slaves embraced it with an exultation that often shocked their former owners.

THE decade of the 1830s was a dynamic time in Alabama. It included Indian removal, the growth of towns and schools, expanded cotton production, strengthened slavery laws, the first railroads, and the emergence of the state's first real two-party political system. In the decade after the 1821 defeat of the Broad River group, virtually all Alabama politicians were Democrats who claimed allegiance to Andrew Jackson. Competition for elective office was between factions of Jackson supporters, and planters had no separate party of their own.

By the early 1830s, however, a new anti-Jackson party began to coalesce. Ironically, Jackson's efforts to follow legal procedures in removing the Indians created an opportunity for his opponents. Some Alabamians who denounced him for delaying state access to Indian land joined others who supported government aid for economic development and a national bank. United by their opposition to Jackson, they created the Whig Party in Alabama, which quickly became the voice for the state's planter interests.

The great economic collapse of 1837 further eroded support for Jackson's party. Democrat Martin Van Buren succeeded Jackson as

Old State Bank Building at Decatur. This branch office of the State Bank of Alabama was built in 1833. It was fortunately preserved by the people of Decatur and is the only one of the state bank buildings that has survived.

president, but he was unable to right the foundering national economy. When the state-controlled Bank of Alabama began to fail, investigations revealed questionable practices by Democratic politicians that further strengthened the Whig opposition.

Before 1837, the state bank's profits provided enough revenue to pay the costs of operating Alabama government. State taxes were actually abolished. But when the bank failed, taxes had to be re-imposed to keep the state afloat. The fact that the new taxes included levies on luxury items and slaves—and thus were paid by the planters and the wealthy—showed that yeoman farmers still dominated state government. They remained virtually untaxed.

Alabama Whigs never won the governor's office or full control of the legislature, but planters gained political strength as prosperity returned in the late 1840s. Large planters, who made up less than ten percent of the legislature in the 1830s and 1840s, were almost twenty-five percent of its membership by the late 1850s. Initiatives during the 1850s such as railroad construction, expanded public schools, improvements in the criminal justice system, and better treatment of the insane, all reflected the increased influence of the planters.

Although Democrats dominated Alabama politics through the entire antebellum period, they were divided into factions. Planters could occasionally win some Democrats over to their ideas, especially

Top: Capitol Park in Tuscaloosa. After the capital moved to Montgomery, the old Capitol building served as Alabama Central Female College until it burned down in 1923. The site was excavated starting in 1989 and is now a city park. Above: Desk from the state Capitol at Tuscaloosa.

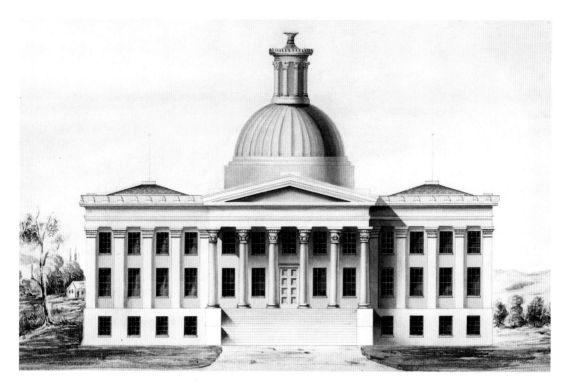

the new generation who lived in towns. In other cases, planters could sometimes tilt the balance in the Democrats' internal struggles.

Another change in Alabama through the 1830s was the shifting of the population center of the state, as more settlers moved into former Indian land in the east. After residents from the new counties complained about the long trips to Tuscaloosa, a statewide referendum allowed the legislature to relocate the capital. Several towns competed for the honor, but the legislators decided on Montgomery.

As part of its incentive package, the city of Montgomery presented the state with a beautiful new Capitol building, designed by Stephen Button, a famous architect of the time. The first legislative session convened there in December 1847, but two years later the building burned to the ground. The replacement structure built by the state in 1851 was much less ornate. The building is still in use, but it has been expanded and renovated several times since then.

Stephen Button's design of the first Capitol in Montgomery. The building burned to the ground on December 14, 1849, two years after it was built and thirty years to the day after Alabama became a state.

POLITICS IN THE 1850s AND GROWING
SECTIONAL TENSION

ALTHOUGH the Mexican War of 1846–1847 usually receives only passing attention in American history, it was a pivotal event. Initiated by Democratic President James Polk, it was popular in Alabama because it raised the prospect of adding more cotton land and slave states to the Union. However, the war also intensified sectional tensions that the nation's political leaders had generally kept tamped down until then.

The national Whig Party split as a result of the war. Northern Whigs, who opposed the war and the prospect of any expansion of slavery into the West, could no longer pull in harness with southern Whigs, who remained committed to slavery. (Methodist and Baptist churches in the South had already split from their national denominations over the issue of slavery in 1844 and 1845, respectively.)

In August 1846, Congressman David Wilmot of Pennsylvania attached an amendment to a war appropriations bill, the Wilmot Proviso, to prohibit slavery in any new territory won from Mexico. The proviso inflamed southern politicians, especially Alabama's William Lowndes Yancey, who insisted that southerners' constitutionally protected rights of property allowed them to carry slaves into any U.S. territory.

Yancey quickly emerged as one of the most aggressive and popular advocates of the rights of slaveholding states. When Alabama Democrats gathered in Montgomery to choose delegates to the 1848 national

Alabama State Capitol. This view shows the building much as it would have appeared in 1851, before the wings were added in 1906 and 1912. The clock and the flagstaff on the dome were also added later.

convention, Yancey proposed the Alabama Platform. It called on the Democratic Party to adopt a platform plank affirming slaveholder property rights in any territory acquired from Mexico and to reject any national candidate who supported the Wilmot Proviso.

Democratic candidates in the North, who did not want to appear to be controlled by slaveholder interests, saw the Alabama Platform as a dangerous political liability. When moderate Democrats at the convention prevailed and avoided addressing Yancey's proposal, he and a supporter walked out. The rest of the Alabama delegation, however, led by future governor John Winston, remained.

William Lowndes Yancey. After a turbulent childhood and a brief career in South Carolina, Yancey moved to Alabama in 1837. He was a planter, newspaper editor, lawyer, and politician who emerged in the 1840s as one of the most outspoken advocates of southern rights.

This growing sectional struggle was the backdrop against which Alabama politics played through the 1850s. In the early part of the decade, moderate Democrats who accepted compromise with northern interests continued to hold power in the state, sometimes with the help of former Whigs. A moderate Democrat from Alabama, William Rufus King, was even elected vice president of the United States in 1852, though he died of tuberculosis shortly after taking the oath of office.

That same year, Yancey's opponent from the 1848 Democratic convention, John Winston, won election as Alabama's governor. Once in office, Winston became a hero of old-line yeoman-farmer Jacksonians by repeatedly vetoing legislation that provided state aid for railroad construction. Winston denounced the bills as an attempt to use taxpayer money for private business interests.

During the 1850s, cotton prices remained strong, while the number of bales produced in Alabama nearly doubled—an increase resulting in part from ever more aggressive pressure on enslaved people to increase their pace of work. As planters plowed their profits back into buying more land and slaves, those prices increased as well, contributing to an expanded sense of wealth and well-being. Buoyed by their rising prosperity, white Alabamians grew even more attached to and confident of their way of life.

Opposite page: William Rufus King. A former member of Congress from North Carolina, King moved to what became Dallas County in 1818 and represented Alabama in the U.S. Senate for thirty years. In 1852, he was elected vice president of the United States, but he died of tuberculosis within six weeks of taking the oath of office. Below: Silver bowl of William Rufus King. This ornate vessel was part of an elaborate set of silver, china, and crystal King acquired while serving as the U.S. minister to France in the mid-1840s.

Yet, the question about slavery expanding into the western territories continued to simmer and soon grew to a full boil. In 1854, Senator Stephen A. Douglas of Illinois secured passage of the Kansas–Nebraska Act, incorporating into law the idea of "popular sovereignty." Under the act, residents of each territory would decide for themselves at the time of statehood whether their state would be slave or free. But under the Missouri Compromise of 1820, the area that would become Kansas had already been designated a permanently free territory. The Kansas–Nebraska Act removed the old restriction, allowing owners to take enslaved people into the territory, at least until the citizens there voted to reject slavery.

Within months of the passage of the act, Kansas became a battleground. Pro-slavery groups, including some from Alabama, rushed there to establish a foothold from which they could fight for slavery. Anti-slavery settlers also rushed in, trying to ensure they had enough

votes to guarantee a free Kansas. A small civil war erupted between the two factions, and scores of people were killed. Meanwhile, a group of northern Whigs who opposed the Kansas–Nebraska Act joined in 1854 with some breakaway Free Soil Democrats to establish a new political party, which they called Republican.

News reports from Bleeding Kansas enraged people on both sides of the struggle. And the controversy merged with other slavery-related disputes, such as enforcement of the fugitive slave law, proposed

additional territorial acquisitions, the *Dred Scott* decision, and John Brown's raid into Virginia. As sectional lines hardened, political passions in America rose to a pitch that often choked off civil discourse.

The increasing sectional bitterness helped William Lowndes Yancey achieve a political recovery. Yancey actually represented a new kind of Democrat in Alabama, more urban and more comfortable with government assistance for internal improvements. He even supported increased protections for the rights of women. But Yancey appealed to the larger Democratic base by claiming to defend the South's rights against the threats of abolitionists and the rising Republican Party.

Though yeoman farmers resisted planter domination, most of them supported the institution of slavery. For them, enslaved people performed menial labor that might otherwise fall to working-class whites. Also, yeoman farmers could not envision any form of emancipation they thought would be workable. The idea of former slaves as their partners in local communities of mutually dependent equals was virtually unimaginable to them.

As national tensions rose, more Alabamians began to agree with Yancey. The right of southerners to carry slaves into the West became a matter of both law and honor. The U.S. Supreme Court's 1857 *Dred Scott* decision actually supported Yancey's arguments. In it, the court ruled that African Americans, whether enslaved or free, could not be citizens of the United States within the meaning of the Constitution and that the federal government had no authority to prohibit slavery in western territories.

Bust of Governor Andrew B. Moore, by Henry Dexter. Dexter was preparing an exhibit in Washington showing busts of all current U.S. governors when the Civil War interrupted his project. Governor Moore secured this plaster copy of the bust Dexter sculpted of him.

While most white southerners hailed the *Dred Scott* decision, many northerners resented it deeply as the work of a cabal of slave-holding interests. As northern resentment grew, white southerners felt even more isolated. Since the adoption of the U.S. Constitution in 1789, claims about the right of states to secede had surfaced in a number of disputes. Yancey had talked about it since 1848. But as the 1860 elections approached, the issue became immediate and real.

In 1860, Alabama governor Andrew B. Moore, previously a moderate Democrat, began taking steps to expand, equip, and train the state's militia. Alarmed by John Brown's raid at Harper's Ferry the previous October, Moore thought Alabamians should be able to defend themselves if necessary.

When the Democrats held their national convention in Charleston in April 1860, Yancey again tried to pass a platform provision calling for the protection of slavery in the western territories. When the convention again rejected Yancey's proposal, the entire Alabama delegation walked out in protest, and they were joined by delegates from six other southern states.

The remaining Democratic delegates in Charleston, unable to agree on a nominee, adjourned the convention. When they later reconvened in Baltimore, they chose Stephen A. Douglas as the party's presidential candidate. Most southern Democrats, however, continued to reject Douglas, and as the 1860 national elections approached, a majority of them rallied behind John C. Breckinridge of Kentucky.

In the fall 1860 elections, both Yancey and Douglas undertook futile efforts to win over the other side. Yancey campaigned in the North, hoping to persuade northern Democrats of the merits of the South's position. Douglas spent the last days of his campaign in Alabama, trying to keep southern Democrats in the party. In Montgomery, he spoke from the steps of the state Capitol, where just a few months later Jefferson Davis would be inaugurated president of the Confederacy. Douglas wound up his campaign in Mobile, having gained little for his efforts in the South beyond the knowledge that he had tried his best. The national Democratic alliance that Andrew Jackson had created decades earlier split in 1860, leaving the way open to the new Republican Party led by Abraham Lincoln.

Lincoln was not even a candidate in Alabama in 1860, since there was no Republican Party in the state to offer a slate of electors. He was elected with only forty percent of the national popular vote. But his Electoral College count of one hundred eighty was well above the one hundred fifty-two needed for victory. He carried all the free states except New Jersey, appearing to confirm white southerners' fears that the rest of the nation was uniting against them.

Nine months before the election, in February 1860, Yancey had persuaded the Alabama legislature to adopt a resolution requiring the governor to call a state convention if the Republican nominee won in November. In accord with the resolution, Governor Moore set December 24, 1860, as the date for electing convention delegates. The one hundred men chosen that day would gather in Montgomery on January 7, 1861, to decide Alabama's future.

Flag of the Young Men's Secession Club in Mobile, which met before the war to promote the cause of secession.

CHAPTER 4

CIVIL WAR AND RECONSTRUCTION

1861 to 1875

T HE MONTH AFTER ALABAMA SECEDED, *delegates from the first seven seceding states gathered in Montgomery and established the Confederate States of America. A year later, Federal troops entered Alabama, seizing large parts of the Tennessee Valley. For three long years, bitter fighting devastated much of northern Alabama. The southern three-fourths of the state escaped major military action until the last months of the war. Ultimately, thousands of Alabamians were killed or maimed, the economy was wrecked, and the institution of slavery—which Alabama had seceded to protect—was abolished.*

Reconstruction brought still more conflict, almost as bitter as the war itself. White Alabamians continued to hold power, but they were divided by old enmities and a staggering array of problems. The hopes of freedmen brightened for a few years, but they were eventually stifled in a series of defeats that ultimately deprived African Americans of any meaningful political voice. The legacy of the Civil War and Reconstruction would weigh on Alabamians for generations afterward with leaden hands.

Above: Old House chamber of the Alabama Capitol. The Alabama Secession Convention met in this room and voted to secede from the Union. Opposite page: Private John Pace Alldredge poses with his Model 1842 rifle musket. Alldredge served in Company A of the 48th Alabama Infantry Regiment. The company was raised by his father, Major Enoch Alldredge of Brooksville, Blount County, and a veteran of the Creek War. John Alldredge died on August 19, 1862, ten days after the regiment saw its first action at the Battle of Cedar Run in Virginia. He was thirty-four years old.

SECESSION

ON January 7, 1861, one hundred delegates elected from across Alabama assembled in the House chamber of the state's Capitol. Baptist minister and former University of Alabama president Basil Manly opened the convention's first session with a prayer, appealing to God "to protect us in the land Thou hast given us, the Institutions Thou hast established, and the rights Thou hast bestowed."

After Manly's invocation, coalitions fell quickly into line. William Lowndes Yancey and his supporters urged immediate secession. Their opponents, who were called "cooperationists," argued that Alabama should first establish an alliance with other southern states.

The cooperationists actually represented a wide range of opinions, but they were joined together in opposition to Yancey. Many old Jacksonian Democrats in north Alabama and a substantial number of former Whigs still felt a strong sense of attachment to the Union, and they were reluctant—in varying degrees—to part from it. One strategy for them was to try to buy time, to keep open a little longer the possibility of a grand compromise, as had taken place in the 1820 Missouri Compromise and the Compromise of 1850. Other cooperationists supported secession but wanted to separate themselves politically from Yancey. Most of the immediate secessionists were from the southern half of Alabama. The cooperationists were primarily from the northern half.

In the convention's first vote, Yancey supporters prevailed fifty-three to forty-five, and a Yancey ally was elected its president. Yancey himself chaired the Committee of Thirteen, which drafted the Ordinance of Secession, and he introduced it on the convention floor. The Ordinance was approved on January 11, with sixty-one delegates voting in favor and thirty-nine opposed. It declared Alabama a "Sovereign and Independent State," summarizing its reasons for secession in the preamble:

Above: Jeremiah Clemens, in his Mexican War uniform. A cousin of Mark Twain, Clemens was a delegate from Huntsville who initially opposed secession, but then signed the Ordinance of Secession. After the arrival of Union troops in north Alabama in 1862, he reaffirmed his anti-secession views and became a staunch Unionist. Opposite page: Alabama's Ordinance of Secession, adopted January 11, 1861.

The election of Abraham Lincoln and Hannibal Hamlin . . . by a sectional party, avowedly hostile to the domestic institutions and to the peace and security of the people of the State of Alabama . . . is a political wrong of so insulting and menacing a character as to justify the people of the State of Alabama in the adoption of prompt and decided measures for their future peace and security.

After the final vote, which was taken in closed session, the doors of the chamber were opened to the public. William R. Smith, a delegate from Tuscaloosa who kept a record of the debates, wrote that "the cheering became now deafening for some moments. It really seemed that there would be no end to the raptures that had taken possession of the company."

A few days before the convention began, Governor Andrew B. Moore had already ordered the militia to seize federal facilities in Alabama. They included forts Morgan and Gaines at the mouth of Mobile Bay, the Mobile customs house, and the federal arsenal at Mount Vernon. Outgoing President James Buchanan, who would continue in office only three more months, did little to resist, and compliant federal officials surrendered facilities in Alabama without a struggle.

In the weeks after secession, the majority of white Alabamians rallied to support their newly independent state. Newspapers reported

ecstatic celebrations and jubilant throngs of people. The excitement
was so great that, in parts of Alabama, remaining opponents often felt
compelled to hold back their criticisms and even their words of cau-
tion. Heightened fears of slave uprisings raised tensions and actually
led to several mob lynchings of suspicious outsiders.

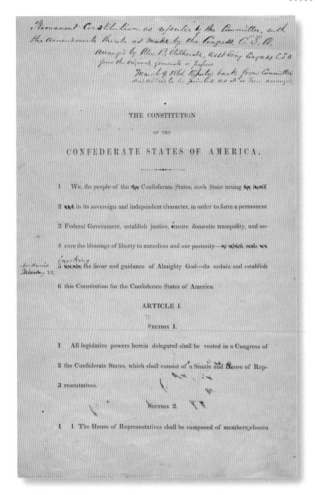

Page one of the mark-up draft of the Confederate constitution. A working copy of the proposed constitution was printed for review by the delegates. This page shows mark-ups made by the secretary, A. B. Clitherall, in the course of the deliberations. The final version was prepared from his notes.

ALABAMA'S Ordinance of Secession included a paragraph inviting other slave-holding states to send delegates to a gathering in Montgomery on February 4. They were to consult with one another "as to the most effectual mode of securing concerted and harmonious action in whatever measures may be deemed most desirable for our common peace and security." The calculated vagueness of the wording did not conceal from anyone the meeting's purpose: to create a new nation.

On February 4, delegates from six states— Alabama, Florida, Georgia, Louisiana, Mississippi, and South Carolina—met in the Senate chamber of the Alabama Capitol. The Texas representatives had not yet arrived, and the upper South states of Virginia, North Carolina, Tennessee, and Arkansas had not yet seceded. The delegates hoped the slave-holding border states of Delaware, Maryland, Kentucky, and Missouri would also join them, but they counted on the upper South states.

The delegates worked quickly and prepared a provisional constitution based on the U.S. Constitution. The few changes they made included a six-year term for the president and a section specifically authorizing "the institution of negro slavery as it now exists in the Confederate States" in any new territories that might be acquired. The delegates chose a Mississippi Democrat, Jefferson Davis, as the Confederacy's provisional president and a Georgia Whig, Alexander H. Stephens, as vice president.

President-elect Davis arrived in Montgomery on the night of February 16, after a long, circuitous trip that illustrated to the world the inadequacies of the South's rail system. At the Exchange Hotel, Yancey joined Davis on the balcony, with a large, welcoming crowd assembled below in Montgomery's Court Square. He commended Davis to the crowd in brief remarks that concluded: "The man and the hour have met. We may now hope that prosperity, honor, and victory await his administration."

Two days later, on Monday, February 18, a band played *Dixie* as Davis's procession climbed Market Street (now Dexter Avenue) to the Capitol. Lacking a Confederate national anthem, the band chose

Inauguration of Jefferson Davis as Provisional President of the Confederate States at Montgomery, Ala., February 18th, 1861.

Left: Photograph of the inauguration of Jefferson Davis. This reprint of a rare photograph was also used for a number of sketches published in magazines of the time. Below: Alabama's State Bible. Acquired for the governor's office by Governor John Winston in 1853, it was used by Jefferson Davis to take the oath of office as president of the Confederacy. It has been used as well by most subsequent Alabama governors for their inaugural oaths.

to play *La Marseillaise*, the anthem of the French Revolution, as Davis stepped from his carriage. Standing at the top of the Capitol steps with his left hand on Alabama's State Bible, Davis swore to "faithfully execute the office of President of the Confederate States," an oath almost exactly the same as that prescribed in the U.S. Constitution. Two days later, he wrote to his wife: "Upon my weary heart was showered smiles, plaudits, and flowers; but beyond them I saw troubles and thorns innumerable."

The provisional government of the Confederacy worked through a formidable list of tasks. It had to establish a military, a currency, a postal system, a diplomatic corps, courts, laws, customs offices and rules, and the means to support and sustain itself. When Abraham Lincoln was sworn in as president of the United States on March 4,

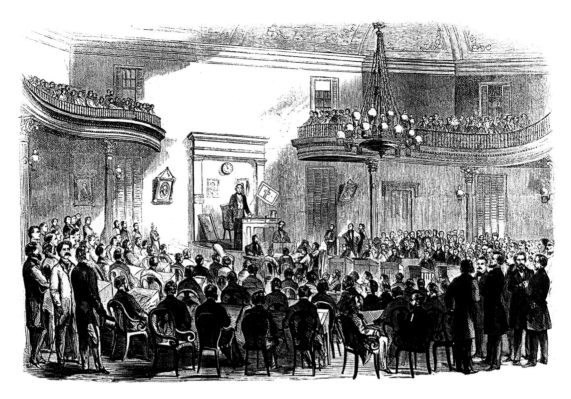

Harper's Weekly print of the Alabama Senate chamber. Delegates from the seceding states met in this room to establish the Confederacy. Later, the Confederate Senate met here.

the Confederacy offered a competing publicity event—the raising of its new flag at the Alabama state Capitol.

Though state and Confederate officials had seized most Federal installations in the South by the time of Lincoln's inauguration, two forts remained in Union hands: Pickens at Pensacola and Sumter at Charleston. The Confederates regarded the continued presence of Federal troops inside their borders as a violation of their national sovereignty. One of Lincoln's first decisions as president was to hold the two forts.

The new Confederate secretary of war was Leroy Pope Walker, grandson of Huntsville's founder, Leroy Pope, and son of John Williams Walker, who had presided over Alabama's 1819 constitutional convention. On April 11, after weeks of posturing and maneuvering by both sides, Walker telegraphed General P. G. T. Beauregard at Charleston, authorizing him to "reduce" Sumter if the demand for surrender was refused. Sumter's commanding officer, Major Robert Anderson, had been one of Beauregard's teachers at West Point. Anderson refused his former student's demands, and Confederate artillerymen began their bombardment early the next morning.

Lincoln responded to the firing on Sumter by calling for volunteers to suppress the rebellion. After that call by Lincoln, Virginia, North Carolina, Tennessee, and Arkansas seceded, bringing the number of Confederate states to eleven. Through great effort and adroit maneuvering, Lincoln was able to keep all the border states in the Union and to peel off the western part of Virginia as a new state.

After admitting the upper southern states, the Confederate Congress voted to relocate the new nation's capital from Montgomery to Richmond. The move acknowledged Virginia's great importance to the Confederacy and also the state's historic status as the home of so many of America's leaders. It also brought Confederate leaders closer to the site of possible future military action.

In late May, Confederate officials in Montgomery packed their records, closed their offices, and unceremoniously departed. In a matter of days, the world spotlight turned away from Alabama. Although the state rarely made the front page of newspapers after that, the next four years was a time of remarkable struggle, hardship, and upheaval that would change many elements of life in Alabama forever.

A first national flag, sometimes referred to as the "stars and bars." Its eleven stars show that it was created after May 20, 1861, when North Carolina, the last of the upper South states, joined the Confederacy. Its resemblance to the U.S. flag prompted Confederate military commanders to use other designs for battle flags.

ALABAMA MOBILIZES FOR WAR

ALABAMA'S Secession Convention continued as a body until late March, selecting Alabama's representatives to the Confederate Provisional Congress, adopting measures for the state's defense, and ratifying the new Confederate constitution. It also revised the state's 1819 constitution, to reflect first Alabama's withdrawal from the Union and then its membership in the Confederacy.

In the months immediately after secession, while the Confederate government was still in the process of formation, individual states launched their own mobilization efforts. Across Alabama, community-

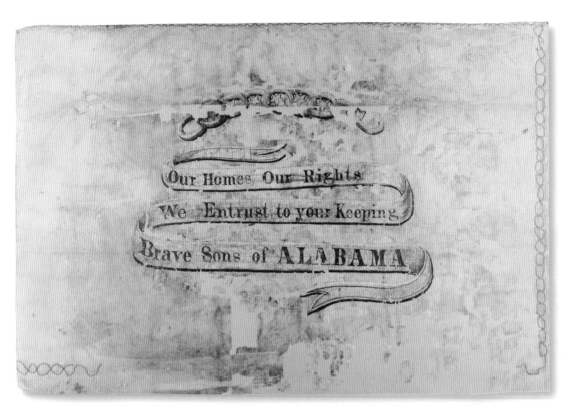

Above: Flag of the Hayneville Guard, presented by the ladies of Hayneville on February 28, 1861. The reverse features an image of the Goddess of Liberty breaking her chains and the inscription: "Tyrany [*sic*] is Hateful to the Gods." Opposite page, above: Tannehill Furnaces, Jefferson County. Built as the Civil War began, at their peak, the Tannehill furnaces produced 22 tons of pig iron a day to supply the Confederate factories in Selma. Opposite page, below: Telegram from J. W. Lapsley to Collin McRae, February 6, 1862. Lapsley informs McRae how much iron he can provide each week to the foundry at Selma and also mentions nearby coal fields.

based militia units sprang up, their equipment and provisions usually supplied by volunteers. For many young men and for the young women who cheered them, the call to arms fired their sense of adventure. Most expected a short, glorious, and relatively painless war.

After early Confederate defeats in Missouri and West Virginia, Alabamians were thrilled by news in July 1861 of a major victory at Manassas, Virginia. In the wake of that battle, however, both sides realized they faced fighting on a scale far beyond their original expectations. By this time, the Confederate government was moving as quickly as it could to create a national army supported by a nationwide infrastructure. The Confederacy could not expect to survive on the voluntary contributions of private citizens and individual states.

One of the Confederacy's great handicaps was the lack of an adequate manufacturing base. Through the 1850s, a number of southern writers had urged economic diversification so that the South would not be so heavily dependent on imports. In Alabama, some rail lines and a few textile mills and iron furnaces were built, but most of the state's wealth had been plowed back into buying land and slaves to produce more cotton.

One of President Lincoln's first actions after Fort Sumter was to order a naval blockade of southern ports. As outside supplies were choked off, the war years became a time of improvisation, adaptation, substitution, and deprivation for Alabamians. They were unable to meet their basic needs for paper, salt, railroad cars and engines, textiles and shoes, machines to make machines, and metal products, including steam engines, tools, and even sewing needles. Railroad tracks were pulled up from lines of low strategic value, such as the one leading into Cahawba, and used to support more critical routes.

Probably the most dramatic example of war mobilization in Alabama took place at Selma. In less than two years, this prosperous cotton town was transformed into the Confederacy's second largest production center of weapons and other military supplies. Starting early in the war, private contractors in Selma began producing uniforms, shovels, and other equipment needed by soldiers. In 1862, Josiah Gorgas, chief of the Confederate Bureau of Ordnance, relocated machinery there from the old Federal arsenal at Mount Vernon and began large-scale production of cannon, shot, and powder. During the last two years of the war, Selma produced almost two-thirds of the Confederacy's ammunition. By 1864, as many as ten thousand people worked at more than a hundred manufacturing facilities in Selma, more people than the entire 1860 population of Montgomery.

Before the war, a few small iron furnaces had been established in Shelby, Bibb, Tuscaloosa, and Jefferson counties. The Civil War pushed Alabama's fledgling iron industry into operations on an entirely new scale and spurred other industries as well. Coal mines expanded to provide fuel for steam boilers. In Clarke and Washington counties, large works were developed for boiling brine from an underground salt dome to extract salt. In the years before refrigeration, salt for curing pork was a necessity for almost all Alabamians.

In February 1862, a flotilla of Federal gunboats steamed up the Tennessee River, landing unchallenged at Florence. Union troops seized Huntsville in April and soon controlled much of the Tennessee Valley. By taking north Alabama, the Union also gained control of the strategic Memphis and Charleston Railroad, a key east-west link for the Confederacy.

For the next three years, Confederate forces would struggle to regain north Alabama. Local guerilla units sprang up to support them, drawing many civilians into the fighting. But Federal forces held at least parts of the Tennessee Valley for the rest of the war. Gaining confidence from the presence nearby of Federal troops, many local people who had opposed secession came out in active support of the Union. The First Alabama Cavalry of the U.S. Army was formed from white Alabama Unionists.

Searching for rebels in a Cave. This print may seem fanciful at first glance, but northern Alabama is one of the most cave-rich parts of the United States, and soldiers and guerilla units fighting Union troops very likely used caves for sanctuary, as Indians had thousands of years earlier.

The combination of occasional regular combat and guerilla warfare was a destructive brew for north Alabama. After a battle, victors often punished their defeated enemies. When the victors were later overthrown, the formerly vanquished exacted their revenge. In some areas, such as parts of Lawrence County, control changed hands more than fifteen times, and cycles of retribution grew more vindictive. Neighbors and even family members were pitted against one another. In addition to the number of people killed, the loss of buildings, crops, and livestock wasted large areas of north Alabama.

Above: Federal troops occupying Stevenson, Alabama. This *Harper's Weekly* print, published in December 1863, shows the Memphis and Charleston Railroad being used to support Union rather than Confederate troops, assisted by African American workers. Left: Nathan Bedford Forrest by Nicola Marschall. Forrest spent a significant part of the war in Alabama. He was an extraordinary battle leader, but his military reputation was clouded by charges that he and his troops committed racial atrocities.

One of Alabama's most famous battles was a series of skirmishes in late April and early May of 1863. Confederate troops under General Nathan Bedford Forrest chased a raiding party of Federal soldiers led by Colonel Abel Streight eastward across northern Alabama. Because of a temporary shortage of horses, Streight's men rode mules, while Forrest's smaller force chased them on horseback. After Forrest fooled Streight into surrendering, the Alabama legislature and state newspapers showered special praise upon a young woman, Emma Sansom, who had helped guide Forrest in a tactical maneuver across Black Creek in Etowah County.

CONFEDERATE WOMEN IN THE WAR

SANSOM was hailed as a heroine, yet many Alabama women performed heroic work. Some women, like Mobile's Kate Cumming, broke tradition and became nurses. They attended patients in conditions that are almost unimaginable today—amid mangled bodies, floors soaked in blood, swarming flies, groans of the dying, and suffocating stench. Their work was also dangerous. Infectious diseases of sick soldiers sometimes killed the people who attended them. Especially in the early months, female nurses faced substantial male resistance—doubts that they were sturdy enough and objections that such work was inappropriate for ladies. But the pressing needs and the nurses' obvious effectiveness soon overcame all but the most entrenched opposition.

While Kate Cumming served close to the battlefield, many other nurses attended soldiers sent home to recover. Women also labored in war industries, including thousands working at the factories in Selma. In rural Alabama, wives of planters frequently took over the duties of plantation management, under conditions far harder than their husbands had known. Their diaries and letters are filled with stories of shortages, rising prices, unruly slaves, refugees, growing disorder, and sickness and death all around them.

Wives of yeoman farmers often bore even more crushing burdens. Unless they had family to fall back on, they had to plow, plant, harvest, cut wood, make repairs, and tend animals, in addition to their already substantial duties of keeping house, cooking, and raising children. Alabama's state and county governments established relief programs for needy families, but the scarcity of supplies and lack of funds meant that the help was never enough.

Kate Cumming. Born in Scotland but reared in Mobile, Cumming served as a nurse with the Army of Tennessee for much of the war. She kept a diary and in 1866 published a book taken from her diary entries.

THE war's impact on slavery was even more disruptive to Alabama's traditional social order. The Confederate government pressed thousands of enslaved people into war service. They were forced to maintain railroads, build fortifications, and labor at munitions plants, iron furnaces, and salt works. Their owners were paid for their work, but many owners complained about both inadequate payments and injuries to their workers. Also, in the dislocations of the times, many impressed slaves escaped and fled.

When Federal troops first entered northern Alabama, U.S. law still allowed slavery. To avoid the legal obligation to return enslaved people to their owners as private property, Union officers declared them *contraband*—a legal term for material that could be seized because it helped the enemy make war. Based on this justification, federal officials in north Alabama provided protection and often employment to slaves who escaped during the early part of the war.

The Emancipation Proclamation made the legal hairsplitting unnecessary. After January 1, 1863, Union armies treated all enslaved people in areas of active rebellion as free. Now all who escaped into Union-held areas not only achieved freedom, they could even join Union forces in the struggle to end slavery. By the war's end, six regiments of United States Colored Troops, totaling almost 7,300 men,

African American workers building Union fortifications. This image could also have been used to depict work on Confederate fortifications, because enslaved people were impressed to help in their construction as well.

had been raised in Alabama. Many other former Alabama slaves enlisted in units raised outside the state.

Because the new black troops were inexperienced—and perhaps because of some degree of discrimination in the Union army—most African American regiments were initially assigned to guarding railroads or holding captured territory. By the end of the war, however, some of these units were joining in hard combat and earning the respect of white fellow soldiers for their fighting ability and courage. Even the Confederate government, desperate for soldiers as the war entered its last months, began considering the use of black troops.

Despite the Federal occupation of north Alabama, most enslaved people in the central and southern parts of Alabama remained at work, helping their owners survive and trying to survive themselves. Some even accompanied their soldier-owners to war, assisting as servants. But as a clearer understanding of the war's meaning and progress spread through black communities, old systems of discipline began to fray. Slaves who did not run away often became more independent in their conduct. They were slower responding to orders, and they pressed their own claims more aggressively. Many white owners grew increasingly apprehensive as they felt their control slipping away.

Above: Lawson Coffee, a corporal in Company A of 110th U.S. Colored Infantry Regiment. Coffee was born in Lauderdale County around 1845 and may have been a slave of the John Coffee family. He enlisted on May 19, 1863, was wounded in battle at Rome, Georgia, and was honorably discharged at Huntsville on April 16, 1866.

ALABAMA SOLDIERS AT WAR

For four long years, almost one hundred thousand Alabama soldiers—Confederate and Union, white and black—fought on, despite seemingly unbearable hardships. For the poorly supplied Confederates, conditions were particularly harsh, but soldiers on both sides faced similar miseries. They often slept on hard ground with no shelter. They suffered lice, crude and inadequate health care, poor food, and sometimes no food. They slogged through miles of forced marches with full packs and weapons—shoes falling apart, and in snow, mud, or scorching heat—all for the opportunity to charge into the murderous fire of their enemy.

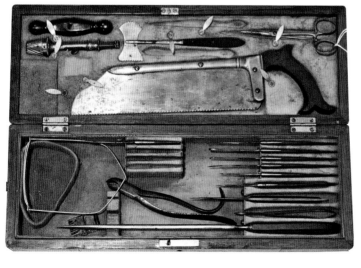

Amputation kit of Dr. Hugh Caffey of Collirene in Lowndes County. Dr. Caffey served as a surgeon in the Army of Northern Virginia.

As the war progressed, clever engineers devised ever more lethal ways of killing. Finely made rifles could strike down approaching soldiers at a thousand yards. Exploding artillery shells ripped through whole ranks of charging infantry. As troops drew closer, artillerymen switched from shells to canisters—cans of iron or lead balls that sprayed out of cannon barrels, tearing bodies apart. For soldiers who were captured, prison conditions on both sides were often horrendous. Waves of disease, from measles to dysentery to typhus, swept through both prison and regular army camps, ultimately claiming more victims than the fighting.

For the survivors of a battle, time for recovery was usually brief. They had to pick themselves up, haul off their wounded comrades, bury their dead ones, and prepare to fight again—and again. In addition to incredible deeds of valor and heroism, the Civil War brought suffering and sacrifice on a massive scale. It is no wonder that stories from the war live on, even today, with power and poignancy.

John Pelham, in his West Point uniform. Rising to the rank of major in the Confederate Army, Pelham was probably Alabama's most famous Civil War hero. He commanded the "horse artillery" under J. E. B. Stuart and was killed in action in March 1863, at the age of twenty-four.

WAR TAKES ITS TOLL

As the Confederate government grew desperate for men and supplies, it established a compulsory draft, raised taxes, impressed more slaves, and restricted economic activity. Although the Confederacy was created in part to safeguard states' rights, the wartime Confederate government was far more intrusive than anything Alabamians had experienced in the Union. After losses at Vicksburg and Gettysburg in July 1863 dimmed the Confederacy's prospects, the demands of Richmond seemed even more onerous.

Partly because the Federal blockade cut off regular imports of food supplies, some parts of Alabama began suffering from food shortages. State and Confederate officials tried to persuade farmers to switch from cotton to food production, but for people whose lives had

Top: Print depicting Mobile Bread Riot in September 1863. Above: CSS *Tennessee*. Built in Selma and floated down the Alabama River to Mobile Bay, the *Tennessee* was the flagship of Confederate Admiral Franklin Buchanan in the Battle of Mobile Bay on August 5, 1864.

centered on cotton for more than forty years—and who expected or hoped for a quick victory—the change was hard, and some refused. Mountains of cotton bales began piling up while many people went hungry. Improvised substitutes for imported items such as coffee, sugar, and even medicinal herbs were poor alternatives at best.

In the spring of 1862, protests over shortages in Tuscaloosa required officials to impose martial law to restore order. Because many men who would have been tending farms were away at war, the shortages grew ever worse. In September 1863, women in Mobile rioted because of shortages and rising prices. *Harper's Weekly* reported the next month: "The rioters openly declared that 'if some means were not rapidly devised to relieve their suffering or to stop the war they would burn the city.' The suffering in Mobile is said to be very great."

Although the *Harper's Weekly* report may have been designed to encourage hopes in the North, large parts of the state, especially north Alabama, did face starvation conditions. Blockade runners continued

to supply a few critically needed items, but the blockade tightened a little more each month. As prices for
basic supplies climbed and almost no cotton was sold,
four decades of accumulated wealth leached away.

In August 1863, Alabama held state elections, and
most politicians who had been elected in 1861 because of their support for secession were defeated.
Historian Ben Severance has recently pointed out that
soldiers away fighting were not able to vote and that
their votes would likely have tilted the balance toward
pro-war candidates. Nevertheless, some new legislators who were regarded as peace candidates were elected, along with
other officials who focused more on states' rights and home defense
than on support for the Confederacy.

**Top: The remains of Fort Morgan,
a site operated by the Alabama
Historical Commission, still show
many features of the Civil War fort.
Above: Fort Morgan, as it appeared
in 1865, when it was re-occupied
by Federal troops after the Battle
of Mobile Bay.**

Although central and southern Alabama avoided Federal attack
for more than three years, in July 1864, General Lovell Rousseau drove
south through the state from the Tennessee Valley to destroy thirty miles
of railroad track between Montgomery and Opelika. The raid cut off
supplies needed by Confederate troops defending Atlanta against General William T. Sherman. The next month, Admiral David Farragut led a
Union naval force into Mobile Bay, which was defended in part by floating mines called torpedoes. Farragut overwhelmed the Confederate

Top: Ruins of the ordnance works in Selma after Wilson's Raiders passed through and destroyed them in April 1865. Above: General James Wilson, who led 13,000 Union troops on a path of destruction through Alabama in early 1865.

defenders, and he earned a kind of immortality with the order later attributed to him: "Damn the torpedoes! Full speed ahead!"

Following these Confederate defeats—and with the toll of destruction continuing to mount—the peace movement in Alabama grew stronger. In September 1864, the state legislature began debating a resolution urging Confederate officials to explore negotiations with the Union. Despite his many other burdens, Jefferson Davis traveled to Montgomery to speak directly to the legislature and urge perseverance: "There is but one duty for every southern man. It is to go to the front."

As Alabama's economy unraveled and resources continued to be drained, law and order at home began to break down. Fearing for the survival of their wives and children, numbers of soldiers began to desert. Since deserters faced capture and punishment, they often banded together for self-protection, sometimes joined by men who had fled their homes to avoid the draft.

In the piney woods along the Alabama–Florida boundary and in large areas of north Alabama, bands of deserters and draft dodgers were sometimes large enough to defeat home guard units sent to suppress them. In their desperate need for supplies and food, some of these bands also plundered and terrorized helpless civilians. Growing numbers of escaped slaves, who also had to find ways to feed themselves, added to the chaos.

Despite the mounting disaffection, many white Alabamians shared President Davis's determination to fight on. Governor Thomas Watts,

elected in 1863, sometimes favored Alabama's rights and its self-defense ahead of support for the Confederacy, but he resisted invading Federal armies with all the energy he could muster until the last days of the war.

THE END OF THE WAR

CONFEDERATE determination alone, however, could not hold back Federal armies. In the spring of 1865, more than 13,000 Union cavalrymen swept through central and western Alabama in an offensive known as Wilson's Raid. They destroyed iron furnaces in Shelby, Jefferson, Tuscaloosa, and Bibb counties, and they burned the University of Alabama and the Confederate manufacturing complex in Selma. They met only ineffective resistance because there were simply not enough Confederate troops left to mount a serious defense.

After Selma, Wilson's forces turned toward Montgomery. The former Confederate capital surrendered without any struggle on April 12, three days after Lee surrendered at Appomattox and four years to the day after the bombardment of Fort Sumter began. Alabama's last pocket of organized resistance was in the southwestern part of the state. An overwhelming Union force captured Fort Blakely on April 9, but Confederate troops continued maneuvering until May 4. That day at Citronelle, General Richard Taylor surrendered the Department of Alabama, Mississippi, and East Louisiana—the last Confederate army east of the Mississippi River to lay down its arms.

Top: Confederate fortifications at Fort Blakely. The fort was captured on April 9, 1865. Above: Sword of Major Thomas Goode Jones. With a white napkin tied on this sword, Jones rode to Union lines to ask for the meeting at which General Robert E. Lee surrendered at Appomattox. Below: General Richard Taylor, the son of President Zachary Taylor, surrendered his army at Citronelle on May 4, 1865.

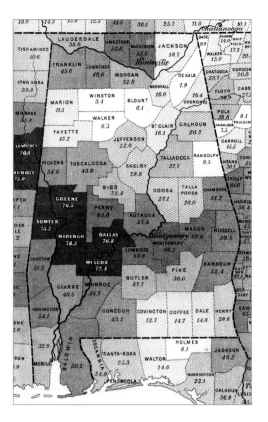

WITH the great engines of war finally stilled, it was time for relief, restoring order, and rebuilding. But Reconstruction was in many ways a continuation of the war. The aims of the North had broadened during the war, from merely preserving the Union to abolishing slavery, and then to less clear ideas about protecting the rights of former slaves. Many former Confederates, on the other hand, continued to struggle after the war, with whatever tools they could find, to preserve as much as they could of their old way of life.

The 1870 census recorded approximately 475,000 black residents and 521,000 white residents in Alabama. Former slaves, now called freedmen, and the handful of black Alabamians who had been free before the war made up almost forty-eight percent of the state's population. At the war's end, they sought to take their place as new citizens, burdened by the legacy of generations of repression and in the face of a deep-rooted white resistance.

Slavery map of the South. This cropped view of Alabama was taken from a larger map prepared by the Census Department in 1861, showing the percentage of slaves in each county of the South.

In his last speech, on April 11, President Lincoln talked about the great challenges of "the re-inauguration of national authority." He wanted a speedy return of rebellious states to "their proper relation with the Union." He also urged that some blacks be granted the right to vote. A restoration of national unity that achieved both of Lincoln's goals would have been difficult even for a president of his extraordinary skill. Unfortunately for the nation, Lincoln was shot on April 14 and died the next day. Leadership of the rebuilding effort fell to hands far less skillful.

The new president, Andrew Johnson, had been a Unionist Democrat from Tennessee, but he had also owned slaves. Lincoln had chosen him as his vice presidential nominee in an effort to create national unity, not because the two men agreed on the same policies. As president, Johnson followed Lincoln's lead by insisting on the abolition of slavery and protection of freedmen's property rights. But he rejected the idea of full citizenship for freed slaves, and he undercut most efforts to help the freedmen establish themselves independently in the postwar world.

Alabamians after the war faced two massive sets of problems that were interconnected. One was addressing their staggering racial and political issues. The other was rebuilding their shattered economy. The sale of cotton had been the foundation of Alabama's economy since the state's creation, but the system of slavery on which cotton production and the entire economy had depended no longer existed.

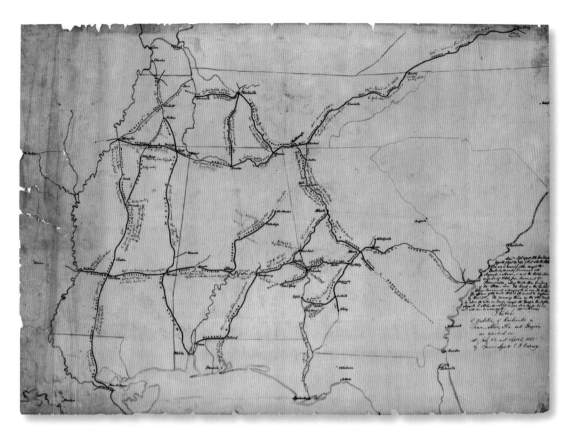

The ten years of Reconstruction in Alabama can be divided into three broad phases, based on changing federal policies. In the first part, until 1867, President Johnson led in setting the terms for Reconstruction, which were surprisingly lenient to former Confederates. The second phase began in March 1867, when Congress wrested much of the power from the president and set a course that actively sought to protect the rights of freedmen. The third phase began in 1874, when the Federal government essentially gave up on further exertions to protect freedmen and white Democrats in Alabama were able to regain political power, bringing Reconstruction to an end.

Railroad map of Alabama, September 1865. This sketch shows the condition of Alabama railroads at the end of the Civil War, but it also illustrates the limited service of Alabama railroads at the time of the Civil War.

PRESIDENTIAL RECONSTRUCTION (1865 TO 1867)

SINCE Congress was out of session at the end of the war and did not return until December, initial responsibility for Reconstruction efforts fell to President Johnson. Under the terms he set, most white men in the South could have their citizenship rights restored merely by signing an oath of allegiance to the U.S. Constitution. All Alabama laws in effect in 1861, with the exception of those regarding slavery, remained in force, and local officials continued in office.

Before adjourning in March 1865, Congress had set up the Bureau of Refugees, Freedmen, and AbandonLands—known as the Freedmen's

Print from the August 11, 1866 edition of *Harper's Weekly*, entitled "Alabamians Receiving Rations."

Bureau—to help deal with postwar problems in the South. The Bureau's most pressing immediate challenge in Alabama was providing food for hundreds of thousands of people facing starvation. Because of the devastation in north Alabama, Bureau officials in the state ultimately distributed more food to needy white people than to freedmen.

The great work of restoring the economy and aiding freedmen in finding their new place in society was far more difficult than providing relief. At the war's end, many freedmen abandoned their homes to find family members from whom they had been separated. Others followed Federal troops. Still others moved to towns in search of new opportunities. But many also remained where they lived as slaves, or returned there when they could find no means for supporting themselves elsewhere. Congress had debated proposals to provide land for the freedmen, but in the end, it did not set up any systematic program to help them become self-supporting.

The work of the Freedmen's Bureau in assisting former slaves was the first large-scale social services program in American history. Bureau officials had no earlier experiences to draw on and very limited resources. With no way to provide work or land for the freedmen, the Bureau's only practical option was to encourage freedmen to resume work as employees of the cotton planters. The Bureau did try to protect the rights of these new employees by requiring written labor contracts that were approved by its officials.

Starting in the latter part of 1865, many freedmen did begin returning to the cotton fields under the new labor contracts, but they quickly found the new arrangement unacceptable. Pushing for maximum production, with attitudes little changed since slavery, planters often treated their employees as they had their slaves, housing them in former slave quarters and working them in gangs. Some planters still used whips to coerce production.

Former slaves, fully conscious of their new freedom, resisted what they saw as merely a modified version of slavery. As the freedmen grew more resistant, planters were forced to accommodate them. The labor contracts were converted into a new arrangement in which individual families of freedmen worked separate tracts of land on which they lived—a system that would come to be known as sharecropping. While its faults would become more apparent over time, in the 1860s sharecropping offered freedmen far more independence than they had known under the old system of gang labor.

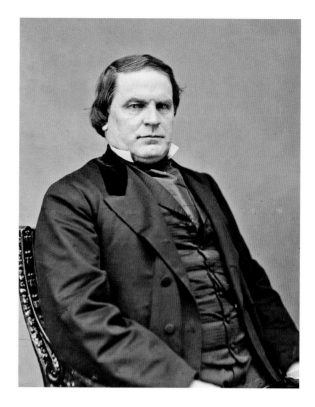

Governor Lewis E. Parsons. Parsons led in the rebuilding of the Democratic Party after the war, but he switched to the Republican Party in 1869 because he believed that cooperation with federal Reconstruction made more sense than continued opposition.

Like their counterparts across the South, Alabama freedmen embraced new opportunities for education with an enthusiasm stoked by many years of dreams long denied. Some black communities built their own schools, and others were established by the Freedmen's Bureau. Some of the most successful schools, such as Lincoln Normal School in Marion and Talladega College, were started with assistance from northern religious groups, particularly the Congregationalist Church's American Missionary Association. Freedmen also began creating other social institutions of their own, such as churches, where they were no longer subject to oversight by whites.

To restore state government, President Johnson, in June 1865, appointed Lewis Parsons of Talladega as Alabama's provisional governor. Parsons, a grandson of the famed New England evangelist Jonathan Edwards, was a former Whig who had opposed secession. In 1863, he had been elected to the state legislature as a peace candidate. At President Johnson's direction, Parson called for elections in August 1865 to choose delegates to a new state constitutional convention that was set for September.

With old laws and officials still in place, the August elections were run by, and only open to, white men. Neither state officials nor President Johnson took any step toward Lincoln's goal of including at least some African American voters in the election process. The southern states were not unique in this refusal; many northern states at the time also denied black residents the right to vote.

The delegates who gathered in Montgomery that September knew they were being carefully watched. They tried to minimize overt actions that would antagonize their recent conquerors, and they formally acknowledged that "the institution of slavery had been destroyed in the state of Alabama." But they avoided taking any position regarding the rights of freedmen. Instead, they directed the next legislature to "pass such laws as will protect the freedmen of this state in the full enjoyment of all their rights of person and property, and guard them and the state against all evil that may arise from their sudden emancipation."

The emphasis on "rights of person and property," as opposed to the larger rights of citizenship, was a critical one. Citizenship rights included voting, jury service, and eligibility to hold public office, which members of the convention did not envision for freedmen. When a group of African Americans in Mobile petitioned the convention for "the right of suffrage and other rights and immunities of citizenship," the petition was tabled without discussion by a unanimous vote.

White Alabamians had justified slavery for decades on claims of black racial inferiority, and they had seen abolition as an impossibility because they could not imagine a society in which white and black people lived together as equals. After four years of war caused in part by those ideas, most white Alabamians remained incapable of suddenly regarding former slaves as social or political equals. So, while outwardly accepting slavery's demise, convention delegates began strengthening indirect tools that would help them re-assert control over the freedmen, and guard "them and the state against all the evil that may arise from their sudden emancipation."

Another feature of the September convention was a renewal of the conflict between yeoman farmer–dominated north Alabama and planter-dominated south Alabama. Yeoman farmers in northern counties had suffered severely in a war they blamed on the planters. They felt it was now their turn to lead the state. Resentments from the war added new grievances to an antipathy that reached back for decades.

Labor contract between J. Miller and William B. Hall of Benton, Alabama, January 11, 1867. Miller agreed to "hire my time" for the year 1867 and "to labor faithfully and yield obedience," for the sum of $144 and rations.

Planters of Whig background made up the largest faction at the constitutional convention, but most of them had also opposed secession. Some had supported the Confederacy after the decision to secede, but many others had sat out the war or even supported the peace movement. These planters, too, had suffered from a war they had generally not wanted.

Both north Alabama farmers and Republican leaders in Washington tended to see the resurgence of these former Whigs as a return of the old planter aristocracy, which in some ways it was. But the planters had not controlled Alabama in the prewar period, and they had not been leaders in the drive for secession. Regardless of who actually deserved blame for the war, old tensions between planters and yeoman farmers quickly revived.

The legislature that was elected under the new constitution convened in Montgomery on November 20, 1865. As a condition for readmission to the Union, it ratified the Thirteenth Amendment to the U.S. Constitution, which prohibited slavery. But, like other state legislatures in the former Confederacy, it also passed a set of bills known as the *Black Codes*, which would have severely restricted the rights of freedmen. When Alabama's new governor, Robert Patton, vetoed the legislation, enough legislators changed their positions to sustain his veto, and

Talladega College, 1907. This photo shows a view of the college forty years after its founding, by which time it had grown into an important center of African American education.

Phillips Memorial Hall, one of the surviving buildings of the Lincoln School in Marion. Founded in 1867, the Lincoln School became an educational center for African Americans in the Black Belt. The normal school that was part of Lincoln moved to Montgomery in the 1880s and eventually grew into Alabama State University. Coretta Scott King was a graduate of the Lincoln School.

the Codes failed to become law. Some yeoman-farmer representatives began to fear that the Codes' provisions might be used against them.

Even though Alabama ultimately rejected the kind of harsh Black Codes that were enacted in other former Confederate states, Alabama's criminal code contained an array of tools that white officials could use to re-establish their control. Legislators strengthened the law against vagrancy, setting a fine of fifty dollars and allowing local officials to hire out offenders to work. The constitutional convention had already raised the cap on cases handled by justices of the peace to one hundred dollars, giving them increased authority free from the burden of formal jury trials.

Vagrancy laws were especially effective as a tool of racial control when they were combined with new stock laws. Before the Civil War, tens of thousands of white yeoman-farmer families were able to subsist on public land, letting their livestock graze on the open range. After the war, the legislature began authorizing counties to require that farmers fence their livestock. By 1880, half of Alabama's counties had enacted stock laws, including all Black Belt counties. Black people who lived in those counties and owned no land could no longer support themselves on the open range the way their white counterparts had for generations before. Vagrancy and stock laws worked together to force most freedmen back to the cotton fields. (Most of the counties with large yeoman-farmer populations refused to adopt the stock laws, and open-range grazing continued in many of those counties into the early twentieth century.)

CONGRESSIONAL RECONSTRUCTION
(1867 TO 1874)

To many Republicans in the North, the treatment of freedmen in the former Confederate states was an offense, if not an outrage. The "Radicals," a growing faction in the Republican Party, pressed vigorously to protect freedmen's rights, despite President Johnson's resistance. During the 1865 to 1866 Congress, the Radicals lacked the votes to overrule Johnson, but they did have the votes to deny seats to the newly elected senators and representatives from old Confederate states. When the new members of Alabama's delegation arrived in Washington in December 1865, Congress refused to seat any of them.

As accounts of the mistreatment of freedmen spread across the North, resentment against President Johnson increased. In the November 1866 elections, Radical candidates asked their constituents if they had waged such a costly and bloody war for such paltry results. The answer was a resounding "No!" After decisive Radical victories at the polls, most Republicans in Congress turned against President Johnson.

When the new Congress convened in March 1867, the Radicals held supermajorities in both houses and could override most presidential vetoes. They immediately passed a series of laws that took control of Reconstruction away from the president and set a dramatically different course. Congress abolished the provisional state governments Johnson had authorized and set up a system of military rule. It also established a new voter registration process that would enroll black men for the first time. After the new registration was completed, new state constitutional conventions were to be held in which freedmen would be able to participate. The registration law also included a mandatory oath designed to exclude from voting all those who had held office "in any State engaged in insurrection or rebellion against the United States, or given aid or comfort to the enemies thereof."

One source of the Radicals' political power was the Union League, a group of clubs that had begun in the North during the Civil War to support President Lincoln. By 1866, Unionist whites in Alabama, mostly in northern hill country, also began forming League clubs. Some of the members had served in the U.S. Army and fought for the Union. League members in Alabama opposed the leadership of the planters in the state's first Reconstruction government, and they also objected to being slighted in postwar relief programs.

Noah Cloud, in the 1850s. A physician, planter, and prominent Whig in Macon County before the Civil War, Cloud published a magazine promoting progressive farming practices. After the war, he joined the Republican Party and was elected state superintendent of education in the 1868 Republican sweep.

The initial relief supplies provided by the Freedmen's Bureau were often distributed by county officials, most of whom had served or supported the Confederacy. Alabama Unionists watched in rage when these officials used food from the Freedmen's Bureau to help former supporters of the Confederacy rather than those who had suffered during the war to maintain the Union. Complaints by Alabama Union League members to Republican leaders in Washington helped spur congressional support for more aggressive measures of Reconstruction.

As the congressionally mandated voter registration began in the summer of 1867, thousands of black Alabamians also joined the Union League. The League quickly grew to include white Unionists from north Alabama, freedmen, and northerners who had arrived in the state after the war, such as workers in the Freedmen's Bureau. It became a powerful political force behind the Republican Party in Alabama, which held its first organizational meeting in June 1867 in Montgomery.

Black men voted for the first time in Alabama in the October 1867 elections of delegates to the new constitutional convention. Of the one hundred delegates elected, historians have been able to document the backgrounds of all but a few. Native-born white Alabamians made up the majority, about fifty-four, but that majority was divided into two rival groups—the hill-country Unionists and the planters.

The other white delegates, approximately twenty-eight of them, were northerners who had moved to Alabama after the war. Many were teachers, preachers, or workers for the Freedmen's Bureau who hoped to build a new Alabama that would include blacks as full citizens. Democrats scornfully referred to these northerners as "carpetbaggers." They called the Alabama-born Republicans "scalawags." Despite the image portrayed in later years of black dominance during Reconstruction, only about seventeen of the one hundred delegates were African Americans.

Almost all the delegates were Republicans, however, so the convention debates reflected the divisions inside the Republican Party—between north Alabama small farmers and former-Whig planters, native Alabamians and newcomers, and whites and blacks. Often, factions were divided among themselves. Many black delegates, for instance, differed with each other over how aggressively to pursue the issue of equal rights. Native-born whites, the most conservative of the delegates, generally held the upper hand in convention voting.

Despite the divisions among delegates and their conservative positions on many issues, the new constitution they drafted marked a sweeping break from the past. It openly declared that "all men are created equal," and it provided for universal male suffrage. It also incorporated a host of progressive features, such as a statewide school system led by a strong state board of education, earmarked funding for schools, increased debtor protections, assistance to the poor, the popular election of judges, property rights protections for women, modernized corporation laws, and a new bureau to promote industrial development.

The constitution also included an unprecedented voter registration requirement. Before anyone would be allowed to vote in Alabama, he

Opposite page: Benjamin Turner, one of the most prominent freedmen leaders in Alabama; photo by Mathew Brady. Turner reportedly learned to read alongside the white children with whom he grew up. As a slave in the 1850s, he managed a hotel in Selma and ran a livery stable. In 1870, he became the first African American from Alabama elected to the U.S. House of Representatives. Above: Jeremiah Haralson, by Mathew Brady. Also a former slave from Selma, Haralson was elected to the Alabama House of Representatives in 1870 and the Senate in 1872. Two years later, he was elected to the U.S. House of Representatives, serving one term.

first had to swear that he rejected the idea of secession and accepted "the civil and political equality of all men." Despite their progressive stance on many other issues, convention delegates shied away from any steps to desegregate public schools or public facilities.

WHITE REACTION

DEMOCRATS also began rebuilding their party in 1867. At first, they called themselves the Conservative Party, to avoid alienating former Whigs. Later, they changed their name to the Democratic and Conservative Party, but by the 1870s, they were again simply Democrats. Like the Republicans, the Democrats were also divided internally. A major issue for them was whether to cooperate with congressional Reconstruction or to pursue all-out resistance. Some Democratic leaders even sought to appeal to black voters, though the party itself was overwhelmingly white.

Under the 1867 Reconstruction Laws, new constitutions in the former Confederate states were to be approved in referendums that required a majority of all *registered* voters, not just a majority of those voting. Alabama Democrats saw that requirement as an opportunity to prevent ratification, and they called on whites to boycott the February 1868 ratification referendum. Following a racially charged campaign, the proposed constitution failed to win the necessary majority.

Radical Republicans in Congress, however, were unwilling to let the document die. In an act passed in June 1868 over President Johnson's veto, Congress accepted the Alabama constitution despite the election failure and admitted the

James Holt Clanton. A former Confederate general, Clanton helped rebuild the Democratic Party in Alabama during Reconstruction and became chairman of its executive committee. He was also alleged to have been the head of the Ku Klux Klan in Alabama.

state back into the Union. Congress's only other requirement was that the legislature ratify the Fourteenth Amendment to the U.S. Constitution, which granted citizenship and all its rights to all persons born in the United States. Earlier during Presidential Reconstruction, the Alabama legislature had rejected the amendment.

The new state legislature elected under the 1868 constitution convened in Montgomery in July. Because Democrats had boycotted the elections, all elected state officials were Republicans. As they turned to the work of rebuilding the state, the new leaders had to find ways to fund the programs that the new constitution mandated. Lacking many options the state had relied on before the war, such as taxes on slaves, Republican leaders turned to the one reliable source of taxation that

A Prospective Scene in the "City of Oaks," 4th of March, 1869.

"Hang, eurs, hang! * * * * * * *Their* complexion is perfect gallows. Stand fast, good fate, to *their* hanging! * * * * * If they be not born to be hanged, our case is miserable."

Left: Woodcut print from the *Tuscaloosa Monitor*, September 1, 1868. This image was published as a threat to Noah Cloud, who was ex officio head of the University of Alabama's board of regents, and to Rev. Arad Lakin, a "carpetbagger" who had just been appointed the university's president. Below: Two men in Klan regalia. This print was based on a photo of two U.S. soldiers modeling seized Klan costumes and was published in an 1884 book about the Klan.

remained; they increased the property tax rate from two to seven and a half mills.

Although freedmen were now citizens and entitled to state services, few of them owned land, which meant the new taxes were paid almost exclusively by whites. Alabama landowners, both large and small, soon found themselves paying far more in taxes for virtually no increase in services for themselves. Racial relations were already strained, but the increased taxes during hard economic times stoked general white resentment and ratcheted racial tensions to a higher level.

From the last months of the Civil War and into Reconstruction, Alabama was an extraordinarily violent place. Many people were murdered for a wide variety of reasons. Law enforcement, if present at all, was weak and uneven. And the large number of desperate people without resources gave rise to widespread theft, especially of livestock, crops, and tools. In some parts of Alabama, local white vigilante bands began organizing to protect their property and restore order. As white resentment grew against black voting, the tax increase, and the new Republican government, this white vigilantism grew into an insurgency.

Secret paramilitary groups such as the Ku Klux Klan (KKK) first emerged in 1867 and 1868. They launched systematic campaigns of intimidation especially targeting Republican Party and Union League leaders, both black and white. People who did not heed Klan threats were often beaten or even murdered. The files of Republican governor William H. Smith (1868–1870) are filled with letters, reports, and pleas for help from people all across Alabama who were victims or witnesses of the violence. In December 1870, Mary Pond, a northern teacher working in Selma for the American Missionary Association, wrote to a friend in Connecticut: "It is estimated that more than 1300 persons have been killed since Gov. Smith was inaugurated."

There are no systematic records to document her claims, but the violence was so widespread that it prompted widely publicized congressional hearings. Those hearings, held in early 1871, led to new federal anti-Klan legislation and increased intervention. The threat of more federal troops being sent into Alabama and examples of aggressive prosecutions of the KKK in other states caused the Alabama Klan to disband in the early 1870s. But local vigilante groups and sporadic mob actions continued for decades afterward.

A message to President Ulysses Grant submitted by a meeting of African American citizens in Montgomery in 1874 provides an example of the intimidation. In the state elections a month before, a Republican worker was sent from Mobile to Washington County with printed "tickets for them [local Negroes] to vote." On the train "he was met…by a democrat, who warned him that if…he went there to do anything in connection with inducing or enabling negroes to vote, he would be killed on the spot." The Republican worker returned to Mobile, and no one else could be persuaded to "peril his life in repeating the attempt." Out of a hundred Republicans in this particular Washington County precinct, "not one of them voted or could have voted."

Railroad bridge at Florence around 1870. The original bridge was destroyed by Confederate troops in 1862 to deny its use to the Union army. The new replacement bridge opened in 1870, and portions of it still stand.

REBUILDING THE ECONOMY

ONE lesson both Republican and Democratic leaders in Alabama drew from the Civil War was that the state's economy must become more diverse. Though the state had some mills, mines, and furnaces before the war, the value of all Alabama's manufacturing facilities in 1860 was only about five percent of the value of its farmland. The number of employees in manufacturing was less than one percent of the state's population.

Even before the Civil War, the state of Alabama had provided some aid to encourage railroad development. As Alabamians began rebuilding after the war, most political leaders of both parties agreed that

more railroads were a critical need. Farmers and manufacturers alike would be able to ship their products to market, and improved access to railroads could support development of the mineral belt in north-central Alabama.

The distinguished British geologist Charles Lyell had visited Alabama in 1846 and described the state's abundant coal and iron deposits. The first entrepreneurs trying to develop these resources, however, were hamstrung by limited rail service. The growth of the Confederate ordnance works at Selma was possible in part because of a recently completed portion of the Alabama & Tennessee River Railroad, which linked Selma to Talladega and passed through the southern part of the mineral belt. For Alabama's Reconstruction leaders, expanding the state's iron and coal industries was also a top priority.

To foster railroad expansion, white Democrats during the Presidential Reconstruction period began providing state guarantees for bonds issued by railroad companies, at a rate of $12,000 per mile of track built. Republicans later raised the amount to $16,000 per mile. As railroad assistance and other programs of the Reconstruction legislature expanded, however, the state's revenues could not sustain them.

Also, controls over state expenditures were grossly inadequate, especially in the aid to railroads. Officials in both parties were induced to guarantee bonds for lines that were not economically viable, and they sometimes paid for miles of track that were not even built. Some counties offered their own programs, most of which were also poorly managed.

Members of the Alabama Legislature, 1872, standing in front of the state Capitol. Although African Americans were elected to the Alabama legislature during the years of Congressional Reconstruction, they remained a relatively small minority.

In 1871, the Alabama & Chattanooga Railroad failed, despite having received almost $7,000,000 from the state in direct support and bond guarantees. After taking over the railroad, the state ended up paying an additional $1 million to get rid of it. When the international economic Panic of 1873 hit, other railroads faltered, and Alabama state government faced financial disaster as the debts ballooned. The costs of interest payments alone threatened to consume all of the state's revenue. Some counties had to declare bankruptcy.

Randolph County Railroad Bond. This eight percent bond was part of a $100,000 issue by Randolph County approved on December 31, 1868, to support the Eufaula, Opelika, Oxford, and Guntersville Railroad.

THE 1874 ELECTIONS AND THE END OF RECONSTRUCTION

The financial and racial problems of Reconstruction reached a crisis in the 1874 state elections. Higher property taxes, increasing demands for civil rights, massive state debt, and the effects of an international financial panic all fueled a new surge of hostility against the incumbent Republican-led government. In a partnership previously rare in Alabama politics, substantial numbers of yeoman farmers and planters joined together in a push to overturn Republican rule.

In a racially charged and bitter campaign, Democrats attacked the Republicans over the state's financial condition, even though they had participated in many of the policies and practices that helped cause it. Democratic newspapers cried out against Republican fraud and mismanagement. Rampant corruption in President Grant's administration in Washington seemed also to reinforce the Democrats' charges that the Republican Party represented big taxes, irresponsible spending, graft, and "Negro rule."

At the same time, divisions inside the Alabama Republican Party worsened. Radical Republicans sought more public offices for black candidates and increased efforts to guarantee civil rights, such as prohibiting segregation in public accommodations. Most Alabama-born, white Republicans vigorously opposed these measures, and the two factions undercut each other.

Yet another major change by that election cycle was that northern support for freedmen was beginning to weaken. More U.S. soldiers were being withdrawn from the South and sent west to fight Indians. Also, the Panic of 1873 shifted national attention to problems of the economy. Many northerners simply grew weary of trying to force change on intractable white southerners. A considerable number of northerners, in fact, shared the racial attitudes of southern whites.

The Democratic gubernatorial candidate in 1874 was George Smith Houston, from Athens. Riding a broad surge of white support and aided by intimidation and fraud at the polls, Houston defeated the moderate Republican incumbent David P. Lewis, 107,118 votes to 93,934. Democrats also won solid majorities in both houses of the legislature. After Congress adjourned the following March without disallowing the election results, Alabama Democrats felt at liberty to move forward with their agenda.

Their first big step was to call a new constitutional convention, which convened in the House chamber of the Capitol in the spring of 1875. With a commanding majority of the delegates, Democrats elected as their president Leroy Pope Walker—the former Confederate secretary of war who had authorized the firing on Fort Sumter. No one in Alabama could have better symbolized the old order.

The new 1875 state constitution brought another sharp turn in Alabama government. It replaced the statement in the 1868 state constitution that "all men are created equal" with "all men are equally free and independent." It abolished the state board of education, the office of lieutenant governor, and the office of commissioner of industrial resources. It also eliminated earmarked funding for education, prohibited support for private business undertakings by either state or local governments, discarded the 1868 voter registration oath, made it easier to remove local officials, and established strict new limits on taxation by state and local governments.

For generations afterward, the overthrow of Republican rule in 1874 would be hailed by Alabama Democrats as the Redemption, and the leaders in the effort were called the Redeemers. White Alabamians were again firmly in control, and they would gradually tighten their grip in the decades to come. Alabama was entering a new era of government austerity, with low taxes, strict limits on spending, and minimal state services, as Alabama's industrial economy began to expand and the economy of rural Alabama deteriorated.

Leroy Pope Walker. Walker's remarkable career ranged from leading the Alabama delegation's walkout of the Democratic Convention in 1860 to securing the acquittal of outlaw Frank James, who was tried for a Muscle Shoals robbery in 1883.

CHAPTER 5

MINES, MILLS, AND MULES

1875 to 1914

FROM THE LATE 1800s *into the early 1900s, Alabama became the most heavily industrialized state of the old Confederacy. Production of lumber, textiles, coal, and iron soared. Birmingham grew so quickly it became the "Magic City." Rural Alabamians, however, remained locked in the annual cycle of cotton production. With crop prices depressed for most of this time, tens of thousands of farm families struggled against grinding poverty. Residents in the small towns that supported the farmers usually fared better. Some did quite well.*

While government leaders kept taxes low, unmet social needs sparked periodic protests and calls for reform. New laws for preserving white control created a repressive and awkward system of racial separation known as segregation. By the early 1900s, automobiles, electricity, and telephones were becoming part of daily life for more fortunate Alabamians—mostly urban dwellers—widening the gulf between them and their rural fellow citizens.

INDUSTRIALIZATION AND BIRMINGHAM

FROM the beginning of Reconstruction, state officials embraced railroad building as their top economic development priority. Although state aid initiatives were often poorly managed, they did help spur growth. As rail expansion proceeded in the early 1870s, two lines took on particular importance. The South & North Railroad, from Montgomery to Decatur, would complete a link connecting the Gulf of Mexico to Nashville and beyond. The Alabama & Chattanooga Railroad would run from Meridian, Mississippi, to Chattanooga, Tennessee, along the same basic route as today's Interstate 59.

TCI plant in Ensley, circa 1910. From the ruins of Civil War iron works, Alabama's coal, iron, and steel industries grew to the point that by 1910, Birmingham was a national center of iron and steel production.

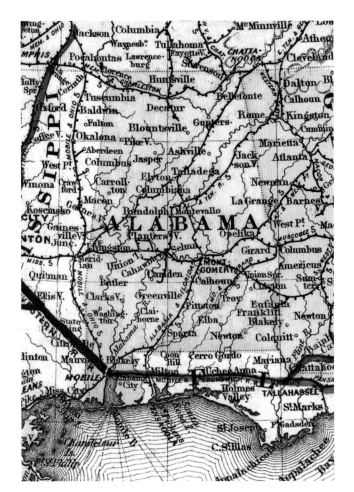

To developers and speculators, it seemed clear that the point in the mineral belt where these two lines crossed would become a valuable site. While final route plans were still in flux, leaders of the two companies competed for control over land around the prospective junction. In December 1870, businessmen connected with the South & North Railroad met in Montgomery to form the Elyton Land Company. They were able to buy the land they wanted and planned a new town at the site, which they named Birmingham, dreaming that it would soon grow to rival its English namesake.

The company sold its first lots in the summer of 1871, and Birmingham was

Left: 1871 railroad map, showing the beginning of the postwar rail expansion in Alabama. The South & North line was still under construction, reaching from Montgomery to Elyton, which became Birmingham the year the map was published.

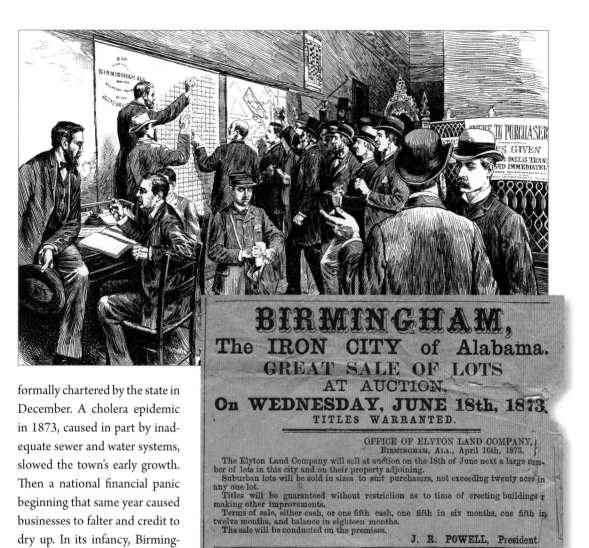

BIRMINGHAM,
The IRON CITY of Alabama.
GREAT SALE OF LOTS
AT AUCTION,
On WEDNESDAY, JUNE 18th, 1873.
TITLES WARRANTED.

OFFICE OF ELYTON LAND COMPANY,
BIRMINGHAM, ALA., April 16th, 1873.

The Elyton Land Company will sell at auction on the 18th of June next a large number of lots in this city and on their property adjoining.

Suburban lots will be sold in sizes to suit purchasers, not exceeding twenty acre in any one lot.

Titles will be guaranteed without restriction as to time of erecting buildings r making other improvements.

Terms of sale, either cash, or one fifth cash, one fifth in six months, one fifth in twelve months, and balance in eighteen months.

The sale will be conducted on the premises.

J. R. POWELL, President

formally chartered by the state in December. A cholera epidemic in 1873, caused in part by inadequate sewer and water systems, slowed the town's early growth. Then a national financial panic beginning that same year caused businesses to falter and credit to dry up. In its infancy, Birmingham caught its first taste of the boom-and-bust cycle that would become part of the rhythm of its life.

The town's iron and coal men, however, were a resilient lot, and they pushed on despite the downturn. Henry F. DeBardeleben, son-in-law of antebellum cotton gin manufacturer Daniel Pratt, was one of the early leaders—a fitting indicator of the strategic shift by business into the new economy of coal and iron.

The early iron furnaces in Alabama were fueled by charcoal, made from wood. Coal was used then mostly for steam engines and in stoves for heating. From the 1850s into the 1870s, lumbermen cut great swaths of forest across the mineral belt to make the charcoal needed by Alabama's growing iron industry. In 1876, engineer Levin Goodrich developed a process for converting local coal into coke, which could replace charcoal in the smelting process. The enormous quantities of coal around Birmingham would be able to support iron production far into the future.

Opposite page, below: The earliest known photograph of Birmingham. Several buildings in this 1873 photograph are numbered and identified as follows: 1. First Presbyterian Church, 2. First Baptist Church, 3. First Methodist Church, 4. Birmingham Water Works, 5. T. L. Huggins's home, 6. Colonel Terry's home. Top: Scene in a Birmingham land office. The first lots were sold in 1871 by the Elyton Land Company. Note the map with lots on the wall. Above: Land sale notice by Elyton Land Company, 1873.

Ironworks at Ironton as seen from the Hotel Looking South of West

Photo taken around 1872 of new works at Ironton, known better later as Oxmoor, which were then under construction. An earlier furnace there had been destroyed by Wilson's Raiders in late March 1865, but in the early 1870s, the facilities were rebuilt and expanded by Daniel Pratt and his son-in-law, Henry Debardeleben.

In 1876, DeBardeleben and two other industrial pioneers, Truman Aldrich and James W. Sloss, established the Pratt Coal and Coke Company to take advantage of the new coal technology. Two years later, DeBardeleben completed the first Alabama coke-burning furnace at Oxmoor, just a few miles south of today's downtown Birmingham.

When workers tapped molten iron from these furnaces, they channeled the flow across a large, open sand floor into molds where the liquid cooled into individual ingots. Because the rows of ingots resembled sets of suckling piglets, the iron was called pig iron. The particular mineral mixture of Alabama's iron ore did not readily produce high quality steel, but it was nearly perfect for making cast iron products, such as cooking pots, wood stoves, and water pipes. Foundries that reheated and molded the pigs into these cast iron products became an important related industry, also fueled by local coal.

Soon after DeBardeleben built his furnace, his old partner James Sloss built another, closer to downtown Birmingham, and other companies joined them. Through the 1880s and into the early twentieth century, coal mines also grew to support the expanding furnaces and foundries.

Ironton Hotel—Operatives' Houses—Shades' Mountain—S. & N. R. R.—Coal Ovens & Coal-wood-yard

Looking East

All this growth transformed Birmingham. The Magic City grew from a drawing in 1871 to a town of 3,086 people in 1880; 26,179 in 1890; and 38,415 in 1900. By 1910, Birmingham was a major "New South" city of 132,685 people, and still growing. The haze of smoke that increasingly shrouded Birmingham was a sign of its progress. Many people came from far away to work in the new industries, not only from northern states, but from eastern and southern Europe as well.

Because of the lack of local capital, Alabama entrepreneurs usually had to find out-of-state investors to help fund their projects. As new companies rose and challenged older ones, those with better access to capital often absorbed companies that lacked it. In this process, corporations and investors from outside Alabama gradually won control of many of the state's coal mines, furnaces, and railroads. Although jobs and administrative positions remained in Alabama, a substantial part of the profits flowed to the outside owners.

Alabama owners of the South & North Railroad (S&N), for example, ran out of money in 1872, before their line reached Decatur. Funding from the more financially secure Louisville & Nashville Railroad (L&N) helped the S&N finish building the line, but brought the struggling

Ironton coal ovens, circa 1872. The mound structures are ovens where wood from the great pile of logs in the foreground was converted into charcoal, referred to simply as "coal" in the photo label.

Workers channeling molten iron across a sand floor for cooling into ingots, called pigs.

company into the L&N system. The L&N then provided critical investment funds for developing Birmingham, and the railroad's profits from Alabama in turn helped the L&N extend its system outside the state.

The Tennessee Coal, Iron and Railroad Company—based in Chattanooga but with funding from northern investors—moved into Birmingham in the mid-1880s. By buying up competitors and consolidating operations, it grew in little more than a decade to be Alabama's dominant industrial corporation. Known as TCI, its holdings included those developed by DeBardeleben, who lost out to the company in a power struggle. In the 1890s, TCI developed new processes for producing steel from local ore, strengthening its position as a major U.S. metals producer. In 1907, tycoon J. P. Morgan engineered a takeover of TCI by U.S. Steel, neutralizing TCI as a competitor.

Although Birmingham was the center of Alabama's coal and iron industry, many other towns were part of the story. An arc of iron production stretched across the state's mineral belt from Gadsden and Anniston in the east, through Ensley and Bessemer, and on to Sheffield in the northwest. Alabama's production of pig iron soared from 62,000 tons in 1880 to 2.1 million by 1920, making the state the fourth largest producer in the nation.

Railroad construction continued as well. Before the Civil War, the state had less than 800 miles of track. By 1880, the total had risen to 1,800 miles, and by 1910 to more than 5,000 miles. Railroads supplanted rivers as the state's principal transportation arteries, and railroad companies became a powerful economic and political force in Alabama as well.

Top: Birmingham skyscrapers in 1915. This view looks south on 20th Street from 3rd Avenue North to what was then proudly called "the heaviest corner on earth." **Above:** Sloss Furnace, a National Historic Landmark, in Birmingham. The remains of the great furnace operations are now a historic site and museum.

LUMBER AND TEXTILE MILLS

A Basil Hall sketch of a longleaf pine forest, 1828. Hall, a British naval officer and world traveler who made sketches with a camera lucida, described a "vast ocean of trees, stretching, without a break, in every direction, as far as the eye could reach; and I remember, upon one of these occasions, thinking that I never before had a just conception of what the word forest meant."

BEFORE the first Europeans arrived in the 1500s, forests covered approximately ninety percent of Alabama. More than half of this forest was a unique ecosystem in which tall, stately longleaf pines shared the soil with a complex meadow understory that was refreshed regularly by fire. Reaching heights sometimes exceeding one hundred twenty feet and diameters of three feet, these pines were a valuable resource for the early settlers at Mobile, who used them for ship masts, lumber, and tar.

The forests provided Alabama settlers with wood for building their homes, cooking their food, and warming themselves in the winter. Wood also fueled the boilers of riverboats, made ties and trestles for railroads, and became charcoal for the first ironworks. For most farmers,

though, the trees were an impediment, and they were simply killed and burned to carve out new cropland. Despite fifty years of consumption and clearing, however, large parts of Alabama were still covered by virgin forests when the state began rebuilding after the Civil War.

Starting in 1850, the federal government began granting rail companies sections of land from the public domain as a construction incentive. Hundreds of thousands of acres of Alabama forests passed into corporate ownership as rail lines expanded through the state. New lines in turn allowed the lumbermen who cut the forests to ship their wood to distant customers.

New steam-powered machines, such as band saws and skidders for pulling logs out of the forests, made the lumber industry more efficient. Companies built their own temporary rail lines as they cut their

Above: Logging train in Autauga County, about 1920. The only person identified in the photo is the man standing on the left, James Jordon Golson. Left: The Kaul Lumber Company mill in Tuscaloosa. In 1912, owner John Kaul built this mill and Kaulton, a company town embodying what Kaul described as a "new welfare emphasis in the southern lumber industry."

way into new sections of forest. When they reached a natural barrier or property line, they pulled up the tracks behind themselves as they backed out and moved to clear another area.

Lumber from longleaf pines often hundreds of years old became one of Alabama's most important exports. In 1869, Alabama produced 86 million board feet of lumber. By 1899, the total had increased to almost 1 billion. Through the early 1900s into the late 1920s, production averaged over 1.5 billion board feet a year. Enough wood to circle the earth with a walkway one inch thick and eleven feet wide was cut from Alabama forests every year for almost three decades. In the 1910 census, 22,409 of Alabama's 72,148 wage earners cut or milled wood, far more workers than in any other industry.

All of this wood—approximately ninety percent of it longleaf pine—went to build structures not only in Alabama but also in the northern United States and Europe. A recent book about southern longleaf pines by Bill Finch, Beth Maynor Young, Rhett Johnson, and John C. Hall notes, "The walls and floors of Balmoral, Prince Albert and Queen Victoria's royal castle in Scotland, were built with longleaf pitch pine." Little is left in Alabama today of these great old forests, though a number of landowners are now trying to restore tracts of longleafs and re-establish the unique habitats of which they were a key part.

Alabama's textile industry also began rebuilding and expanding after the Civil War. Growth surged in the 1880s when manufacturers from the Northeast started building mills in the South. The southern mills were closer to the supply of cotton and had ample access to waterpower to run their machines. But, most important, wage rates in the South were far lower than in the Northeast. By

Above: Turner Terminals in Mobile circa 1925. The holds of both ships in the foreground are being filled with lumber. Right: Company town at Lanett, taken in 1901 for a promotional book about West Point and Lanett. The tracks of the Chattahoochee Valley Railroad and the fence of the Lanett Bleachery and Dye Works are in the right foreground.

1910, textile manufacturing had become Alabama's second largest industry, based on the number of workers employed—12,731—and the number was increasing each year. One-third of these workers were women, a high percentage compared to other industries.

In all these early industries, work was long, hard, and often dangerous: cutting, moving, and milling huge trees; hacking ore or coal from seams deep in the earth; tending furnaces of hot, deadly, molten iron; or running powerful spinning or weaving machines in noisy, lint-filled factories. No industrial safety agency existed to record the deaths and injuries from accidents or other causes, such as lung disease, broken bones, or damaged muscles and joints. No worker's compensation agency existed to assist the injured or aid the families of workers who lost their lives. The 1910 census reported that seventy-one percent of Alabama's wage earners worked sixty hours a week or more.

But while work in the new industries was hard, so was farm work. And, though industrial wages were usually low, those jobs nevertheless paid more than sharecropping. Often the industrial jobs also included company-provided benefits, such as housing, education for children, and medical care. Company towns became worlds unto themselves for thousands of Alabamians, where work, home, social activities, recreation, shopping, and church life all were centered in one tightly bound community. Thousands of Alabama sharecroppers left their farms behind to take jobs in Alabama's growing industries.

Young girl working at the Barker Cotton Mill in Mobile, taken by Lewis Hine, 1914. Nationally known photographer Lewis Hine traveled around the nation documenting child labor conditions. His other Alabama photographs, available online at the Library of Congress, show conditions considerably worse than this image indicates.

RURAL ALABAMA

DESPITE the state's mushrooming industrial growth, Alabama remained overwhelmingly rural. In the 1910 census, only seventeen percent of the population lived in a town or city of 2,500 people or more. Of the state's 2.1 million citizens, eighty-three percent were classified as rural, and, with depressed cotton prices, the conditions in which they lived were generally bleak.

Year after year, the system of sharecropping and tenant farming expanded, from fewer than 69,000 farms in 1880 to approximately

155,000 in 1910. That same year, eighty-five percent of all Alabama farms operated by blacks and forty-three percent of those operated by whites were classified as either tenant or rental. Many descendants of the proud and independent yeoman-farmer settlers of early Alabama became locked in bonds of debt dependency that would have appalled their forebears.

Sharecroppers paid for their use of land by pledging in advance a portion of their crop at harvest time. Tenant farmers paid cash rent for the tract they farmed and usually had more independence than sharecroppers. But both groups worked land they did not own, and

Cotton picking near Furman, Alabama, early 1900s. Mary Simpson, a teacher and the daughter of a Wilcox County planter, took photographs that lovingly documented life around her, though the names of the subjects are not recorded.

Top: Workers' shack from a farm at Furman, Alabama, in the early 1900s, taken by Mary Simpson. Above: Children with a goat, another photo from Furman in Wilcox County by Mary Simpson.

landowners usually had the upper hand in setting the terms of their agreements.

Sharecroppers often depended on landowners to advance at least part of what they needed for the coming crop year, such as seed, a mule, fertilizer, and even provisions to live on. The cost of these advances was taken from the farmer's share of the proceeds when the cotton was sold. With depressed cotton prices through most of the late 1800s, sharecroppers often ended the year in debt, with the balance due rolled over to the next year's loan.

The loan agreements sharecroppers signed in order to receive their advances were often backed up not only by pledges on their crops, but by their livestock, plows, or household possessions. Chattel mortgage books kept by county probate judges were filled with page after page of these loan documents. Each one told a personal story of struggle and debt. Often, the landowners and merchants themselves were in debt to their banks and suppliers, which might in turn be obligated to other banks and suppliers, usually outside the state. Everyone in the system was locked into cotton because it was the only farm product for which banks and merchants would lend money.

The sharecropping system was rife with abuse and exploitation. Interest rates on loans and supplies were usually high, often usurious. Farmers might be required to buy and sell only with the merchants or landowners who extended the loans, at prices set by the lenders. Since many of the sharecroppers, both black and white, were illiterate, they were at a great disadvantage if they tried to mount any kind of challenge. Courts and law enforcement officials usually supported the landowners and merchants.

One of the best accounts ever written of a sharecropper's life is *All God's Dangers*, in which a black Tallapoosa County farmer, Ned Cobb, tells his life's story. The book is drawn from extensive interviews with Cobb, although names and places were altered when it was published in 1974 because Cobb's family was still fearful of reprisals.

Cobb, the son of a sharecropper, became a sharecropper himself in the early 1900s, and he continued farming into the 1960s. When he was interviewed late in his life, he could still recall specific details about how much cotton he made in a particular year, his mules and their personalities, and people he worked for and with.

Although Cobb took pride in his own thrift and hard work, he reported that his father had squandered the little money he earned. Cobb explained the behavior, in part at least, by the number of black farmers his father had seen "cleaned up," who had lost all they owned when their property was seized under some type of legal claim. Cobb recalled that his father was "cleaned up twice."

One of Cobb's stories was about "old man Henry Kirkland," whose

son had "pretty good book learnin'" and began keeping a record of Kirkland's debts. At settlement time, Kirkland took his son and the record book with him to challenge the landowner's figures. According to Cobb, the owner "flew into a passion over that book business and throwed that pistol on old Uncle Henry and deadened him right there." He also shot the son, who survived. Although the landowner was jailed, "the company in Opelika that furnished him" and "had a mortgage on everything he had" got him out with no further penalty. All surviving members of the Kirkland family eventually left the county.

One of the times Cobb's father was cleaned up took place around 1900. The father had worked hard to accumulate five or six head of cattle, on which a white man held a lien. When someone offered to

Basket weaver at Clayton, Alabama, 1915. This basket maker had learned his craft as a slave and was teaching others when this photo was taken.

buy one of the cows, the lienholder gave Cobb's father oral permission to sell it, but then afterward sued him for an unauthorized sale.

Cobb's father was jailed and then released to the custody of the man who had killed Henry Kirkland. Every member of the Cobb family worked particularly hard, and in fear, for the next year, receiving nothing for their labors but meager supplies of "sorghum syrup and corn meal." In desperation, Cobb's father struck a deal with the landowner. In addition to their other work, the family made a large number of split-oak cotton baskets the landowner could sell, which won Cobb's father his freedom. Both black and white sharecroppers were subject to this kind of treatment, but blacks had even fewer resources with which to protect themselves.

With the spread of tenant farming and sharecropping, the size of Alabama farms decreased. In 1860, the average size was 347 acres. After the Civil War and five years of Reconstruction, it fell to 222, and it continued falling to 126 acres in 1890 and 79 by 1910. These numbers show individual farm operations, not ownership. Often one person owned many farms, as old plantations were divided into multiple sharecropper tracts. Historian Gavin Wright points to the decrease in farm size as another indicator of rural poverty. With labor so cheap,

Gathering the Fleecy Staple. **Despite the lilting label, cotton picking was hard, hot, back-breaking work for thousands of Alabama farm families, black and white, for generations.**

GATHERING THE FLEECY STAPLE.

Farmers with wagons of cotton waiting to be baled at Furman, Alabama, in the early 1900s.

people could be pressed into more intensive cultivation of smaller plots.

An additional victim of tenant farming and sharecropping was the land itself. Even before the Civil War, most Alabama farmers used practices that quickly depleted the soil's nutrients. Rather than mulching, composting, and rotating crops to renew soil fertility, farmers found it easier to clear more forest or simply move on when the soil "played out." In the postwar era of tenant farming and sharecropping, those who worked the land had little incentive to protect or restore it. The extra effort made no sense to a sharecropper working someone else's land, which he might not even farm the next season.

Both prewar and postwar farming practices resulted in decades of terrible erosion, a massive loss of topsoil, and decreased fertility. Before the 1830s, Alabama rivers and streams had run clear. Rainfall soaked into the forest floor and then percolated through the soil into the water table below, emerging in pure springs to feed the creeks and rivers. By the end of the 1800s, most Alabama waterways had become muddy channels of flowing topsoil, the runoff of each new rainstorm.

In 1896, when botanist George Washington Carver first arrived at Tuskegee Institute from Iowa to head the school's Agriculture Department, he was appalled by the "devastated farms, ruined estates, and a thoroughly discouraged people, many just eking out a miserable sort of existence from the furrowed and guttered hillsides and neglected valleys called farms."

George Reynolds and family, along with an African American boy, in front of their home in Clayton, Alabama, around 1900.

Although Alabama farmers enjoyed occasional years of improved cotton prices in the early 1900s, for decade after decade their primary experience was impoverishment. Wage rates remained low in Alabama's industries because so many poor farmers were always available to fill each job vacancy. Through this entire period, per capita wages in Alabama remained at about fifty percent of the national average.

Life was somewhat better in the hundreds of small towns that served Alabama farms. At intervals along railroad lines, especially at junctions and strategic crossings, towns grew up or expanded to provide local farmers with services, supplies, and markets for their produce. These towns were home to doctors, lawyers, bankers, and merchants, and to schoolteachers, preachers, blacksmiths, craftsmen, and laborers. Harper Lee, who grew up in Monroeville in south Alabama, portrays life in one of these towns in her novel *To Kill a Mockingbird*.

CULTURAL VARIETY

BECAUSE images of white and black communities are so strong in Alabama history, there is a tendency to overlook smaller immigrant and ethnic communities that were also an important part of life in the state. The stories of these people reveal a greater complexity than is portrayed in the standard narrative. For example, because of the area's rich cultural history, some counties around Mobile maintained three separate school systems into the mid-twentieth century—for black, white, and Creole students.

Jewish immigrants, mostly from Germany, began arriving in Alabama before the Civil War. Their numbers increased into the early 1900s, with many of the later arrivals from Eastern Europe or Mediterranean countries. Jewish businessmen often became leaders in towns and cities across the state, and some built companies of national importance. The international financial firm Lehman Brothers, for example, was formed in Montgomery. Just before the Civil War, the brothers opened a branch in New York, and the branch soon outgrew the home office in Alabama.

Italian and Slavic immigrants worked in mines and at furnaces around Birmingham. A community of German farmers settled in Cullman County, and other Germans settled in Baldwin County, along with groups of Greeks, Italians, Scandinavians, Poles, Bohemians, and even a community of social progressives from the Midwest who built the town of Fairhope. Over time, the ethnic distinctions gradually faded, and most of the immigrant groups began to blend into the larger community, while perhaps still keeping the religious affiliation and a few traditions of their forebears.

Above: Temple Mishkan Israel, Selma. Selma boasted an active Jewish population from the late 1800s through the first half of the 1900s, including several mayors. By 2010, only about a dozen members remained in Selma, most of them elderly. Left: A family of Slovak immigrants, Brookside, Alabama, near Birmingham, in the early 1900s. Many Slovaks came to Brookside in Jefferson County to work in the coal mines.

RECONSTRUCTION-era Republicans, whom the Democrats called carpetbaggers and scalawags, had tried to disparage the Democrats by calling them "Bourbons." The Republicans thought a comparison to the French aristocrats who had returned to power after Napoleon was an insult. Some Democratic leaders, however, liked the name. In many ways they *were* attempting to restore the old order in Alabama, just as the Bourbons had sought to do in France.

Alabama's Bourbon leaders were united on two basic priorities: They wanted to reestablish white political control and to run a frugal government with low taxes. They held up these goals in proud contrast to what they decried as the excesses of Republican corruption and Negro misrule during Reconstruction.

Republicans did not deserve all the blame for Reconstruction problems or receive adequate credit for their accomplishments. And Negro legislators never approached majority control in either house of the Alabama legislature. But the Republicans, with overwhelming support from Negro voters, had been the dominant party between 1868 and 1874, when the state lost control of its finances. And there had been corruption, though Democrats had been at least partial participants in that, as well.

When Governor George Smith Houston took office in late 1874, state expenditures far exceeded revenues. Interest payments alone threatened to consume the entire state budget, leaving no money to operate the government. Houston set up a commission to negotiate with bondholders and reduced the debt from approximately $30 million to around $9 million. Through his administration and those that followed, improvements in managing the tax system actually increased revenue, so the remaining debt could be gradually be paid down.

The lack of adequate funds, however, meant that Alabama schools, human services programs, public health, and the justice system struggled to function at even a minimal level. In 1900, for example, per pupil expenditures for education in Alabama were seventeen percent of the national average. In many ways, the Bourbon leaders' indifference to education was entirely consistent with the needs of a low wage, physical labor economy. In comments about a federal education bill in 1887, Alabama congressman and future governor William C. Oates declared:

Governor George Smith Houston. A long-time congressman from Limestone County, Houston was a Jacksonian Democrat before the war and openly opposed secession. After the war, his work as an attorney associated him with railroad interests, helping him to bridge both factions of the Democratic Party. The last county created in Alabama was named for him.

It is not the duty nor is it in the interest of the State, to educate its entire population beyond the primaries. Universal experience teaches that if a boy, without regard to his color, be educated beyond this point, he declines ever to work another day in the sun.

Over the course of four decades, the neglect of education, public health, aid to the infirm, internal improvements, and economic development inflicted long-term damage on Alabama society. Illiteracy increased, and poverty and disease wrecked the lives of thousands of people. One particularly destructive consequence was the convict lease system.

Even before the Civil War, Alabama had put convicts to work to help cover prison costs. In response to the chaos and violence after the war, state and local governments had cracked down severely on criminal activity, though the crackdowns were sometimes hard to distinguish from the effort to reestablish white control. Soon the state's prisons were filled, mostly with black inmates.

To relieve overcrowding and help with the state's budget woes, officials in 1875 began leasing convicts to work for private businesses. The system quickly took on a life of its own. Because businesses using convict labor enjoyed huge profit advantages over those paying wage-workers, some public officials were able to extort money or other benefits in return for granting leases. Robert McKee, the secretary to Governor Edward O'Neal, wrote to a friend in 1882 that "the 'penitentiary

A scene from a convict camp in Bullock County. The pen behind the prisoners was on wheels so that it could be moved from site to site.

NAME: *Harrison Grant*   COUNTY *Montgomery*

ring' is a power in the [Democratic] party, and it is a corrupt power."

Working conditions for leased convicts were often brutal. Many were kept in chains or pens at night and beaten with whips during the day to force them to work harder. The state's leasing program included some controls and inspections to protect inmates, but similar city and county programs had virtually no oversight. The death rate for state prisoners regularly exceeded five percent a year, but it was higher for prisoners leased by local governments. Convict leaseholders, unlike antebellum slave owners, had no vested interest in the health of their workers, and conviction for a petty crime might in effect become a death sentence.

Another corrupting factor in the system grew out of the way county officials were paid. For many office holders, their pay consisted of the money they collected. When a convicted person could not pay his fees and fines, an individual or company could step in, make the payments, and then lease the convict for a term of labor. From the perspective of local officials, the more people they arrested and leased, the more money they made. At the state level, the leasing of convicts became a major source of revenue for operating state government.

As the convict lease system expanded, agents actually began buying prisoners from local officials and selling them to companies. In some cases, convicts were procured on demand. When more laborers were needed, officials could simply arrest whomever they wished on

Top: Convict stockade at Banner Mine, Pratt Consolidated Coal Company, Birmingham. On April 8, 1911, 128 miners, all but three of them convicts, were killed in an explosion, the worst mine disaster in Alabama history. Above: Entry for Harrison Grant from the Convict Register of Montgomery County. An eighteen-year-old with no education, Grant was sentenced on August 7, 1909, to serve a year and a day for burglary and grand larceny. He died from falling rock in the Pratt Mines just a few months later.

whatever charges they might contrive, and then sell their victims to waiting agents.

Convict leasing shattered the lives of thousands of innocent people and families. Because the system was so heavily directed at blacks, it became yet another tool of racial control and repression. Douglas Blackmon, a writer for the *Wall Street Journal*, won a Pulitzer Prize in 2009 for his study of convict leasing in Alabama, *Slavery by Another Name: The Re-Enslavement of Black Americans from the Civil War to World War II.*

Another corrupt aspect of Alabama politics in these years was voting fraud. In 1874, Democrats had used ballot manipulation to help regain political control. Over the following decades, especially in counties where black voters were in the majority, white officials perfected techniques for managing the election results. A separate ballot box prepared in advance could be substituted for the real one. Extra ballots could be slipped in during the counting process, and valid ballots for opponents thrown out. Final tally sheets could be falsified.

Russell Cunningham of Birmingham, who was president of Alabama's senate in 1901 and a future governor, referred to the system of voting fraud as "the best and cheapest method of swindling [that] the white people have ever devised for the maintenance of white supremacy." Vote counters in the Black Belt—not the voters themselves—not only determined who won local elections, but they often provided the winning margins in congressional and statewide races as well.

Ballot box from Perote in Bullock County used during Reconstruction.

PROTESTS, POPULISM, AND REACTION

BOURBON Democrats dominated Alabama politics from 1874 into the early 1900s. Republicans during this period remained divided into the two factions that had formed during Reconstruction. The "Black and Tans," mostly African Americans, continued calling for protection of the rights of people of color. The "Lily Whites," virtually all white, resisted the push for civil rights, arguing that a focus on the rights of African Americans meant political suicide for the Party.

Lily White Republicans continued to win local offices in some north Alabama counties into the twentieth century. In state races, they often supported independent candidates who occasionally sprang up in opposition to Bourbon rule. But for the next century, Republicans failed to pose any serious statewide challenge to the Democrats. They were more notable as bogeymen for Democrats to denounce.

The Greenback Party was the first major independent political movement in Alabama in the post–Civil War years. It called for relieving poor farmers' debt burdens by printing more money, "greenbacks," to force interest rates down and to create enough inflation to reduce the relative value of old debts. Attacking bankers, industrialists, and other moneyed interests, the Greenback Party appealed especially to small, hill-country farmers of the old Jacksonian tradition. The movement resembled the political battles of their forebears—a fight against an entrenched, moneyed elite whom they saw as exploiting the common people.

The Greenback Party waned in the mid-1880s, but a new, more potent movement followed it. Through the 1870s and 1880s, a series of national organizations had emerged to help farmers improve their conditions. By 1889, two of these were very strong in Alabama. The Farmers' Alliance was an all-white organization, claiming about 120,000 members; the Colored Farmers' Alliance claimed about 50,000 members. The farmers' alliances initially provided services such as educational programs and cooperative buying and selling enterprises to help members get better prices. By the early 1890s, however, they began turning toward political action.

In 1892, members of the two farmers' alliances joined with labor union members to form the Populist Party in Alabama. Unions were then organizing in reaction against wage reductions and increasingly aggressive work regimens that were being imposed by the newly consolidating coal and railroad companies. The Populist Party was unusual for the time in trying to unite working-class people who were black and white, urban and rural.

Reuben Kolb of Barbour County, candidate of the Populist Party for governor in 1892 and 1894.

Reuben Kolb of Barbour County was Alabama's most prominent Populist leader. Kolb had been the state's agriculture commissioner and had run for governor as a Democrat in 1890. He felt he was cheated in the state Democratic convention that year, and after his supporters were denied seats in the 1892 state convention, Kolb bolted from the party. He ran in the general election as the candidate of a new splinter party he helped form, the Jeffersonian Democrats. The Populist Party in Alabama endorsed Kolb as its candidate as well. The platform of the new coalition called for better schools, improved roads, the popular election of railroad commissioners, opposition to trusts and national banks, "abolition of the present convict lease system," "the protection of the colored race in their political rights," and "a fair ballot and honest election count."

Many Alabama historians believe Kolb would have won the 1892 election if so many fraudulent votes had not been counted against him. Outside the Black Belt, his majority was more than 15,000. But in the fifteen counties of the Black Belt, incumbent governor Thomas G. Jones won by more than 30,000 votes. One historian, Bill Rogers, concluded that "fraud on such a scale had not been seen since Reconstruction." Another historian, Malcolm McMillan, observed how ironic it was that "the Democratic Party, which claimed to be 'the white man's party of Alabama,' remained in power by using the bulk of the Negro votes."

Kolb ran again as a Populist candidate in 1894 and lost again, though some counties did manage to elect Populist legislators and two Populists were elected to Congress. But after Kolb's two successive defeats, his campaign and the Populist Movement as a whole lost energy. In 1896 and 1900, the Democrats chose William Jennings Bryan as their presidential nominee, and Bryan's popularity as an advocate of farmers and workers drew many Alabama Populists back into the Democratic fold.

SEGREGATION

Most of the laws used by Alabama whites to regain control immediately after the Civil War, such as vagrancy and stock laws, were indirect and not overtly racial. Bourbon leaders continued to fear renewed federal intervention if they went too far in openly limiting the rights of African Americans. Through the 1870s and 1880s, however, a series of

Brierfield train station, with separate entrances for black and white passengers. Edna Bayne Pfaff and her son, Ross, wait on the steps.

decisions by the U.S. Supreme Court severely weakened the Fourteenth and Fifteenth amendments. Then in 1896, in *Plessey v. Ferguson,* the Court accepted a Louisiana law mandating "separate, but equal" accommodations for black and white people. The decisions of the Supreme Court, along with the national Republican Party's growing indifference to civil rights, emboldened southern whites to tighten their control.

In the late 1800s and early 1900s, state and local governments across the South began to adopt laws formally separating black and white people in public places. In rural areas where people knew each other and where whites held almost complete economic and legal control, there was little need for additional government intervention. But controls did seem necessary in Alabama's growing towns and cities, where crowds of people were thrown together in casual, often anonymous contact. The new laws required segregation in public transportation, restaurants, lodging, theaters, parks, swimming pools, libraries, hospitals, stadiums, prisons, waiting rooms, and restrooms.

Rules for social interactions between black and white people were unwritten, but they were usually well understood by people of both races. Blacks had to act deferentially to whites and stay within the boundaries of conduct expected of them. Since whites controlled most businesses, most land, public offices, the legal system, and the criminal justice system, overlapping structures of enforcement helped them ensure compliance.

In addition, self-appointed individuals and groups often acted as enforcers of racial control outside the law, using intimidation and violence. Public officials exerted few restraints to their actions, and sometimes acted in concert with them. Mobs were also a danger. A 2015 study by the Equal Justice Initiative, a non-profit civil rights organization in Montgomery, identified three hundred twenty-six recorded lynchings of African Americans in Alabama between 1877 and 1950.

THE CONSTITUTION OF 1901

By the 1890s, voting fraud played such a glaring role in Alabama elections that it attracted congressional investigations and embarrassing articles in national newspapers. At the same time, candidates in Alabama who lost statewide races because of voting fraud in the Black Belt threatened to stuff their own boxes in the white counties where they had support. The editor of the Mobile *Register* worried that "the practice of ballot box stuffing" might spread "until elections will have lost all respect and legality."

With the federal government's abandonment of civil rights protection in the late 1800s, Alabama political leaders saw a possible solution. If black voting was eliminated or radically reduced, fraudulent

Governor William J. Samford. Samford won election in 1900, pledging to support a new constitutional convention. His death during the convention caused the delegates to restore the office of lieutenant governor, which had been removed in the 1875 constitution.

Constitutional Convention of Alabama, 1901.

Copyright by W. JEROME CHAMBERS.

Photographs by W. JEROME CHAMBERS,
Studio 17 Dexter Avenue, Montgomery, Ala.
Orders Filled for Individual Pictures.

manipulation would no longer be needed. White Alabamians could then resume honest elections among themselves. By 1900, four other southern states had already adopted constitutions that disfranchised most of their black residents, and the U.S. Supreme Court had already accepted the restrictions in Mississippi's plan.

The idea of changing Alabama's constitution to limit black voting merged with other constitutional concerns that were surfacing in the 1890s. Alabama needed to build and maintain highways, yet the 1875

Composite photograph of the delegates to the 1901 constitutional convention. John Knox of Anniston, pictured in the center, served as the president.

constitution did not allow the state to pay for internal improvements. In addition, the constitutional limits on taxation severely restricted the ability of municipalities to sell bonds for paving streets, buying fire equipment, expanding water systems, or making other needed improvements. The taxation limits also undercut efforts by Alabamians trying to improve education.

Another set of restrictive barriers built into the 1875 constitution was tight state control over local governments. To provide backup protection in counties where black politicians might be elected, the constitution required legislative authorization for many basic functions of local governments. By the 1890s, there was almost no chance that black candidates could win political control of a major local government in Alabama, but the legislative controls remained in place. The requirements for legislative approval created long delays and formidable legal barriers to many important local actions. For growing Alabama towns and cities, the process was becoming a major impediment. For the legislature itself, the press of local bills was often so great that legislators could not attend to general issues of statewide concern.

After years of discussion, the legislature set a statewide referendum on the question of a constitutional convention for April 1901. Voters approved the proposal and elected delegates in the same election. When the delegates gathered in Montgomery in May, the convention's president, John Knox of Anniston, laid out his view of their mission:

Constitution of 1901. Alabama still operates under this constitution, although some provisions have been overturned by court rulings and it has been amended 892 times as of 2015.

And what is it that we want to do? Why it is within the limits imposed by the Federal Constitution, to establish white supremacy in this State. . . . But if we would have white supremacy, we must establish it by law—not by force or fraud. . . . If you teach your boy that it is right to steal votes, it is an easy step for him to believe that it is right to steal whatever he may need or greatly desire.

The work of the convention fully achieved Knox's goal. The new constitution drastically reduced the number of registered black voters through a blend of residency, property, employment, character, and educational requirements. It established a cumulative poll tax and set a broad list of crimes that meant automatic disqualification. And it set up county boards of registrars, appointed by state officials, which were granted full authority over the voter registration process.

To reduce the number of poor white voters who would be disfranchised—and to lessen their resistance to ratifying the constitution—a temporary provision permitted registration by any man who had fought in any of the nation's wars or was a descendant of a war veteran. This "grandfather clause" was in effect until January 1, 1903, after which white and black applicants were subject to the same requirements.

The cumulative poll tax was especially important in its later impact on poor white voters. It was a voluntary tax; payment was necessary only if a person wanted to vote. Because it was cumulative, each year's unpaid balance was added to the next year's amount due. Over time, the $1.50-per-year tax could grow into a major financial hurdle for a cash-starved farmer or millworker, just for the right to cast a ballot.

The convention kept a verbatim record of its deliberations, which affords a unique view of Alabama's political landscape. In the end, Black Belt politicians surrendered their ability to run up large totals of fraudulent votes, since most black residents would no longer be able to vote. However, black residents were still counted in setting legislative and congressional districts. Thus, white voters in predominantly black counties enjoyed proportionately more political heft than their fellow citizens in predominantly white counties.

The fight over ratification of the proposed constitution was lively and vigorous. To drum up support, the Democratic Party appointed a committee of respected leaders chaired by a rising young political star from Birmingham named Oscar W. Underwood. The committee's slogan was "White supremacy! Honest elections! And the new constitution! One and inseparable!"

An opposition effort emerged that called on working-class whites to defeat the constitution because it threatened their future right to vote. That fear would later prove to have been well founded. In the decades after 1901, the names of tens of thousands of poor white men would disappear from Alabama voting rolls as the burdens of the poll tax mounted and other restrictions were applied as well. For conservative leaders of the Democratic Party, reducing the old Populist voting base was another significant achievement of the convention.

In the ratification election, the constitution was narrowly rejected by voters in Alabama's white-majority counties. But it won approval statewide by almost 27,000 votes, with the victory margin of nearly 31,000

Poll tax receipt of Rosa Boyles, October 22, 1920. The 1920 general elections were the first in which women could vote. The tax forms still said "due by him" and had not yet been changed to acknowledge participation by women voters.

votes coming from Black Belt counties. In a bitter irony, thousands of black Alabamians were fraudulently counted as approving the document that led to their disfranchisement. By January 1, 1903, only 2,980 of the state's nearly 200,000 black men of voting age were registered to vote.

Most of the reform-minded supporters of the 1901 constitutional convention were sadly disappointed by its final product. Some limits on government activity were relaxed, and more funds were earmarked for education. But the new constitution continued to be severely restrictive overall in limiting tax increases and in maintaining state control over local governments. The U.S. Supreme Court rejected a case from Alabama that challenged the constitution's disfranchisement provisions.

Coffin of Jefferson Davis, lying in state at the Alabama Capitol. In May 1893, Davis's body was removed from its grave in New Orleans and transported by train for reburial in Richmond. On May 29, the train stopped for part of the day in Montgomery, and the casket was carried to the Capitol in a ceremonial procession. Davis's body laid in state there, where mourners paid their respects.

WHITE UNITY

THE next year, in 1902, the Democratic Party began holding primary elections in which black men were not allowed to vote. The Party maintained that, as a private organization, it had the right to limit its membership, and it identified itself as the party of white Alabamians. White Democrats who voted in the primaries were expected to remain loyal and vote for the Party's all-white nominees in the general election.

The Party leadership stressed the need for white unity as both a political and a historical imperative. Loyalty to Democratic candidates would ensure continued white control and prevent a return to the evils of Reconstruction. This argument was buttressed by new initiatives then underway to reshape the interpretation and teaching of Alabama and American history.

By the 1890s, a new generation of white southerners had grown up in the shadow of the Civil War—their values powerfully marked by its stories. As they took up the reins of leadership, they sought ways to pay homage to the heroes of what they saw as a great and valiant effort, one that had failed only because of the overwhelming numbers and resources of the enemy. They expressed their devotion by building monuments, joining patriotic societies, holding memorial ceremonies, and promoting the teaching of a version of history they felt properly honored the men of the Confederacy.

Starting in the 1890s, the United Confederate Veterans, the United Daughters of the Confederacy, and the Sons of Confederate Veterans undertook active campaigns to restructure the teaching of history in schools. They pressured state legislatures and school boards to reject textbooks they felt were insulting to the South and its defenders, and they developed their own historical interpretation that textbooks had to conform with in order to be adopted.

Their interpretation was built on a basic framework of sequential, interrelated claims. It characterized slave owners as generally benevolent. It focused on broad sectional differences rather than slavery as the cause of the Civil War. It emphasized the unity of white southerners in support for and loyalty to the Confederacy. It portrayed Reconstruction as a time when vindictive Radicals had forced a corrupt and destructive outside government on Alabama. And it depicted the conservative Democrats who ended Reconstruction as Redeemer heroes.

Although specific historical examples could be produced to support each of these claims, as a whole they amounted to a rewriting of history that distorted it in fundamental ways. This interpretation minimized and largely ignored the brutality and destructiveness of slavery, as well as its importance in causing secession. It exaggerated white unity by omitting substantial voices of white dissent before, during, and after the Civil War. It misrepresented the story of Reconstruction, portraying it as a simple struggle between honest and corrupt people. And it glamorized the brutal violence and fraud the Redeemers used to end Reconstruction.

Since American textbook publishers did not want to produce separate books for the North and the South, this revised interpretation soon became standard in most schools across the United States. It also drew support from prominent national historians of the time, such as Ulrich B. Philips at Yale University and William A. Dunning at Columbia University, both of whom were highly sympathetic with the views of white southerners. This general portrayal continued to be the dominant national interpretation of the Civil War, at least in white America, until after World War II, when a new generation of historians began pointing out its inaccuracies and distortions.

Official symbol of the Alabama Democratic Party from the late 1800s into the mid-twentieth century.

For the Democratic Party, this view of history served to confirm its role as the defender of white interests and good government in Alabama. The state party's symbol from the late 1800s into the 1950s was a rooster with the words "White Supremacy for the Right." During these years, white political allegiances, power alignments, racial attitudes, and history instruction all worked together to support the Democratic Party's dominance in Alabama. Loyalty to the party and

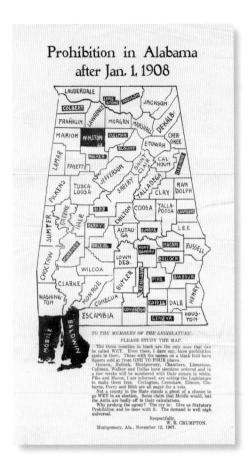

Prohibition in Alabama
after Jan. 1, 1908

Map showing the status of alcohol restrictions by county in 1907. W. B. Crumpton, who led the Anti-Saloon League in Alabama, was pushing at the time this map was prepared for statewide, statutory restrictions on the manufacture and sale of alcohol.

the ideas it represented was synonymous with good citizenship and civic duty for many white Alabamians. And winning Alabama's Democratic primary became "tantamount to election," a phrase that continued for generations in the state's political lexicon.

REFORM MOVEMENTS

ONE of the ironies of Alabama's 1901 constitution is that it was portrayed as a reform initiative. In the early 1900s, in Alabama as across the nation, new groups were springing to life seeking to rid the country of such social ills as political corruption, alcohol abuse, business monopolies, child labor, and impure food and drugs. These reformers also sought to strengthen education, assist the urban poor, build libraries, improve public health, preserve sites of natural beauty, and secure for women the right to vote. Historians call this new era of reforming zeal the Progressive Movement.

The fight against alcohol was a centerpiece of Progressive Era efforts in Alabama. With roots reaching back to the antebellum period, the temperance movement had re-emerged in Alabama in the 1880s, especially with the arrival of the Women's Christian Temperance Union (WCTU). The temperance campaign enjoyed considerable success through the 1890s in county-based local option votes to prohibit alcohol sales.

In 1904, a new organization, the Anti-Saloon League, joined the WCTU in an expanded political campaign for prohibition, not just temperance. Supporters believed that eliminating alcohol entirely would free thousands of people from the curse of drunkenness, strengthen religious lives, safeguard families, produce better workers, and make society more orderly and wholesome.

The prohibition campaign in Alabama had a major success in 1907. Led by Governor Braxton B. Comer, the legislature adopted a new local option act, and by the end of the year, twenty-four counties had joined the previous twenty in banning alcohol sales. This success led to a new act that made it illegal to produce or sell alcoholic beverages anywhere in Alabama beginning in 1909. Feeling the wind in their sails, Alabama prohibitionists decided to press on for a constitutional ban instead of relying merely on statutory law. The defeat of their proposed amendment in a statewide referendum was a temporary setback, but the prohibitionists pressed on with their efforts.

The WCTU was important as well for giving women a chance to engage openly in public policy issues. In towns and cities, increasing numbers of men worked in offices while women remained at home, often with maids and free time. The WCTU served as a training ground for women in organizational leadership. Its religious origins helped make their social activism acceptable in the otherwise conservative political environment of Alabama.

Women's clubs were another source of reform energy. The Alabama Federation of Women's Clubs, formed in Birmingham in 1895, linked local women's groups across the state. In 1898, Margaret Murray Washington, wife of Tuskegee Institute's Booker T. Washington, led in forming the Alabama State Federation of Colored Women's Clubs. One of its major projects was to organize and build a school for delinquent youth at Mount Meigs, now a major facility of the State Department of Youth Services.

Women's clubs tended to focus on education, a close second to prohibition in reform priorities. Reformers pushed to increase school funding, expand course offerings, and add more days to the school year. They also sought to professionalize the education system by improving teacher training, establishing credential requirements for teachers, standardizing textbooks, and strengthening the curriculum. In 1907, the legislature increased school funding significantly and stipulated for the first time that there would be a high school in every county, though by 1911 only about half of Alabama's counties actually had them.

Julia Tutwiler is remembered today, for good reason, as the most famous of Alabama's reformers, but her story also illustrates how the Progressive Movement grew and its initiatives intertwined. She studied at her father's famous Greene Springs School in Hale County, at a boarding school in Philadelphia, at Vassar, and in Europe before returning to Alabama to teach. In the winter of 1879–1880, she helped found the Tuscaloosa Benevolent Association to improve deplorable conditions in the city's jail. She later led prison reform efforts statewide for the WCTU, traveling throughout Alabama and even lobbying the legislature.

Tutwiler also focused on education for women. She helped found what became the University of West Alabama and was chosen its

Julia Tutwiler. In addition to her career of service in education and social reform spanning more than four decades, Tutwiler also wrote Alabama's official state song.

president in 1890. She also assisted in founding the Alabama Girls' Industrial School, now the University of Montevallo. In 1893 she secured admission for the first women students to the University of Alabama, one year after the Alabama Polytechnic Institute (now Auburn University) had admitted its first coeds. Tutwiler also fought against

the convict lease system, supported women's suffrage, and helped start the first reform schools for juveniles in the South, which included assisting Margaret Murray Washington's efforts at Mount Meigs.

Through their years of effective involvement in a range of reform initiatives, Alabama women gained more confidence as participants in the public arena, and more of them began calling for the right to vote. They argued that their participation in elections, in addition to being a matter of fairness, would also improve state politics. In 1912, women from suffrage organizations in Birmingham and Selma met with attendees from several other towns at the Church of the Advent in Birmingham to form the Alabama Equal Suffrage Association (AESA).

The ASEA initially sought legislative authorization of a referendum to amend Alabama's constitution to allow women the

Left: Booker T. Washington. After the death of Frederick Douglass in 1895, Washington became the best-known African American leader in the United States. Opposite page, above: Margaret Murray Washington, wife of Booker T. Washington, was an educator and served as the Lady Principal at Tuskegee. She was also a leader in African American women's organizations and was active in a variety of reform initiatives. Opposite page, below: Booth of the Alabama Equal Suffrage Association at the 1915 Alabama State Fair in Birmingham. Seated on the left is Patti Ruffner Jacobs, president of the Alabama Equal Suffrage Association and a national leader in the women's suffrage movement.

right to vote. In 1915, the Alabama House of Representatives refused to authorize the referendum, despite an energetic campaign by the AESA. Frustrated, some of the women turned instead toward the effort to amend the U.S. Constitution. Enfranchisement for women nationwide would bring victory in Alabama, despite the legislature's opposition.

And they won. In June 1919, Congress passed a resolution to amend the U.S. Constitution so that women could vote. In August 1920, the Nineteenth Amendment became part of the Constitution after receiving approval by the required three-fourths of the states, but without that of Alabama. In that fall's elections, Alabama women voted for the first time. The Alabama Equal Suffrage Association celebrated its success and changed its name to the League of Women Voters.

Battles to improve education were fought across a broad front. Alabama's best known educator was Booker T. Washington, who led Tuskegee Institute from 1881 until his death in 1915. With funding from prominent northern philanthropists, some support from the state, and the work of faculty and students, Washington built Tuskegee into a national center of African American education.

George W. Carver. Like Washington, Carver sought to find practical ways of helping improve the lives of black people in the South. His appreciation of the complex interconnectedness of the natural world was far ahead of his time.

Washington's emphasis at Tuskegee was on self-improvement and practical skills. He believed that as African Americans became successful workers, grew more secure financially, and managed their affairs capably, they would earn their seats at the table of citizenship. Critics such as W. E. B. Du Bois chided Washington for his restraint in not openly opposing segregation, but Washington was careful to avoid offending the white power structure of Alabama. In a very difficult environment, he struggled to supply his students with practical tools to help them succeed. He hoped, through their success over time, to improve conditions for all African Americans.

George Washington Carver was another famous Tuskegee Institute educator. Carver taught thousands of students at the school, and he worked directly with farmers, traveling across the state to promote crop diversification, methods of soil renewal, scientific farming, and self-sufficiency.

Higher education across Alabama also became more professional during this period. Universities recruited faculty members with Ph.D. degrees and became centers of research and scholarship. Alabama native Eugene Allen Smith earned his doctorate in Germany and returned to serve as a professor of science at the University of Alabama. He also became the state geologist and systematically studied Alabama's natural resources, seeking ways to use them to build the state's economy. George Petrie, a historian at Auburn, had studied at Johns Hopkins University in the modern Germanic system of research scholarship. He became one of Auburn's most beloved and respected teachers, and the coach of its first football team.

In the late 1800s, *normal* schools emerged in different parts of the state, mostly with church sponsorship, to help educate teachers. By the early 1900s, some received state funds, including schools at Florence (now the University of North Alabama), Normal (now Alabama A&M University), Jacksonville (now Jacksonville State University), Montgomery (now Alabama State University), Livingston (now the University of West Alabama), and Troy (now Troy University).

Perhaps the most successful Progressive Era reforms were in public health. One of the most widespread afflictions in Alabama in the early twentieth century was hookworms. A 1910 study estimated that forty percent of the South's population was afflicted with them. Hookworm larvae lived in the soil, spread from unsanitary outhouses, and entered human bodies through lesions in bare feet. They became resident parasites, causing anemia, weakness, stunted growth, bloated bellies, digestive problems, and sometimes death. Hookworms were a millstone dragging down the entire region.

In 1910, the Rockefeller family made a million-dollar gift for a campaign to attack the hookworm infestation in the South. Working with the public health departments of Alabama and eight other states, the Rockefeller Sanitary Commission organized programs of intensive health education and treatment. Despite initial resentment by many Alabamians at the intrusion by meddling outsiders and the implicit insult of their sanitary practices, the commission achieved such dramatic success that most critics were at least silenced, if not converted.

The reduction of the hookworm infestation improved the lives of hundreds of thousands of people who were finally rid of the debilitating parasite. The campaign also gave state health officials new confidence and credibility, and the techniques they learned became part of the core practice of public health work in Alabama.

In 1900, many Alabama deaths resulted from illnesses that could be addressed by improved public health practices. Almost twenty percent of recorded deaths were caused by tuberculosis, seven percent by malaria, six percent by diarrhea, and thirteen percent by typhoid fever. Since poor sanitary practices were a major contributing cause of deaths from diarrhea and typhoid fever, new public water and sewer systems were major life-saving advancements. And public health officials would soon turn their attention to reducing tuberculosis and malaria deaths.

Examples of the effects of the hookworm parasite from the Annual Report of the Alabama Department of Public Health for 1914.

YEARS OF INNOVATION AND GROWTH

THE 1800s began with a technological innovation that shaped the future of that century, the cotton gin. As the 1900s opened, a cluster of new technologies was spreading across Alabama, including electricity, telephones, automobiles, and airplanes. The combined influence of these innovations would be as powerful in the new century as the cotton gin had been in the previous one.

In the late 1800s, a few entrepreneurs began producing electricity for local use, mostly with small, coal-fired generators. In 1906, William Patrick Lay formed the Alabama Power Company in Gadsden, Alabama, with an ambitious plan to build a dam on

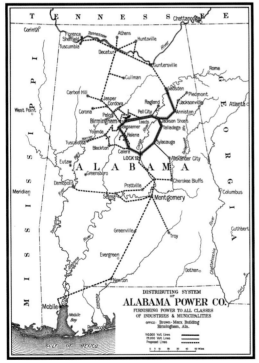

the Coosa River. When Lay was unable to secure adequate funds for such a massive project, as frequently happened to Alabama entrepreneurs, he sold his company in 1912 to James Mitchell, a Massachusetts engineer who had access to British financing.

Mitchell hired a Montgomery attorney, Thomas Martin, as his legal counsel, and with Martin's advice acquired other companies that held promising dam sites across the state. In late 1913, the company completed its first dam, now known as Lay Dam, at the Lock 12 site on the Coosa River. By the following summer, the dam's generators, backed up by two steam plants, provided electricity for a loop that included Birmingham and Gadsden. This service was in place just in time to support the area's industrial build-up for World War I, and it marked the beginning of a service system that would grow to expand across the state.

Alabamians begin using telephones in the late 1800s. The first phone companies were usually small, local operations where switchboard operators connected lines by hand to link callers. In Fort Payne, for example, a local company opened in 1900 with thirty-seven customers. By 1904, it had grown to sixty-six subscribers when Southern Bell bought the company and took over operations. As telephone networks spread, Alabamians were linked for the first time in almost instantaneous contact.

Even before automobiles appeared in Alabama, there was a push for improved roads. Among other benefits, they would help farmers, manufacturers, millers, and lumbermen get their products to market. In 1898, Congressman John H. Bankhead of Jasper and publisher Asa Rountree, of Hartselle and then Birmingham, created a good roads association to promote highway development in north Alabama. In 1906, Rountree helped found the Alabama Good Roads Association.

Their collaboration bore fruit the next year, when Alabama voters ratified the first amendment to the 1901 constitution. It relaxed the restrictions against state support for internal improvements to let the state build "public roads, highways and bridges." The money for the work was to come from convict lease funds. In 1911, the legislature created the Alabama Highway Commission to coordinate road building across the state.

When John H. Bankhead was elected to the U.S. Senate in 1907, one of his first achievements was securing a $500,000 appropriation to test the idea of national highways. That test program helped prepare the ground for the 1916 Bankhead-Shackleford Act, which formally launched the U.S. highway system. When the first two transcontinental highways were completed a few years later, the northern route from New York City to San Francisco was named the "Lincoln Highway." The southern route, which ran from Washington, D.C. down through Alabama and west to San Diego, was the "Bankhead Highway."

As the 1900s began, individuals and communities across Alabama were being knit together into new networks—of highways, schools, public health initiatives, electrical service, telephones, and even volunteer organizations. Industrial and economic growth, new technologies, and the work of reformers were improving life for many Alabamians, especially in the towns and cities. The great majority of Alabamians, however, still lived and worked on farms, locked in their own older networks of depressed cotton prices and debt. But beginning with World War I, a series of new encounters with the world outside accelerated the pace of urban changes and eventually extended these changes across the state through rural Alabama.

Above: Photo without identification from the papers of John H. Bankhead. The banner on the car reads: "Official Car Bankhead National Highway," and it may have been making an inaugural transcontinental crossing. Opposite page, above: Lay Dam hydroelectric plant of the Alabama Power Company, on the Coosa River near Clanton. Opposite page, below: Map showing the service grid of the Alabama Power Company in 1914. Red lines show the core loop then in service; broken lines show planned expansions.

CHAPTER 6

SHAKING THE FOUNDATIONS

1914 to 1955

S TARTING IN THE MID-1910S, *Alabamians entered a time of acceler-*
ating change. World War I brought a surge in the economy and new
engagement with the world outside Alabama. The use of automobiles
and electricity spread and became part of daily life, especially in Ala-
bama towns and cities. Through the 1920s, urban Alabama enjoyed at least
some of the exuberance of the Jazz Age. During those same years, rural Ala-
bama sank even deeper into poverty as prices for cotton fell to prewar lows.

Then the Great Depression, the New Deal, and World War II all jolted
the state in a reeling series of disruptions that peaked in the 1940s in the all-
out efforts of a nation at war. By 1955, many aspects of Alabama life were
radically different from what they had been in 1914. Hundreds of thousands
of Alabamians had moved from farms to cities. The economy was far more
prosperous. The character of government itself, and of its relationship to the
people, had changed. The social and political system that had emerged after
Reconstruction remained largely intact, but the disruptions of the previous
four decades had shaken its foundations.

WORLD WAR I

IN the summer of 1914, the great powers of Europe lined up and tore into
each other with all the destructive might they could muster. The carnage
churned on for more than four years, devouring millions of lives and profoundly altering life for hundreds of millions more. What later became
known as World War I shaped the course of the entire twentieth century,
and it was more important than has generally been recognized for Alabama.

Although the United States resisted entry into the war until April
1917, Alabamians felt its economic repercussions as soon as the first great

**Curbside recruiting, in front of Louis Saks Clothiers, located at the corner of
19th Street and 2nd Avenue North in Birmingham.**

ARE YOU 100% AMERICAN? PROVE IT! BUY U.S. GOVERNMENT BONDS THIRD

THE SPIRIT OF AMERICA

JOIN

World War I liberty bond and recruitment posters. The exertions of war brought a new sense of national unity in Alabama, urged on by energetic campaigns promoting patriotism and service.

guns began firing. Cotton prices initially faltered, but then surged to new highs. Industries ramped up production of coal, iron, timber, and textiles—supplying first the Europeans and then the buildup of American forces. Military bases and war construction brought money, thousands of jobs, and new people to Alabama.

Alabama's National Guard was activated in June 1916, though its first posting was to the Mexican border. Eventually, about 12,000 Alabamians volunteered as Guardsmen or enlistees. Approximately 74,000 more Alabama men, white and black, were drafted under a new selective service law.

In August 1917, the 4th Regiment of the Alabama National Guard was re-named the 167th Regiment of the U.S. Army's 42nd (Rainbow) Division. Although replacement troops from other states were later added, the regiment was a distinctive Alabama unit within the U.S. Army, and Alabamians took pride in its achievements. The 3,677 men of the 167th shipped out from Alabama in August, and, with some pauses for training and organizing along the way, arrived in France in November.

By early 1918, the 167th was in trial service with French units, where the Alabamians proved themselves to be effective fighters. They helped fend off Germany's final great offensive in the spring of 1918, and by July they were charging German lines. That November, the 167th swept into the enemy heartland and became part of the Allied occupation forces.

Alabama soldiers in the 167th and other units earned honors and respect for their fighting skill and courage. A total of 2,401 Alabamians were killed in action, and another 3,861 died of wounds or diseases. Many others returned home maimed in body or spirit. Yet overall, World War I was a great patriotic experience for most Alabamians.

Even before the United States' declaration of war, voluntary organizations had sprung up urging Americans to unite in support of the

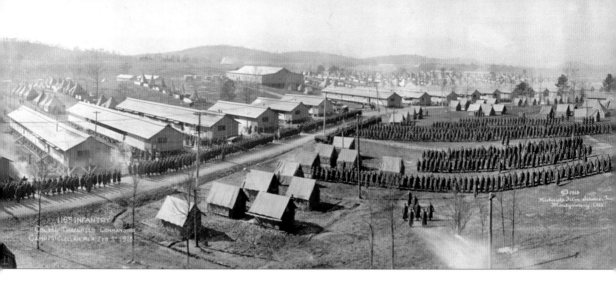

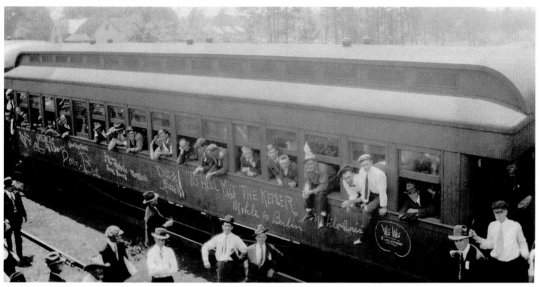

nation's defense and its values. After America formally entered the war, constant promotional campaigns urged citizens to do their part for the war effort. Alabamians knitted socks, conserved gas, planted "liberty gardens," and bought bonds. Though a deep consciousness of the state's Confederate heritage still marked public life—in fact, many former Confederate soldiers were still alive—World War I called forth a new spirit of national patriotic fervor in Alabama.

At the beginning of the war, only the Alabama flag flew over the state Capitol. State law made no provision for the U.S. flag. On April 6, 1918, state officials dedicated a new pole for the U.S. flag on the Capitol's south lawn, paid for by hundreds of individual contributors, including school children. Before the dedication ceremony, thirty thousand soldiers from the Ohio 37th Infantry (Buckeye) Division, then in training at nearby Camp Sheridan, paraded up Dexter Avenue. Huge crowds of Alabamians cheered as the Ohioans—many the

Top: Camp McClellan near Anniston was one of many camps quickly constructed to train American troops for the war. The site was chosen because of the suitability of the surrounding hills for artillery training. In 1929 it was renamed Fort McClellan. Above: Young men depart by train for mobilization, probably to Montgomery. The writing on the side of the car includes "Mobile to Berlin" and "To Hell Mit The Kaiser."

Mortimer Jordan, a physician from Birmingham and an officer in the 167th Infantry. Jordan's warm, witty, and insightful letters back to his wife provide important information about life in the 167th from the time of Mexican service until his death at the Second Battle of the Marne on July 28, 1918.

grandsons of men who had invaded the South a half century earlier—traced the route of Jefferson Davis's inaugural procession up Dexter Avenue to the Capitol.

Mortimer Jordan of Birmingham, an officer in the 167th, wrote to his wife about being called a "Yank" by people in Great Britain: "Think of it! Southern troops being called 'Yankees'! Am not minding it in the least, either. Surely times do change."

Sometimes, patriotic zeal was tinged with nativism. As proponents extolled what President Woodrow Wilson called "one-hundred percent Americanism," many cast wary eyes at outsiders—including foreigners, radicals, labor union members, and, sometimes, Catholics. In early 1917, the first deployment of the Alabama National Guard's 4th Infantry Regiment after returning from Mexico had been to guard Alabama's critical bridges, railroads, and industrial sites. They were to protect important locations against possible sabotage by German agents or sympathizers in America, perhaps among those immigrants in Baldwin and Cullman counties.

In addition to inspiring a new patriotic spirit, World War I opened doors of opportunity to jobs, training, travel, money, and a broader world of experiences. Many farmers abandoned their plows to work in war industries. Approximately 150,000 white and 85,000 black Alabamians left the state during the war years. Southern blacks moved north in such numbers that their exodus came to be called the Great Migration. It would continue for three decades, altering the population profile of Alabama, as well as that of the North.

Increased shipping and shipbuilding propelled Mobile into a new era of development. With a wider recognition of the harbor's potential benefits for the entire state, Alabamians amended the state constitution in 1921 to create a docks commission in order to improve further the shipping facilities there.

At Muscle Shoals, Congress authorized mammoth construction projects that would eventually help reshape the future of north Alabama. Two enormous plants were built to make nitrate for ammunition, and construction began on a great dam across the Tennessee River to supply the plants with electric power. The first nitrate was not produced until November 1918, the month the war ended, and Wilson Dam was not finished until 1924.

The question of who would control these great resources became a national political issue. The Alabama Power Company had donated the dam site to the nation for the war effort and hoped afterward to acquire the dam or at least its electricity. Henry Ford offered to buy the dam, at a very low price, and to develop the entire area into a major manufacturing center. A few powerful members of Congress, especially Senator George Norris of Nebraska, argued that the dam was a public resource and should remain in public control. The nitrates used to make ammunition also are a major component in fertilizer, so the

Top: Wilson Dam at the end of construction, December 13, 1924. Work would continue on the lift lock on the left until 1927. Above: United States Nitrate Plant No. 2, at Muscle Shoals, Alabama, after World War I.

Victory parade for the 167th in May 1919. After arriving at Union Station in Montgomery, returning veterans marched up Commerce Street under this welcoming arch, greeted by young ladies in white dresses, on their way to the state Capitol.

future of the nitrate plants was important as well to American farmers. The contenders fought each other to a standstill, and nothing was decided through the 1920s.

THE WAR'S AFTERMATH

At the war's end, Alabamians joined their countrymen in long, exultant celebrations. As festivities trailed off, however, the state's booming war economy wilted into a postwar letdown. Military bases cut back sharply in the rush to demobilize. Crop prices plunged to below prewar levels. Industrial demand also faltered, though by the early 1920s conditions for Alabama factories began to improve again.

Alabamians' pride in their war efforts suffered a blow when reports appeared about how many of their men had been declared unfit for military service. The *American Medical Journal* disclosed that in the first half of 1918 more inductees from Alabama were medically unfit than from any other state—more than seventeen percent. This total came after local draft boards had already rejected twenty-four percent of the prospective draftees. Of the Alabama National Guardsmen deployed to the Mexican border in 1916, sixty percent suffered from hookworms.

The fitness reports on Alabama draftees were so dismal and embarrassing that Governor Charles Henderson commissioned a study of the state's social and educational services by the prestigious Russell Sage Foundation. The report was completed as Governor Henderson's term ended in December 1918. In it, the author began by politely applauding the state's contributions during the war, as well as pockets of excellence he found in some state services. But overall, his findings painted a bleak picture of life in Alabama.

The author found that the state's educational system was inferior; almost a quarter of Alabamians over ten years old were illiterate. Pellagra, hookworm, and tuberculosis were still widespread. Child welfare programs, public health, services for the insane or disabled, and prisons were all pathetically underfunded and inadequate. With cutting irony, he noted that the state's most recent budget had allocated $56,000 to eradicate cattle ticks and prevent hog cholera, while only $25,000 went to public health programs for Alabama citizens. Another study that year was similarly damning. Entitled *Child Welfare in Alabama*, it plowed much the same ground as the Russell Sage report but was even more detailed in its findings and recommendations.

Governor Thomas Kilby, seated before the window, in his office at the Capitol with Ira Champion and William Darden, 1919.

Boll Weevil Monument, Enterprise, Alabama. The monument was erected in 1919 to thank the boll weevil for causing local farmers to switch from cotton to peanut production and to illustrate how a disaster can present an opportunity. The monument's boll weevil has been stolen so many times that in 1998 the city replaced the statue with this copy and moved the original to a local museum.

Unlike many reports of this type, these two were not simply shelved. In November 1918, Thomas Kilby, a wealthy iron manufacturer from Anniston, won the election to succeed Henderson. Kilby had campaigned on a call for sweeping reform, and after he became governor, his legislative initiatives were guided by recommendations in the two reports.

Although Kilby was a conservative businessman, he implemented the most aggressive reform agenda Alabama had seen since Reconstruction. He won passage of tax increases to improve education, public health, prisons, social services, and highways. He pushed through the state's first income tax, though the state supreme court later declared it unconstitutional. He established a new department of child welfare, and he created a new state board of education to unify and professionalize public education. Many of the ideals of the old Progressive Movement found their most substantial realization up to that time under Kilby's leadership.

Since Reconstruction, most Alabama public officials had worked to keep taxes low, restrain government spending, and give business a wide berth. Many citizens did not think of social welfare as the responsibility of state government. Another legacy of World War I was a more expansive vision of the role of government.

Although the war and Kilby's reforms brought change, much in Alabama continued as it was before the war. Maintaining segregation remained a priority for virtually all white Alabamians. In fact, by then the system had hardened into a way of life that many Alabamians came to regard as the natural order of things.

In politics, rural counties continued to dominate the legislature despite surging growth in the cities. Under the 1901 constitution, each county had at least one state representative. After each census, thirty-eight additional seats were to be allotted based on county population. Even though this system already skewed power in favor of rural counties, the legislature disregarded the periodic reapportioning requirement. Despite the continued population shift to the cities, the number of legislators for each county remained fixed as it was in 1900. By 1960, Dallas County still had three representatives, while Jefferson County, with more than eleven times the population, had only seven.

Rural counties, however, were still split along cultural lines that dated back to the state's founding. The counties of northern Alabama and the Wiregrass region of southeast Alabama were dominated by descendants of yeoman farmers. Most people there still struggled to scratch out a living from the land, largely with their own hands. They also retained their ancestors' political suspicions of planters and wealthy elites. Rural Black Belt counties, by contrast, were usually controlled by large landowners and the townspeople who were their

suppliers and agents. The conservative alliance between Black
Belt politicians and urban industrial leaders remained a powerful force.

Through the 1920s, the state's
economy continued to suffer its
special bipolar disorder of rural
depression and urban prosperity.
The boll weevil, an insect that destroyed developing cotton bolls,
compounded the woes of Alabama farmers. The weevils first

appeared near Mobile in 1910, and by the early 1920s, they had spread
over the entire state. Although some farmers turned to other crops such
as peanuts, most stayed determinedly with cotton, struggling at first to
kill the weevils by hand and with homemade insecticides.

As more Alabamians were able to buy cars, automobiles became
commonplace after World War I. Increasing numbers of Alabamians
were also able to enjoy electric lighting and the convenience of new
appliances such as refrigerators, stoves, washing machines, and electric

**Top: Interior photograph of the
Alabama Theater in Birmingham.
Above: Montgomery's Dexter
Avenue at night in 1907. The tangle
of wires and the proliferation of
poles were part of the new electrical
lighting that changed the nighttime
for people in Alabama towns.**

irons. Starting in the late 1920s, high school football teams were able to play night games for the first time, thanks to electric lighting. Talking movies first appeared in 1927, and ornate movie palaces, such as the Alabama Theatre in Birmingham, began opening that same year. The lavish structures must have been astonishing to rural Alabamians coming to the city for the first time.

In 1921, Alabama Power Company in Birmingham built the state's first radio station as a way to communicate with its crews. Within months, public interest was so great that the station began to broadcast entertainment programs and local news features. By 1923, the demands of radio service were becoming a distraction for a company whose primary job was electricity, so Alabama Power donated the station and equipment to the Alabama Polytechnic Institute (now Auburn University). Auburn merged it with its own station to create WAPI. In 1928, WAPI affiliated with the National Broadcasting Company (NBC), and Alabamians began to listen for the first time to live national programs of news and entertainment.

Top: Ku Klux Klan Day at the Opelika District Fair, October 29, 1925. Two hundred new members were inducted, and fifteen hundred members paraded during the day's festivities. Above: William J. Simmons, founder of the second Klan, who was born in Harpersville. Above Simmons's desk is a cropped poster of the movie *The Birth of a Nation*, showing a Klansman on horseback brandishing a burning cross.

A PECULIAR POLITICS OF REACTION AND REFORM

THE old issue of prohibition took on new life during and after World War I. In 1915, after several fits and starts over the previous decade, Alabama banned the manufacture and sale of alcoholic beverages statewide. In late 1917, just months after declaring war on Germany, Congress passed a resolution to amend the U.S. Constitution and establish prohibition nationally. The Eighteenth Amendment received

formal ratification on January 16, 1919, and became effective one year later in 1920.

Even after the amendment's enactment, prohibition remained a lively issue in Alabama. The struggles were not just over enactment, but also over implementation and enforcement and, later, calls for its repeal. Supporters of prohibition included a unique mix of old progressives, mainline Protestants, bootleggers who profited from illegal sales, and, by the late 1910s, members of the Ku Klux Klan.

The Reconstruction-era KKK had disbanded in the 1870s. Forty years later, in 1915, Alabama native William Joseph Simmons launched a new version, known today as the second Klan. In a 1917 pamphlet, Simmons wrote that the Klan's mission was "to conserve, protect and maintain the distinctive institutions, rights, privileges, principles and ideals of a pure Americanism."

Simmons himself was a failed medical student and former minister who became involved in some of the patriotic organizations that grew amid the fervor of World War I. On Thanksgiving night in 1915, he led a small group of people to the top of Georgia's Stone Mountain, where they set fire to a large cross to mark the new Klan's founding.

The movie *Birth of a Nation* had premiered earlier that year to massive national audiences. It presented the version of Reconstruction then current in which the South was shown as despoiled by venal blacks and carpetbaggers and then as redeemed by the KKK. White actors in blackface portrayed African Americans as caricatures, while the Klansmen were portrayed as chivalrous heroes.

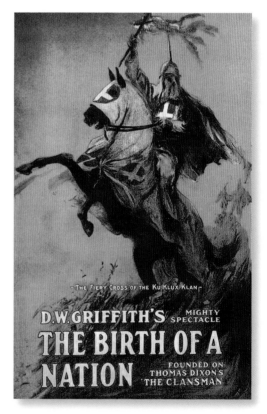

The Birth of a Nation poster. This is the full version of the poster shown in Simmons's office. The star of the movie was Henry B. Walthall from Shelby County, Alabama.

The movie's images, though distorted, would shape many Americans' ideas about Reconstruction for years to come. The burning cross was actually a dramatic element introduced in the movie that had not been a practice of the first Klan. The adoption of cross burning by the second Klan was an early example of how movie images can take on a life of their own.

Membership in the second Klan grew slowly during the war years, but in the early 1920s, its numbers began to soar, especially in the Midwest and the South. The period just after World War I was a turbulent time for the United States. Race riots erupted in many cities. Labor unions called numerous strikes, including a bitter and prolonged one in Alabama by the United Mine Workers.

These upheavals fanned fears that communism and anarchism might spread to America. During the winter of 1919 to 1920, U.S. Attorney General Mitchell Palmer launched a series of raids against suspected radicals and anarchists across the nation, arresting approximately 10,000 people in twenty-three states. Alabamians also read in their newspapers of communist uprisings spreading from Russia into Europe and other parts of the world.

After the tumult of a world war, many Americans and Alabamians longed for a return to the "normalcy" that presidential candidate Warren G. Harding called for in 1920. The Klan's claims of defending "pure Americanism" attracted widespread support. By 1924, the Alabama Klan boasted a membership of approximately 115,000 men, when the total vote in the state's U.S. senatorial election that year was only 159,640.

Unlike the first Klan, the second was centered in towns and cities. It included doctors, lawyers, shopkeepers, and even a considerable number of ministers and law enforcement officers, as well as mechanics, carpenters, and other workingmen. As its numbers grew, so did its political influence. In the 1920 Democratic primary, Klan member Lycurgus Breckenridge Musgrove almost defeated Alabama's powerful incumbent U.S. senator, Oscar W. Underwood.

Senator Underwood had enjoyed a long and distinguished career in Congress, representing the interests of Birmingham's industrial elite. He had even been a candidate for the Democratic nomination for president in 1912, and he would try again in 1924. Musgrove's campaign against him reflected a resurgence in Alabama of the old anti-elite politics of the common man fighting against the special interests. In the 1920 race, Musgrove denounced Underwood for defending "the fossiliferous old asses of reaction" and for not supporting prohibition.

The political force Musgrove represented was less a campaign with a specific agenda than a general reaction against an entrenched power

U.S. Senator Oscar W. Underwood of Alabama. Underwood ran for president of the United States two times, once in 1912 and again in 1924. In 1924, he took an active position against the Ku Klux Klan, but he did not run for office again in Alabama after taking that stand.

structure that ignored the interests of common people. For many working-class white Alabamians, the second Klan provided a way to band together with like-minded neighbors and to assert themselves and their interests in the face of a larger world over which they had little influence.

The new Klan also had a violent side, which, unlike cross burning, did harken back to the first Klan. From its beginnings, leaders of the second Klan denounced people and groups they considered hostile to traditional American values: purveyors of alcohol, immigrants, radicals, Catholics, Jews, immoral people, labor leaders, and disruptive blacks. Starting in the early 1920s, bands of Alabama Klansmen moved from rhetoric to threats and attacks against selected offenders. Their victims were both black and white, since race was just one of the second Klan's many interests.

Grover Hall of the *Montgomery Advertiser*. Hall won a Pulitzer Prize in 1928 for a series of editorials denouncing the Klan.

Their customary attacks were usually what was called floggings, which became commonplace in Alabama through the mid-1920s. One grand jury in 1927 reported at least seventeen in its county, but it also found insufficient evidence for any prosecutions. Law enforcement officers, many of whom were Klan members, rarely arrested Klan vigilantes. When they did, all-white juries rarely returned convictions. The Klan's representation of itself as heirs of those who had redeemed the South and reestablished white supremacy was hard for most white juries to disregard.

By the late 1920s, however, the number and viciousness of Klan floggings drew critical national attention to Alabama. One flogging story after another appeared in major newspapers, reporting gory details that embarrassed many of the state's business and civic leaders. Some Alabama leaders, such as Oscar Underwood, began to speak out against the Klan. Grover Hall of the *Montgomery Advertiser* loosed a string of withering editorials against the Klan, which won him a Pulitzer Prize in 1928.

Despite widespread criticisms of Klan assaults, many white Alabamians remained sympathetic. They dismissed the stories as newspaper exaggerations and the floggings as trivial abuses, or even useful acts of vigilante justice. In the 1926 state elections, three candidates with conspicuous Klan support won office as governor, attorney general, and U.S. senator.

The new governor, Bibb Graves, had long represented the interests of ordinary Alabamians. He had opposed the 1901 state constitution and had supported the reform initiatives of Governor B. B. Comer twenty years earlier. Graves had also commanded a field artillery unit in World War I, and later he was a founding state leader of the politically potent American Legion. Graves is credited with coining the term "Big Mules" to describe the Birmingham industrialists he attacked in his 1926 campaign. He was also a leader of the second Klan, having served as Cyclops of Montgomery Klavern Number 3.

As governor, Graves led an effort to increase funding for education by more than 150 percent over the level of his predecessor. He upgraded the state's mental hospitals and doubled spending for child welfare and public health. And he persuaded the legislature to end the convict lease system. Alabama was the last state in the nation to do so.

Graves, an engineer, became known as "The Builder." With revenue from new driver's license fees and gasoline taxes replacing convict lease funds, he launched a major road and bridge construction program for Alabama. Despite what might have been expected of a former Klan leader, he set up a Division of Negro Education, with a black man as its director. But he remained generally quiet about ongoing Klan violence and did little to prevent it.

Top: The Bibb Graves Bridge crossing the Coosa River at Wetumpka, completed in 1931. Above: Bibb Graves, governor of Alabama from 1927 to 1931 and from 1935 to 1939.

In the same 1926 election, Hugo Black won Oscar Underwood's former Senate seat. Black, too, had been a Klan leader, in Birmingham. As an attorney and politician there, he also had a long record representing working people against big corporations. In the 1930s, Black would emerge as a key ally of President Franklin Roosevelt in the New Deal, and in 1937, Roosevelt appointed him to the U.S. Supreme Court. Black's subsequent thirty-four years of service on the Court were distinguished by his ardent defense of civil liberties.

It may seem ironic that many Alabama Klan leaders of the 1920s became the state's New Deal progressives in the 1930s, but the Klan's

Above: U.S. senator from Alabama, Thomas J. "Cotton Tom" Heflin. A brilliant and colorful speaker, Heflin also helped write the language in the 1901 constitution that disfranchised most African Americans. Below left: Senator Hugo Black of Alabama (left) and Representative William Connery Jr., of Massachusetts, May 24, 1937. They sponsored legislation recommended by President Franklin D. Roosevelt raising the minimum wage to forty cents an hour.

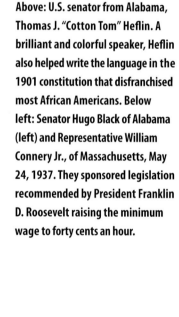

role in representing the interests of marginalized whites had helped attract these men to it. When the New Deal came along, it offered an unprecedented opportunity to improve the lives of working-class Alabamians in a real and substantial way, and these former Klansmen readily embraced the new programs of relief, assistance, and development.

Alabama's other U.S. senator at the time was J. Thomas "Cotton Tom" Heflin. His career illustrates the other face of the Klan, the one that focused on attacking threats to their view of the proper social order. Heflin was said to have been a member of the Klan, and he enjoyed its enthusiastic support throughout his career. He fought vigorously against alcohol, blacks, and Catholics, adding the New Deal to his list in the 1930s. Heflin had also opposed women's right to vote, but he sponsored the 1914 congressional resolution that created Mother's Day. He thought the recognition would emphasize woman's proper role in the home. Ironically, Heflin now lives in history as "the Father of Mother's Day."

THE GREAT DEPRESSION

Bibb Graves' administration began in 1927 in a surge of reform enthusiasm but ended in 1931 in the pall of the Great Depression. The stock market crash of 1929 was one of a series of disasters—including regulatory neglect, monetary policy failures, bank collapses, and rising trade barriers—that triggered a massive international economic downturn. By the early 1930s, commodity and property prices were plunging, and bankruptcies and unemployment rates were soaring around the world.

Walker Evans's photograph identified as Lucille Burroughs, Hale County, 1936. The photographs selected for *Let Us Now Praise Famous Men* focused on the grimness of sharecropper life. This photograph showing a young girl smiling despite the hardship she endured was not used in the book.

For most Alabama farmers, the Depression marked a further descent in a long decline that had continued, with occasional sputters of good times, since the Civil War. Cotton, the great staple of Alabama agriculture, dropped from a high of thirty-five cents a pound in the uptick of World War I to a nickel in 1932. Much of the state resembled a Third World country.

One of the best known books to emerge from the Great Depression was about Alabama. During the summer of 1936, photographer Walker Evans and writer James Agee visited three white farm families in west Alabama. Their book, *Let Us Now Praise Famous Men,* is a sad, poignant depiction of people worn and deeply scarred by poverty.

Alabama's towns and cities, after having enjoyed relative prosperity during the 1920s, were shattered by the Depression. Between 1929 and 1933, half of the state's mines and mills closed. By 1934, a quarter of Birmingham's work force was unemployed, and many who

were employed worked only part time. President Franklin D. Roosevelt called Birmingham the "worst hit town in the country."

Store clerks and construction workers, accountants and architects, laborers and lawyers all found themselves without jobs and with little hope for new ones. As people lost their jobs and cut their spending, business activity wilted. Some companies reduced wages and

Walker Evans's photograph of Floyd Burroughs. Evans changed the names of his subjects for the book. Burroughs's real name was George Gudger, and his daughter, opposite page, was Maggie Louise.

increased production demands on workers, trying to remain competitive by cutting prices.

In 1933, Harry Hopkins, who ran several major New Deal programs, sent a prominent reporter, Lorena Hickok, around the nation and told her to let him know what she found. Hickok reached Alabama in April 1934. Examining conditions faced by "white collar people," she reported to Hopkins about an unemployed musician and his wife and baby, trying to survive on relief payments of $4.80 a week. He could sometimes find an odd job, but they had to pay $3 a week just for rent.

After many months with no steady work, the man told Hickok: "We've pawned everything we have—my wife's engagement ring and all her other trinkets, all our silver, all my instruments, my watch and other jewelry, and most of my clothes." He said that by the end of each week they usually did not have enough money left for food. Their diet consisted primarily of bacon and flour. "My wife is losing all her teeth. I got a relief order for her to go to a doctor. He said it was due to bad and insufficient diet. Well, she's still nursing the baby, for one thing. Because we cannot afford to buy milk."

Hickok's letters tell one story after another like that. The correspondence files of Alabama governor Benjamin "Meek" Miller, who succeeded Graves, contain many more. Private charities, churches, businesses, local governments, and the state were all overwhelmed by the numbers of people in need, and their resources were soon exhausted.

Benjamin "Meek" Miller of Wilcox County. Miller was governor of Alabama from 1931 to 1935, through some of the hardest years of the Great Depression. Stacks of letters from desperate people in his gubernatorial files help document today the wretched conditions many Alabamians endured then.

The personal transformation of Governor Miller (1931–1935) is a testament to the Depression's power to alter lives. Miller was a wealthy, conservative landowner and lawyer from Camden who in the 1930 election carried the banner of the Black Belt/Big Mule alliance. His campaign denounced the loose spending of Bibb Graves and the outrages of the KKK. Miller's personal frugality was legendary. He brought his own cow to the governor's mansion so he would not have to buy milk or butter.

But when Miller as governor saw the plight of hundreds of thousands of desperate people, this deeply conservative man changed. In 1931, he persuaded the legislature to authorize a referendum to reimpose the income tax by a constitutional amendment. Miller's tax proposal was so steeply progressive that only a small number of Alabama's wealthiest people would pay anything, yet Alabama voters rejected it in 1931 and again in 1932. Miller persevered, however, and

Alabama voters ratified the amendment in 1933. Many of Miller's former supporters regarded him a traitor.

Conditions were so wretched in Alabama and across the South during these years that the Central Committee of the Communist Party USA saw the time as opportune for a southern organizing campaign. It designated Birmingham as headquarters of a new district of Deep South states, and the first two party organizers arrived there in late 1929. More followed over the next few years.

The Communist Party's Alabama campaign had a dual thrust, one on urban workers and the other on rural sharecroppers. The urban organizers initially tried to build membership by providing assistance to impoverished people and by organizing protests to demand expanded public relief and jobs. They also daringly advocated "Full Rights for the Negro People." In August 1930, the Party began publishing a weekly newspaper, the *Southern Worker*. Though the paper was datelined Birmingham, it was actually printed in Chattanooga because the Birmingham police harassed Party workers so fiercely.

Despite police hostility, by the fall of 1932, the Party was able to mount demonstrations of five thousand or more people, mostly black, outside the Jefferson County courthouse. After New Deal programs began providing more relief and the 1933 National Industrial Recovery Act added new protections for unions, the Party shifted its urban efforts to labor organizing.

In rural Alabama, the Party's first inroads were in Tallapoosa County, where two brothers, Tommy and Ralph Gray, read issues of the *Southern Worker*. The Gray brothers, grandsons of a black Reconstruction-era legislator, liked what they read and organized meetings of a new Croppers' and Farm Workers' Union, which later evolved into the Share Croppers' Union.

In July 1931, at a gathering of about 150 black sharecroppers near Camp Hill, Ralph Gray challenged the county sheriff when he arrived to break up the meeting. The confrontation turned violent, and both Gray and the sheriff were injured. A posse returned, killed Gray, mutilated his body, burned his house, and raided other black homes in the area. An unknown but reportedly large number of people were killed or wounded.

Despite the attacks, the union continued its organizing efforts. Another confrontation occurred near Reeltown in December 1932,

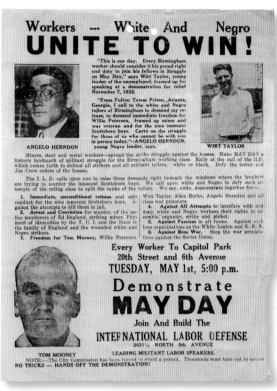

Flier circulated by the International Labor Defense, an organization of the Communist Party, calling workers to a May Day demonstration at Capitol Park, now Linn Park, in Birmingham.

when sheriff's deputies tried to seize the livestock of a union member for a debt collection. A shootout resulted in several people being killed and many arrested, followed by another wave of raids on black homes. Ned Cobb, who described the fight and its aftermath in the book *All God's Dangers*, was arrested and convicted as one of the gunmen trying to fight off the posse. He served thirteen years in Alabama prisons before being released in 1945.

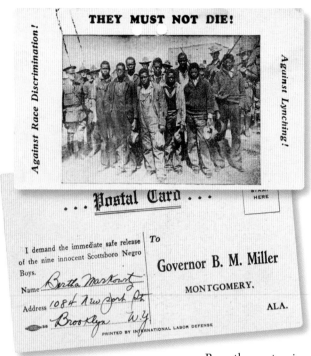

The Communist Party also reached out to black Alabamians through its defense of nine young men who became known as the Scottsboro Boys. Arrested in March 1931, all but the youngest (a thirteen-year-old) were sentenced to death on charges of raping two white women, charges that one of the women later recanted. The convictions were based on scant evidence and were rendered by a hostile court and jury against clients represented by indifferent lawyers. The Communist Party provided lawyers for appealing the convictions, and the cases continued in the courts for years.

Card to Governor Miller from Bertha Markowitz of Brooklyn, New York, calling for the release of the Scottsboro Boys. Governor Miller received boxes of protest cards and letters during the trials.

The Communists made the Scottsboro Boys the centerpiece of an international propaganda campaign. It held them up to the world as an example of the injustices faced by black people in the South and of the Party's vigilance in their defense. The trials also resulted in two major U.S. Supreme Court rulings. One said that defendants in capital cases had to have a lawyer. The other declared that blacks could not be systematically excluded from juries.

Although the Communist Party enjoyed some successes in Alabama, New Deal programs began to provide more relief services by the mid-1930s, weakening the Party's attraction. Tough harassment by law enforcement officers and internal problems also hampered the Party's efforts. Its alien doctrines gained almost no traction among native whites. The greatest part of the Party's success grew out of its early advocacy of civil rights for African Americans.

THE NEW DEAL

EVEN before President Franklin Roosevelt launched the New Deal in 1933, his predecessor, Herbert Hoover, had already tried relief and public works on a scale far beyond any ever undertaken by the U.S. government. But they were not enough. When Roosevelt took office in March 1933, panicked depositors were lined up at banks across the

nation, trying to withdraw their money. Hundreds of the banks had to close. The economy appeared to be in free fall.

Two days after his inauguration, Roosevelt declared a bank holiday, closing all U.S. banks until a rescue plan could be adopted. Three days later, Congress passed the Emergency Banking Act, which allowed the Federal Reserve to step in and assist banks it deemed sound. The act succeeded to a degree that surprised its critics and energized its supporters. Though many banks never reopened, depositors felt safe with the ones that did, and the banking panic ended.

The Banking Act and the rush of other legislation that quickly followed marked Roosevelt's "first hundred days" as a unique time in American history. An unprecedented flood of laws created agencies for relief, securities regulation, public works, agriculture, and labor relations, as well as banking. Although some of the acts were later ruled unconstitutional and all would be modified, they showed a new spirit of hands-on government and a willingness to experiment.

The programs of the New Deal were profoundly important for Alabama. The Agricultural Adjustment Act (AAA) began paying farm owners to take land out of production. Its goal was to reduce crop surpluses and thereby improve prices, but its effects were far broader.

An Arthur Rothstein photograph of a reforestation project in Macon County in 1937, taken for the Farm Security Administration. One of the major initiatives of the New Deal was to protect and restore the land long ravaged by destructive farming practices.

Almost all the money went to landowners, despite efforts by some in Congress to allot a generous portion to the people who worked the land. Since landowners were paid for not growing crops, they no longer needed as many tenants or sharecroppers. Tens of thousands of displaced farm families began to move to towns and cities, or even out of state. Later, many landowners used their federal payments to buy tractors, further reducing their need for farm workers. The AAA launched the federal government into a role of oversight and support of American agriculture that continues today.

The Civilian Conservation Corps (CCC) put tens of thousands of young men to work on public projects in rural areas. CCC-built park facilities, from Monte Sano and De Soto in north Alabama to Chickasaw and Florala in the south, are still core properties in Alabama's park system. Another New Deal program, the Public Works Administration, supported a wider menu of construction projects, ranging from hospitals and airports to schools, military bases, and dams.

Altogether, New Deal projects reached virtually every community in Alabama, and many facilities built then are still in use.

The 1933 National Industrial Recovery Act (NIRA) granted unions expanded rights to organize. It also set minimum wage rates, limited work hours, and expanded government oversight of industries. For many Alabama workers, the NIRA brought the beginning of the forty-hour work week, down from sixty or more just a generation earlier. When the first federal minimum wage requirements went into effect across the nation, they applied in practice mostly to southern workers because northern wage rates were generally above the initial minimum.

Alabama congressman Henry B. Steagall from Dale County co-sponsored the landmark Glass-Steagall Act, which regulated banking. It established the Federal Deposit Insurance Corporation to insure depositors' savings, and it separated investment from commercial banking. For sixty years, its regulatory structure protected the American banking system with an effectiveness previously unknown, until its repeal in 1999.

One of the most important New Deal initiatives for Alabama was the Tennessee Valley Authority (TVA). The TVA act resolved the fate

Opposite page, above: Bunker Tower at Mount Cheaha in the Talladega National Forest. The facilities at Cheaha are among many works of the CCC still in use in Alabama. Opposite page, below: Alabama Department of Archives and History, also known as the War Memorial Building. It houses historical records and artifacts of Alabama, as well as research facilities and museum exhibits. The original portion was completed in 1940 as a WPA project. The wing on the left was added in 1969 and the one on the right in 2005. Below: Wheeler Dam and powerhouse at Decatur. Work on this TVA project began in 1933, and was completed in 1936.

of Wilson Dam by making it part of a unique public entity with a visionary mission of planned development for an entire region. In addition to building dams, the TVA's mandate was to improve navigation of the Tennessee River, establish flood control, begin a program of land conservation, and promote both industrial and agricultural development. When the build-up for a new world war began a few years later, the ready availability of cheap and abundant electricity would give the Tennessee Valley a great advantage in attracting new industries and military bases.

Both the TVA and the AAA included soil restoration as a major goal. It is hard for Alabamians today to imagine the condition of rural land across much of the state in the 1930s. Depression-era photographs showing expanses that resemble lunar landscapes document the effects of years of destructive land-management practices. President Roosevelt, who spent a great deal of time at Warm Springs, Georgia, had seen for himself the wasted barrenness of much of the South's farmland.

To promote soil reclamation, New Deal programs took land out of production and began anti-erosion and reforestation efforts. New types of administrators and technical specialists appeared whose duties were to promote better land management practices. The heirs of this first generation of specialists continue similar work today.

The New Deal created many other programs that aided Alabamians directly. Social Security provided both old-age pensions and unemployment assistance. The Federal Housing Administration underwrote loans to help people buy houses. Other New Deal programs supported the construction of urban rental housing. Alabama's network of rural electric cooperatives also began under the New Deal.

The word *transformative* is often overused, but the changes in Alabama during the 1930s approached that level. New Deal programs touched virtually every person in the state, often in ways that significantly improved their lives. The new relationship it created between citizens and their government also changed the political life of the nation.

New Deal programs attracted the support of many Alabama politicians—not only Bibb Graves and Hugo Black, but also a whole cadre of Alabama congressmen. Some of them became national leaders. Lister Hill, first in the U.S. House of Representatives and then in the Senate, led in passing a variety of New Deal acts. He became a lawmaker of national stature in the area of public health, as John Bankhead had been for highways a generation earlier. Bankhead's son, William Bankhead of Jasper, became speaker of the U.S. House in the late

Opposite page, above: Eroded land on a tenant farm in Walker County, taken by Arthur Rothstein in 1937 for the Farm Security Administration. Opposite page, below: Lauderdale County farmer Julien Case in 1942. Rothstein followed Case around his farm to photograph innovations fostered by the TVA, showing Case here repairing his own transformer. Below: First grade class at Gee's Bend, 1939. One initiative of the New Deal was to establish experimental communities, such as the cooperative farming community in Wilcox County, begun in 1937.

Members of Alabama's powerful congressional delegation in the late 1930s. Seated (left to right): Senator John Bankhead II, Speaker of the House William Bankhead, and Senator Lister Hill; standing (left to right): Representatives Pete Jarman, Frank Boykin, Henry Steagall, Joe Starnes, John Sparkman, Sam Hobbs, and Luther Patrick. Right: Members of the House of Representatives standing in the House Chamber of the U.S. Capitol, with President Roosevelt in his wheelchair, lower right, at a memorial service for Speaker William B. Bankhead of Alabama, September 16, 1940.

1930s, and his other son, John Bankhead Jr., became chairman of the Senate Finance Committee. Alabama's congressional delegation as a whole was one of the most liberal in the South during these years, as a division began to widen in the state between New Deal allies and a growing cohort of conservative opponents.

WORLD WAR II
· · · · · · · · · · · · · · · · · · · ·

DESPITE unprecedented spending and an avalanche of programs, the New Deal did not end the Great Depression. It established a partial safety net and provided relief for millions, but until 1939, prices remained low and unemployment rates stayed high. Then, almost in a matter of months, World War II threw the state's economic gears from sluggish to full throttle.

In early 1939, as Europe teetered on the brink of war, most Americans believed the United States should stay out of another foreign debacle. But after seeing Germany's blitzkrieg invasions of Poland and then France, more American leaders, including many from Alabama, urged greater preparedness. Starting in 1939, orders for new goods snapped Alabama industries into action, and the pace of mobilization only accelerated over the months to come.

Beginning in April 1941, for example, approximately 20,000 construction workers descended on Childersburg, Alabama. In what had been a town of about five hundred people with no paved streets, workers built the Alabama Army Ammunition Plant, the largest powder and explosives plant in the South. At its peak, more than 14,000 employees at the plant produced almost 40 million pounds a month

Electric phosphate smelting furnace used to make elemental phosphorus in a TVA chemical plant near Muscle Shoals, Alabama. Increasing phosphorous production was part of the growing war effort.

of TNT and gunpowder. They also produced heavy water used in the Manhattan Project for making the first atomic bombs.

At the Bechtel-McCone Birmingham Modification Center, another 14,000 employees—about forty percent of them women—modified airplanes for their final deployment. Almost half of America's B-29 bombers went through the Birmingham facilities. Women pilots conducted some of the test flights and also flew some of the planes between facilities, freeing male pilots for combat service.

In the last half of 1941, federal officials bought 35,000 acres of land near the textile and agricultural town of Huntsville and began building a cluster of huge facilities. The Redstone Ordnance Plant produced conventional explosives, while the Huntsville Arsenal made incendiary ordnance and, in case they were needed, chemical weapons. Most of the nearly two million floating smoke pots that screened U.S. ships during the war were made in Huntsville. Within a little more than a year, the number of workers at Redstone and the Arsenal nearly matched Huntsville's prewar population.

In Mobile, two shipbuilding companies employed approximately 60,000 workers, who at the peak of production launched a ship every week. A massive Alcoa plant there produced approximately thirty-four percent of the nation's

Above: Applicants for work at the Childersburg powder plant, registering at the employment office in Sylacauga, May 1941.

aluminum in 1943. Brookley Field became an aircraft-training facility, a refitting and repair center, and a depot, eventually employing 17,000 civilian workers. So many defense workers flooded into Mobile that boarding houses started a hot-bunks system, scheduling rentals so that people not at work could sleep in the beds of those who were.

Historian Allen Cronenberg, in his book *Forth to the Mighty Conflict*, describes the incredible impact of war production on Alabama industries. O'Neal Steel in Birmingham made bombs. Stockham Valves and Fittings produced 4.5 million 75-mm shells, along with millions of grenades. The TCI division of U.S. Steel made helmets, armor plating for warships, and nearly 5 million 155-mm artillery shells. The Gardiner-Waring Company in Florence worked round the clock to produce cotton underwear for the troops, while Avondale Mills in Sylacauga made cloth for sandbags, fatigues, and mattresses. The Goodyear Mills plant in Decatur made canvas, and the old Daniel Pratt cotton gin works in Prattville converted to weapons production.

Alabama also became home to nine major military bases. Maxwell Field in Montgomery trained more than 100,000 airmen, at the site where Wilbur and Orville Wright had established their first flying school just over thirty years earlier. Other air-training

Left: Plant 2 of the sprawling Redstone Arsenal complex, toward the end of construction in the summer of 1942. Above: Moving ordnance outside the manufacturing plants at Redstone.

Above: Women working in the chemistry lab of the Goodyear Rubber plant in Gadsden during World War II. Right: General Benjamin O. Davis (left), commander of the Tuskegee Airmen with pilot Edward Gleed, at an airfield in Italy.

facilities, in addition to Maxwell and Brookley, were at Selma (Craig Field), Courtland (Courtland Field), and Dothan (Napier Field). The nation's principal aviation-training center for African Americans was at Tuskegee, providing the famed Tuskegee Airman their name and a special sense of heritage.

Camp Rucker, a new base in southeast Alabama secured partly through the influence of Congressman Steagall, became a major Army training center. Camp Sibert near Gadsden was a training center for chemical warfare. Fort McClellan, a facility near Anniston established in World War I, became a sprawling induction and training center and then added a depot.

More than 320,000 Alabamians served in the military during World War II, approximately twenty-three percent of the state's male population. They served in every major theater—Mediterranean, European, and Pacific—from the sands of North Africa to the Arctic Sea and from Pearl Harbor to Japan. Many Alabamians won honors and distinctions, but more than 6,000 were killed in action or died of other causes. Thousands more were wounded. For all who served, the war was a life-changing experience, and many Alabamians would remember it as a defining event of their lives.

One of the most highly regarded books about the war was written by Eugene Sledge, a Marine from Mobile who recorded his combat experiences in a small notebook. Years later, while teaching biology at the University of Montevallo, he wrote *With the Old Breed,* describing the vicious battles at Peleliu and Okinawa through the eyes of an ordinary soldier.

Sledge's descriptions are unforgettable—of mangled corpses, a pestilence of flies and maggots, the nauseous stench of death, suffocating heat during the day, and desperate nights in shallow, mud-filled foxholes. Veteran fighters did not even bother to learn the names of replacement troops because they were killed so quickly. Sledge somehow managed to survive, but later he looked back and saw there the death of his "childish innocence that accepted as faith the claim that man is basically good."

Top: Soldiers in combat training at Camp Rucker in Dale County. Above: Members of Company K-3-5 of the 1st Marine Division. Eugene Sledge of Mobile, later author of *With the Old Breed*, is front row center, with his cap pushed back on his head.

By the end of World War II, every person in Alabama had a story to tell. Many were as dramatic as Sledge's, though few people could match his narrative skill. Most stories would have told of major personal struggles—and of change, growth, and exposure to a wider world. Many Alabamians who had left their homes felt a deep desire to return to the life they had known. For many others, the war experiences raised hopes for something better.

From an economic perspective, the war brought unprecedented amounts of money and opportunity to Alabama. A sharecropper who before the war had struggled on the margins of survival might have become a welder at a Mobile shipyard, where he earned more in one year than he had in his entire life. Women who had taken jobs to support the war effort had earned enough money, often for the first times in their lives, to enjoy a degree of financial independence.

African Americans found opportunities as well, though they were routinely frozen out of most highly paid jobs. Black leaders at the national level and in Alabama pressed the Roosevelt administration for fairer treatment. One of these leaders was John LeFlore, the long-time executive secretary of the NAACP chapter in Mobile and a tenacious

Paul Imes, Samuel Watkins, and George Richardson, lab technicians working for the TVA at Muscle Shoals in training for professional positions, June 1942.

advocate for African American rights. LeFlore and his colleagues argued relentlessly that black Americans, too, were fighting to defend the nation and that they deserved to share in the benefits as well as its burdens of that struggle.

In the spring of 1943, President Roosevelt's Committee on Fair Employment Practices heeded the pleas of LeFlore and his colleagues. The committee ordered the Alabama Dry Dock and Shipbuilding Company in Mobile to promote some of its seven thousand black workers to skilled positions. When twelve of them were upgraded to welders, white workers rioted. Officials had to bring in troops from Brookley to restore order.

Opportunities for black Alabamians came in many forms, often unintended. Theodore Roosevelt Clay, a sharecropper with a fifth-grade education, moved to Huntsville when the government bought the land he farmed for the new arsenals. Clay found better work in Huntsville and eventually saw eight of his nine children graduate from college.

Returning veterans such as John Harbert in Birmingham and Winton Blount in Montgomery came home ready to go to work. Both began as small contractors, but by taking on projects of ever-increasing scale, they built major construction companies. Other veterans returned to school, assisted by the recently enacted GI Bill. Alabama colleges, universities, and professional schools were swamped with veterans, often the first in their families to attend an institution of higher learning. Eugene Sledge returned from the Pacific to enroll at Auburn.

At the University of Alabama, veterans attending law school included future governor John Patterson, who had served in North Africa and Italy, and future U.S. senator Howell Heflin, a Marine who fought in the Pacific and earned the Silver Star for gallantry in action. James E. "Big Jim" Folsom returned from the Merchant Marine and resumed his interrupted political career, running for governor in 1946. His

Governor James E. "Big Jim" Folsom, standing in the governor's mansion with an unidentified visitor. Folsom was a larger-than-life figure in many ways. He pressed for one of the most ambitious reform agendas of any governor in Alabama history, but was unable to win legislative passage of most of his proposals.

victory helped launch a new generation of leadership by World War II veterans, who would dominate Alabama politics and business into the 1980s. George Wallace had already finished law school in 1942 when he entered the Army Air Corps. He, like Big Jim, plunged directly into politics when he returned home to Barbour County.

The story for women was more complex. Many had thrived in their World War II jobs and wanted to continue to work, but many others were eager to start families and return to a more traditional life as housewives. So many babies were born after the war that the entire postwar generation would be known as "baby boomers." Many women who did take time off for families would later return to work when their children were older. And they had already proven they could do much more than the kinds of work formerly allotted them.

The war brought many more mundane changes. Government officials promoted frozen rather than canned food during the war to save metal. By the end of the war, frozen foods were part of the American diet. Plywood became a standard building material for the many frantic construction projects of war. After the war, it was used to build the thousands of houses that popped up in towns and cities across Alabama. The GI Bill and the New Deal's Federal Housing Administration helped make the construction of these houses possible. And it was in these modest homes that proud parents raised the children of the baby boom.

Fred Clement, with his Edsel convertible. Automobiles became almost a necessity in the years after World War II, as new housing developments, shopping centers, businesses, and places of recreation relied on people being able to drive their own vehicles.

Having more money also meant that more people could buy cars. Detroit shifted back from war to automobile production, and Alabamians were ready to enjoy the luxury and independence of their own vehicles. Cars let them commute to work from the new suburbs that blossomed around larger towns. Cars also allowed more opportunities for travel, prompting the growth of motels and the development of vacation destinations, such as the beaches of the Gulf of Mexico. New gas and service stations, auto repair shops, parts stores, and dealerships grew to become a major sector of the state's economy.

As the military cut back, Alabama congressmen fought to keep bases in the state open. The efforts of Alabama's junior U.S. senator John Sparkman on behalf of Redstone Arsenal would prove to be crucial for Alabama's future. As an energetic New Dealer and influential member of the House of Representatives during the war, Sparkman had worked to secure Redstone and the Huntsville Arsenal. After the war, as a U.S. senator, Sparkman joined with his powerful colleague Lister Hill to find a new use for the deactivated facility.

In October 1948, pressed by the two Alabama senators, the Defense Department announced that Redstone would be reactivated and that the Huntsville Arsenal property would be added to it. The expanded facility would become home for the Army's guided-missile research. In 1950, the missile research group, which included Wernher von Braun and his German colleagues, was relocated from Fort Bliss, Texas, to Redstone.

Another legacy of World War II was a reinvigorated sense of America as a beacon of freedom to the rest of the world. Both Germany and Japan had subjugated other people based on their claims of racial superiority. President Franklin Roosevelt had set forth America's position against this aggression in his 1941 Four Freedoms speech: "Freedom means the supremacy of human rights everywhere. Our support goes to those who struggle to gain those rights or keep them."

In the Cold War that followed World War II, including the Korean War, America continued to represent itself to the world as the bastion of liberty. But America's leadership in defending freedom abroad cast new light on places at home where freedom was denied. And African Americans, who had supported and fought overseas for their country, were calling, with growing insistence, for their full citizenship rights at home.

Wernher von Braun with Major General Holger Toftoy, in Huntsville before November 1952, with some of the products of their early work. General Toftoy commanded the unit that brought von Braun and his team to the United States, and he directly oversaw the team's work at Huntsville from 1952 until 1958.

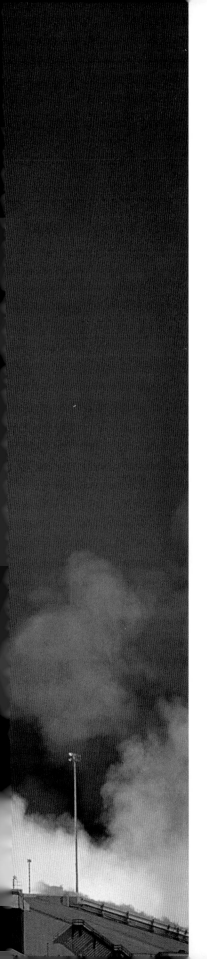

CHAPTER 7

CHANGING TIMES

1955 to 2010

T HE MONTGOMERY BUS BOYCOTT *(1955–1956) helped launch the modern civil rights movement. It was the first of a series of Alabama confrontations, culminating in the Voting Rights March of 1965, that changed the state's and America's history. In the decades after legalized segregation ended, Alabamians had to readjust virtually every area of public life to reflect, for the first time in the state's history, a society in which all citizens were entitled to equal rights.*

Desegregation was part of an even larger set of changes that, upon reflection, are stunning in scope. In less than a lifetime, Alabamians went not only from a segregated to a desegregated society, but from farming with mules to raising genetically modified crops, from sweltering summer heat to air conditioned spaces, and from wire-tethered telephones to portable devices connecting instantaneously to the entire world. Alabamians even helped land the first man on the moon in July 1969. These massive changes brought enormous benefits, but they brought struggle and conflict as well.

THE CIVIL RIGHTS MOVEMENT IN ALABAMA

THE upheavals of the New Deal and World War II threw up new challenges to the South's system of racial segregation. After President Harry Truman ordered the desegregation of the military in 1948, black and white soldiers fought side by side in the Korean War. By the mid-1950s, visitors to Alabama military bases passed from a segregated culture into an integrated one each time they entered a gate.

At the same time, the black middle class in towns and cities across Alabama continued to expand. Their ranks included professionals

Launch on July 16, 1969, of Apollo 11. The Saturn V launch vehicle that helped carry the first human beings to the moon was developed at the Marshall Space Flight Center in Huntsville.

such as teachers, preachers, doctors, and lawyers, as well as business owners, skilled workers, and public employees—some of whom had benefitted from federally funded programs of the New Deal and World War II. Many of them had college degrees, and they were keenly conscious of the inequities they had to endure.

The U.S. Supreme Court during this time began to show that it also recognized the inequities. In *Smith v Allwright* (1944), the court ended the white-only political primaries of the Democratic Party. After that decision, black Alabamians—at least those who succeeded in registering—could vote in the primary that actually determined who held public office in the state.

At the same time, increasing numbers of black Alabamians began registering to vote. John LeFlore in Mobile, for example, and Amelia and Samuel W. Boynton in Selma organized programs to teach applicants how to get around registration barriers. In Montgomery, the number of African American voters grew to make up more than seven percent of the city's 1955 voting rolls. Although the numbers were still relatively small, they were large enough that some white politicians began seeking the support of black voters.

As historian J. Mills Thornton has pointed out in *Dividing Lines*—an extraordinary book about the civil rights movement in Montgomery, Selma, and Birmingham—increased attention by some city officials created new optimism in Montgomery's black community. The city's commissioner for public safety even began hiring black police officers, though they were assigned to work only in black neighborhoods. In an African American voter forum held before the March 1955 city elections, leaders pressed white candidates about their concerns, one of which was the seating system for city buses.

Amelia Boynton speaking at Brown Chapel in Selma, May 1966. A graduate of Tuskegee Institute, Boynton and her husband began organizing African American voter registration efforts in Selma in the 1930s.

Under policies then in effect, Montgomery buses reserved the front ten seats for white riders and the rear ten for black riders. A middle zone of sixteen seats was to be adjusted by the driver based on the ratio of black and white passengers. In practice, however, the adjustment process was applied only against black riders. It was made even more offensive by the drivers' frequent rudeness in ordering riders to surrender their seats and the fact that those riders then usually had to stand.

While African Americans in Montgomery were becoming more hopeful in the early 1950s, white people were growing more anxious. Especially in the wake of the Supreme Court's *Brown v Board of Education* decision in 1954, the question of race relations, never entirely dormant, regained primacy. In the 1955 municipal elections, the commissioner who had hired the black policemen was denounced by his

Mug shot of Rosa Parks. Parks was the long-time secretary of the Montgomery Chapter of the NAACP and knew about earlier protests against Montgomery's system of bus segregation. Her actions on December 1, 1955, appear to have been an informed personal response to the immediate situation rather than a preplanned action.

opponent for soliciting black votes. The opponent's victory set into motion a new political dynamic in which candidates vied to surpass each other in proving their commitment to segregation.

At least two times before December 1955, African American riders had refused to give up their bus seats and had been arrested. One of the arrests, in fact, became an issue in the city elections. When Rosa Parks refused to give up her seat on December 1, she was also arrested. But Parks was the secretary of the local NAACP chapter and was widely known and respected in the African American community. Her arrest triggered a community-wide boycott of city buses.

After the boycott began, its leaders and local officials began negotiating almost immediately, but white officials refused to give any ground. Two months later, Klan members threw a bomb at the home of the boycott's leader, Martin Luther King Jr. The bombing and the intransigence of local officials persuaded the protestors to turn to the federal courts for help.

In their original negotiations with city officials, boycott leaders had only asked that the city adopt the plan of bus segregation used in Mobile. There, white riders seated themselves from the front and black riders from the rear, but the buses had no adjustable section and no one had to give up a seat. In the federal lawsuit they now brought, Montgomery's boycott leaders broadened their complaint. They no longer asked for the Mobile plan but framed their suit as a challenge to segregation itself.

In June 1956, federal judges Richard Rives and Frank Johnson rendered the majority decision of a three-judge panel in favor of the boycotters. The U.S. Supreme Court affirmed that ruling in November. On December 21, after the city's appeals were exhausted, black riders began using the buses again. Now they could sit in any open seat they chose.

The Montgomery Bus Boycott was a major victory, but in the years immediately following it, little else about segregation in Alabama changed. Most white Alabamians united to defend segregation in a strategy of "massive resistance." They hoped that if they held firm and used all the tools at their disposal, including economic pressure, they

Above: Mug shot of Martin Luther King Jr., after he was arrested for violating Alabama's anti-boycott laws. The date of his death was written later on the photo, apparently by a public safety official when the photo was removed from the active file. Right: Handout of Integrated Bus Suggestions. This remarkable document was circulated by the Montgomery Improvement Association and probably written by its president, Martin Luther King Jr. It was fortunately preserved by Inez Jessie Baskin, an African American reporter in Montgomery.

December 19, 1956

INTEGRATED BUS SUGGESTIONS

This is a historic week because segregation on buses has now been declared unconstitutional. Within a few days the Supreme Court Mandate will reach Montgomery and you will be re-boarding integrated buses. This places upon us all a tremendous responsibility of maintaining, in face of what could be some unpleasantness, a calm and loving dignity befitting good citizens and members of our Race. If there is violence in word or deed it must not be our people who commit it.

For your help and convenience the following suggestions are made. Will you read, study and memorize them so that our non-violent determination may not be endangered. First, some general suggestions:

1. Not all white people are opposed to integrated buses. Accept goodwill on the part of many.
2. The whole bus is now for the use of all people. Take a vacant seat.
3. Pray for guidance and commit yourself to complete non-violence in word and action as you enter the bus.
4. Demonstrate the calm dignity of our Montgomery people in your actions.
5. In all things observe ordinary rules of courtesy and good behavior.
6. Remember that this is not a victory for Negroes alone, but for all Montgomery and the South. Do not boast! Do not brag!
7. Be quiet but friendly; proud, but not arrogant; joyous, but not boisterous.
8. Be loving enough to absorb evil and understanding enough to turn an enemy into a friend.

Now for some specific suggestions:

1. The bus driver is in charge of the bus and has been instructed to obey the law. Assume that he will cooperate in helping you occupy any vacant seat.
2. Do not deliberately sit by a white person, unless there is no other seat.
3. In sitting down by a person, white or colored, say "May I" or "Pardon me" as you sit. This is a common courtesy.
4. If cursed, do not curse back. If pushed, do not push back. If struck, do not strike back, but evidence love and goodwill at all times.
5. In case of an incident, talk as little as possible, and always in a quiet tone. Do not get up from your seat! Report all serious incidents to the bus driver.
6. For the first few days try to get on the bus with a friend in whose non-violence you have confidence. You can uphold one another by a glance or a prayer.
7. If another person is being molested, do not arise to go to his defense, but pray for the oppressor and use moral and spiritual force to carry on the struggle for justice.
8. According to your own ability and personality, do not be afraid to experiment with new and creative techniques for achieving reconciliation and social change.
9. If you feel you cannot take it, walk for another week or two. We have confidence in our people. GOD BLESS YOU ALL.

THE MONTGOMERY IMPROVEMENT ASSOCIATION
THE REV. M. L. KING, JR., PRESIDENT
THE REV. W. J. POWELL, SECRETARY

Left: Juliette Hampton Morgan at the Montgomery Library, June 1, 1955. After the Montgomery Bus Boycott began in December, Morgan wrote letters to the newspaper comparing Martin Luther King Jr.'s nonviolence to the tactics of Gandhi. Below: Rosa Parks and Virginia Durr, appearing together in the 1990s. After Parks was arrested on the evening of December 1, 1955, Durr joined her husband, attorney Clifford Durr, and E. D. Nixon, a long-time activist in Montgomery, in securing Park's release on bond.

could fend off the new federal impositions as their forebears had done during Reconstruction.

A corollary of massive resistance was that white Alabamians felt they had to maintain a solid front. Since any acts of conciliation were seen as weakening their united stand, segregationists applied intense pressure against other whites not to break ranks. Their attacks against those who showed signs of cooperating with black protestors were often vicious. When Juliette Hampton Morgan, a white librarian, wrote letters

to a Montgomery newspaper praising the bus boycott, she was harassed and bullied so aggressively that she committed suicide.

Through the late 1950s, segregationists' successes in resisting any more major changes gave them reason to hope their strategy might succeed. Schools and most public facilities remained segregated, and in some Alabama counties, absolutely no African Americans were able to vote. Alabama State College students launched a series of sit-ins in Montgomery in early 1960, but the state's crackdown was fierce. Officials forced the college to expel or suspend many of the student leaders and to fire faculty members thought to have encouraged them. The wall of segregation in Alabama, though under assault, seemed to be holding firm.

Top: The Greyhound bus that carried Freedom Riders burning near Anniston, on Mother's Day, May 14, 1961. Above: Governor John Patterson (left) and Birmingham Public Safety Commissioner Eugene "Bull" Connor (right), attending the opening of Birmingham's new Eastwood Mall in 1960, the first enclosed mall in the Deep South.

Then on Mother's Day, May 14, 1961, two commercial buses, one Greyhound and one Trailways, crossed into Alabama traveling their regularly scheduled routes. A group of black and white riders on each bus intentionally sat in the section customarily used by the other race. The "Freedom Rides" from Washington, D.C., to New Orleans were an initiative of the Congress of Racial Equality (CORE). Their purpose was to test compliance with a recent Supreme Court ruling that had declared segregation unconstitutional in interstate bus seating and terminals.

When the Greyhound bus stopped in Anniston, a member of a waiting Klan mob punctured one of tires. Klan members then followed the bus until it had to pull over outside the town because of the flat tire. As a mob gathered, a Klan member threw a fire bomb into the bus. When smoke and fire began to fill the bus, the mob would not let the passengers out. E. M. Cowling, an undercover state investigator who had been secretly tracking the riders, drew his gun and forced the mob back, allowing the riders to escape asphyxiation.

When the Trailways bus reached Birmingham later that afternoon, a Klan mob attacked the riders at the station. City public safety commissioner Eugene "Bull" Connor had alerted the Klan to the bus's arrival and had directed police to stay away long enough to give the Klansmen a free hand.

After these attacks, most of the original riders were too injured or dispirited to proceed, but new volunteers arrived, organized by stu-

dents at Tennessee State University and Fisk University in Nashville. They joined the only member of the first group to continue, their fellow student, John Lewis, a native of Troy, Alabama. On Saturday, May 20, 1961, this new group of Freedom Riders pressed on to Montgomery.

As in Birmingham, city police stayed away while a Klan-led mob attacked the riders at the bus station. John Seigenthaler, an assistant to U.S. Attorney General Robert Kennedy, was in town that day negotiating with state officials for the safety of the Freedom Riders. When he tried to help two of the riders escape, he was hit on the head with a pipe and knocked unconscious. Floyd Mann, director of Alabama's state police, arrived, drew his gun, and personally protected some of the fallen riders from even more serious injury.

The next night, Martin Luther King Jr. spoke to more than a thousand supporters at Montgomery's First Baptist Church, where civil rights leader Ralph Abernathy was pastor. As the service began, a white mob outside set fire to a car and began throwing objects at the church, threatening to burn it. Governor John Patterson had to call in the

Top: First Baptist Church, Montgomery, where Martin Luther King Jr. spoke to a packed gathering on May 21, 1961. A mob outside compelled Governor John Patterson to call out the National Guard. Above: Montgomery Greyhound Station, where the Freedom Riders were attacked by a Klan mob. The building is now the Freedom Rides Museum.

Right: George Wallace campaigning for governor in 1962. White Citizens' Council members sought to use economic and political pressure to suppress African American activism and to enforce white unity in resistance. Below: President John Kennedy and Governor George Wallace at Redstone Arsenal on May 18, 1963. President Kennedy's visit came literally days after the violent demonstrations in Birmingham and less than a month before Wallace's stand in the schoolhouse door in Tuscaloosa.

National Guard to restore order. News coverage of the attacks against the Freedom Riders again drew national attention to conditions faced by African Americans in Alabama.

President John Kennedy, who had taken office just four months earlier, had been supported in his campaign by many white southern Democrats, including Governor Patterson. Although Kennedy was reluctant to offend his southern white supporters, the violence and open defiance of federal law helped push him into a position of more active engagement in civil rights. In September, the Interstate Commerce Commission issued an order expressly prohibiting segregation in all interstate bus and train terminals nationwide.

The attacks against the Freedom Riders also caused some white moderates in Alabama to break ranks with the strategy of massive resistance. Montgomery businessman Winton Blount called a number of white civic leaders to a meeting at his home on Saturday evening, just hours after the attacks against the Freedom Riders. The group adopted a resolution denouncing "mob violence" and calling for local authorities to maintain "law and order." The following Monday, two local civic clubs and the Chamber of Commerce endorsed the resolution. The white Montgomery Ministerial Association approved an even stronger resolution, and the *Montgomery Advertiser* strongly supported the resolutions editorially.

Birmingham police blocking marchers on sidewalk. The placards read "Open Lunch Counters to All" and "Everybody Wants Freedom."

At the state level, however, white resistance only intensified. George Wallace ran for governor the next year (1962), trumpeting his defiance of the federal government and his determination to defend the southern "way of life." In his January 1963 inaugural address following an overwhelming victory, Wallace proclaimed to the cheering crowd: "Segregation forever!"

Just two months after Wallace's address, however, civil rights activists in Birmingham launched a new campaign. The protest leader, Fred Shuttlesworth, was a local minister whose capacity for defiance fully matched Wallace's. In cooperation with Martin Luther King Jr. and the Southern Christian Leadership Conference (SCLC), Shuttlesworth led a series of sit-ins and demonstrations at downtown Birmingham stores. Other black leaders in the city were then in quiet negotiations with white leaders over efforts to reform city government, which created some divisions in the black community and resentment in the white community over the timing of the demonstrations. Moderates of both races called for calm and for continued talks.

Shuttlesworth and King pressed on with the demonstrations, but after more than a month, they had little to show for their efforts. They raised the stakes by calling on students to join them, and hundreds of young people responded. Police commissioner Connor arrested them by the hundreds. As jails and holding areas filled, the frustrated Connor turned to fire hoses and dogs to try to punish and intimidate the demonstrators. Televised evening newscasts were then becoming standard fare in homes across the United States, and film footage from

Above: Fred Shuttlesworth (left) with Ralph Abernathy and Martin Luther King Jr. in Birmingham, 1963. Shuttlesworth, a Birmingham minister and civil rights leader, was a co-founder with King and others of the Southern Christian Leadership Conference in 1957. He fought fearlessly for civil rights despite a blast of sixteen sticks of dynamite under his bedroom window that virtually destroyed his house (he was in bed then) and a beating by a Klan mob with brass knuckles and chains.

Right: One of the photos taken by investigators in the aftermath of the 16th Street Baptist Church bombing on September 15, 1963.

Birmingham of police dogs biting young men and girls being slammed into walls by powerful jets of water became lead stories.

The violence prompted President Kennedy to send in a mediator, and within weeks Birmingham leaders took the first steps toward desegregating downtown facilities. Just a few months later, however, as Birmingham began desegregating its public schools, Klansmen planted a bomb at the 16th Street Baptist Church. The explosion killed four black girls attending Sunday school—Addie Mae Collins (age 14), Carol Denise McNair (age 11), Carole Robertson (age 14), and Cynthia Wesley (age 14)—and it brought further disgrace to Alabama and to the cause of massive resistance.

In the aftermath of the Birmingham violence, President Kennedy proposed a sweeping civil rights bill to end segregation in employment and public accommodations nationwide. Kennedy himself was assassinated just two months after the bombing, but his successor, Lyndon Johnson, secured passage of the Civil Rights Act of 1964, partly as a memorial to Kennedy.

The passage of the Civil Rights Act of 1964 was another heavy defeat for segregationists in Alabama, but civil rights leaders knew that African Americans still needed to be able to vote to protect their rights. Through 1964, voter registration efforts in Alabama intensified, and a particularly fierce struggle developed in the Black Belt. Sheriff James Clark in Dallas County made national news by his public bullying of hopeful registrants.

After a state trooper shot and killed demonstrator Jimmie Lee Jackson in neighboring Perry County, protest leaders in Selma called for a march on Montgomery. On March 7, 1965, the day after Governor Wallace issued an order forbidding a march, Hosea Williams and John Lewis led about six hundred people toward Montgomery. As the lead marchers crossed the eastern side of the Edmund Pettus Bridge, a waiting force of state troopers, sheriff's deputies, and mounted posse members fired tear gas at the marchers and then charged into them with nightsticks and cattle prods. The attackers beat many marchers to the ground, leaving eighteen who had to be hospitalized.

Images of this attack were broadcast on national television, inspiring thousands of people from across the nation, black and white, to come to Alabama to join the protest. On March 21, after two weeks of legal maneuvers, Martin Luther King Jr. led a new group of marchers across the bridge toward Montgomery. This time they were protected by a federalized Alabama National Guard.

Emergency room logbook from the Good Samaritan Hospital in Selma, listing patients treated there on Bloody Sunday. The entry on the lower part of the right page is for John Lewis, listing a fractured skull.

Martin Luther and Coretta Scott King in center, with Ralph Abernathy's children in front of them and Abernathy on the far left, as they approached the end of the Selma to Montgomery March.

Four days later, approximately 25,000 people swept up Montgomery's Dexter Avenue to the Alabama Capitol. Standing in front of the steps where Jefferson Davis had been inaugurated president of the Confederacy and George Wallace had recently proclaimed "Segregation forever!" Martin Luther King Jr. delivered one of his greatest speeches: "How long? Not long, because the arc of the moral universe is long, but it bends toward justice."

The marches, the attack at the bridge, and the deaths of two protestors—James Reeb and Viola Liuzzo—all helped President Johnson win passage of federal legislation to protect the voting rights of African Americans in the South. That act, passed in August 1965, sealed the fate of legalized segregation in Alabama. As they had in 1867, federal officials came to Alabama to ensure that black citizens could register and vote. But unlike a century earlier, federal support continued for decades afterward, during which time African Americans became ongoing, active participants in the political life of the state.

These four great Alabama confrontations—the bus boycott in 1955–1956, the Freedom Rides in 1961, Birmingham in 1963, and the voting rights marches in 1965—were turning points in the history of America, not just of Alabama. They have attracted so much attention, however, that they overshadow the stories of hundreds of other important local actions that took place all over the state. The relatively peaceful process of desegregation in Huntsville, Mobile, and many other towns, for example, did not make national news. And the focus on famous leaders overlooks the exertions of thousands of ordinary people, including

some whites, who also labored in the face of danger to secure civil rights for everyone. The great successes of the civil rights movement could not have been achieved without thousands of unheralded volunteers.

President Lyndon Johnson hands a pen to Martin Luther King Jr. following the signing of the Voting Rights Act, August 6, 1965. On Dr. King's right is Reverend Ralph Abernathy.

AFTERMATH OF THE CIVIL RIGHTS MOVEMENT

By the mid-1960s, it was clear to most people that legally mandated segregation was at an end. But what was to come next was not so clear. Alabamians had to find ways to move forward as a society in which all citizens had the same legal rights. Yet the actual culture in which they lived was freighted with inequitable practices and ways of thinking that had accrued over many generations. Everywhere people of both races came together, old ways were in conflict with the new legal order.

When did one use Miss or Mister in addressing a person of another race? Who yielded when a black person and a white person arrived together at a door? Did one hold it for the other? What happened when black people moved into a previously white neighborhood? All these questions about personal conduct merged with a knotty list of public policy issues, such as fairness in the allocation of public services, equitable treatment in employment, and, especially, questions about making up for past inequities. Through the decades after 1965, Alabamians had to work through difficult adjustments in virtually every sphere of public life.

Differing expectations complicated the adjustment process. Most civil rights leaders were preachers, and during the civil rights struggles, many had painted visions of the "beloved community" of equality

Sheriff Lucius Amerson (left) and his deputies being sworn in by Judge Preston Hornsby, January 16, 1967. Amerson was the first African American sheriff in the South since Reconstruction.

that they hoped to attain. But for most people, the end of segregation was just the starting point of a process of change, and very little changed right away in the daily lives of either black or white Alabamians. For many African Americans, the fact that so little actually did change left them disappointed and frustrated, and sometimes angry. After such a mighty struggle, the results certainly did not feel like fairness and equality.

Most white Alabamians, however, felt that a great deal had changed. The practice of segregation they had struggled so long to defend had been overturned. And now, many felt it was time to put those conflicts behind them and move on to other matters. They were generally indifferent to what was, from the perspective of African Americans, a long list of issues that still needed attention and remediation. Thus, the years after the civil rights movement continued to be a time of struggle—not as violent as during the decades of protests and demonstrations, but often quite tense and very difficult.

The practice of at-large elections was one example of these friction points. For years, many Alabama communities had set up county and city boards and commissions in which each member was elected by all the voters of that county or city. Under this system, white majorities usually elected all-white governing bodies.

After the Voting Rights Act, black organizations pushed for governing bodies in which members represented separate districts. They took their complaints to federal courts and won most of these battles as well. In newly created districts where black voters were in the majority, African Americans began winning elections. When the new African

American officials took their seats on school boards, city councils, and county commissions, still more adjustment struggles followed.

Alabama's practices for setting legislative districts took a double hit in the 1960s. In 1964, the U.S. Supreme Court struck down the old system for apportioning districts. In *Reynolds v Sims,* a case originating in Jefferson County, the Court ruled that each district had to represent roughly the same number of people, without regard to factors such as geography or county and city boundaries. With the passage of the Voting Rights Act the next year, legislative reapportionment every ten years had to comply with both the new act and the *Reynolds* decision.

Under the old system, counties had been the basis for legislative districts, which made sense in some ways because legislators then represented specific political entities. Now, reapportionment became a far more complicated and more political process. Those who drew the lines determined the makeup of each district down to the street and house, without regard to county or city boundaries. They often were able to tailor districts to elect or defeat particular candidates.

Composite of photos of the members of the Alabama House of Representatives elected in 1970. It includes the first two African American representatives in almost a century, Fred Gray and Thomas Reed, both from Macon County, and one woman, Retha Deal Wynot, from Gadsden.

Reynolds reshaped the Alabama legislature. Jefferson County, for instance, went from having one senator and seven representatives to seven senators and twenty-two representatives. The four counties of Jefferson, Mobile, Montgomery, and Madison came to control forty percent of the seats in the legislature. In the wake of *Reynolds* and the Voting Rights Act, the first African American legislators in almost a century, Fred Gray and Thomas Reed, were elected in 1970.

A major player in the new reapportionment struggles was the Alabama Democratic Conference (ADC), a majority-black wing of the Democratic Party. ADC president Joe Reed was also associate executive secretary of the recently integrated Alabama Education Association, the powerful state teachers' lobby. Reed used the Voting Rights Act to ensure that the percentage of black legislators reflected the black percentage of the state's population. Because all black legislators were Democrats and the Democratic Party held overwhelming legislative majorities, black senators and representatives were soon able to win leadership posts and to wield substantial influence in the legislature.

By far, the most difficult and volatile area of adjustment in desegregation was the public schools. During slavery, black people were systematically denied the right to learn. For the five generations after slavery, black children were shortchanged in educational services. The programs and facilities for black students—from buildings, course

Frank Johnson, judge of the U.S. District Court for the Middle District of Alabama, 1955 to 1979. Johnson was a Republican from Winston County, a descendant of hill country yeoman farmers who had opposed secession and who joined the Republican Party after the Civil War.

offerings, books, and enrichment activities to equipment and maintenance—were almost always inferior to those for white students, sometimes dramatically so.

Many dedicated teachers in black schools worked hard to help their students grow and develop. Black schools often became centers of community and cultural life for African Americans in Alabama. But while some students did well academically, many others did not. Black schools as a whole continued to bear the marks of generations of deprivation.

Since the days of Horace Mann in the 1830s and 1840s, a basic goal of American public education had been to create a unified populace by teaching students a common skill set and a shared framework of values. Public schools had helped integrate one wave of immigrants after another into the life of the nation. In Alabama and the rest of the South, however, black students had always been kept apart from that process of integration.

A help session for Bessemer High School students, held in the basement of St. Paul's Lutheran Church in Birmingham, December 1965.

Because white Alabamians resisted school integration so tenaciously, federal judges, especially Frank Johnson in Alabama's Middle District, grew impatient with the delays. Ultimately, Johnson issued sweeping orders for immediate desegregation in Alabama, which white-dominated school boards had to scurry to implement. Still more years of conflict and struggle followed. Black students generally lost their old schools and many of their community traditions because they were transferred to white schools. Two cultures that had been divided in many fundamental ways for generations were suddenly thrust together with little advance preparation to smooth the process.

In many ways, social class was almost as big an issue as race in this cultural merging. For middle-class black students whose lifestyles resembled those of their white classmates, the chances for success in the new environment were good, though many still experienced galling instances of discrimination. Some black families even began moving to suburbs so their children could attend schools where greater affluence and a largely middle-class student population helped sustain higher academic standards.

In school districts with large numbers of black students who lived near or below the poverty line, white families who were able to do so generally abandoned public schools, either by moving to suburbs or

by establishing private schools. Their departures often triggered a self-reinforcing cycle of public school decline and abandonment. In parts of Alabama, new patterns of school segregation began to reemerge, shaped almost as much by class and income as by race.

As school systems attempted to work through these changes, political questions about education policy and funding took on new importance. Politicians argued over whether the most important need was more money or better administration and enforcement of standards. Those disagreements often became entangled in the interplay of other ongoing interests. One of the difficulties of public policy in the post–civil rights era was that, although most issues were not overtly racial, racial interests were still a factor in many political decisions.

Across Alabama society, adjustments seemed to take place most successfully in the military, athletics, music, and evangelical churches. In these areas where Alabamians joined in a shared mission, their common commitment helped them overcome old divisive barriers from the past. For the state as a whole, the adjustments that followed the civil rights movement proceeded unevenly, and many difficult issues and conflicts remained three generations after the process began, despite the considerable progress.

A CHURNING AND SOMETIMES
SPUTTERING ECONOMY

As Alabama began the process of desegregation in the 1960s, a series of major disruptions in the economy contributed to the state's difficulties. In the years immediately after World War II, economic conditions in Alabama and across the United States had continued to improve. With the rest of the industrialized world devastated by the war, the United States enjoyed economic dominance. American producers supplied countries around the world, as well as the pent-up demand at home.

But this advantage could not last forever. As other nations rebuilt, many installed the most modern and efficient machines available. And because their currencies were cheap compared to the dollar and their wage scales lower, they enjoyed substantial pricing advantages. By the mid-1960s, industries that had been leading sectors of Alabama's economy, such as textiles, coal, iron, and steel, were coming under pressure from foreign producers. To remain competitive, businesses had to invest in new technology, become more efficient, and cut jobs.

Over the next three decades, tens of thousands of Alabama jobs disappeared because of increased mechanization and foreign competition.

Alabama River Pulp Company at Claiborne in Monroe County. Even though paper production was a strong Alabama industry in the last part of the twentieth century, by the early 2000s, many of these plants were struggling as electronic communications displaced paper media.

Tallassee Mill, built 1852–1854. This was once the largest building in Alabama under one roof. It continued in operation until textile production ceased in the 1960s. The building was gutted in the 1990s to salvage the heart-pine lumber that formed the interior structure.

The 1950 census reported that 50,657 Alabamians worked in the lumber and wood products industries. By 2011, the number had fallen to 12,823. These losses were only partially mitigated by employment growth in the state's paper mills, where just over 11,000 Alabamians worked in 2011.

The primary-metals industry, including steel making, suffered similar declines. In 1950, 46,314 Alabamians were employed in primary metals, but by 2011, the number was down to 14,185. Mechanization hit coal mining as well, claiming thousands more jobs.

Of all Alabama industries, losses in textiles were probably the most visible and dramatic. In 1950, 62,023 Alabamians produced cloth or made apparel. By 2011, the number had fallen to 10,037. This decline was especially painful because textile plants were often the main employers in many small towns across the state. Valley, Sylacauga, Alexander City, Monroeville, Fort Payne, and many other towns took terrible blows as their textile plants first began to lay off workers and then to lock their doors.

Other changes also eroded the economies of small towns. National chain stores, usually in larger towns, offered prices that independent local stores could not match, and people who now owned cars could drive farther for better selections and lower prices. Long-established wholesale companies that supplied the small independent stores also began to close. At the same time, new suburban shopping centers drew business away from stores in city centers. Even in larger Alabama cities, parts of the historic downtown business districts looked almost abandoned by the late 1900s.

Changes in Alabama agriculture rivaled those of the textile industry in their impact. The 1954 agricultural census reported 176,956 farms in Alabama. By 2012, the number had fallen to 43,223. In 1930, the state's farmers cultivated 3,566,498 acres of cotton. Those numbers fell to 1,142,480 in 1954 and to 376,464 in 2012. Tenant farming, which included 176,247 farm families in 1935, was no longer even reported in 2012. By that time, farming—the work of most black Alabamians for generations—had become largely a white occupation, supplemented by migrant labor.

Farmers who persevered on the land saw revolutionary changes in agricultural technology. In 1950, only 37,783 Alabama farms had at least one tractor; 173,578 did not have even one. Within twenty years, Alabama agriculture was almost fully mechanized. Manual work continued only for specialty crops such as tomatoes and peaches.

A chemical revolution accompanied the mechanical one, as the expanded use of fertilizers and pesticides brought huge increases in crop yield per acre. By the 1990s, a genetics revolution introduced modi-

A chicken farm in Monroe County, 2010. Photo by Carol Highsmith. These chickens are egg layers.

fied plants that were either more disease resistant or productive —or both. With all these advances, yields per acre for some crops were as much as ten times higher than they had been sixty years earlier.

Hog production, by contrast, fell from 871,566 in 1954 to 446,448 in 2012, despite a fifty percent increase in the state's population. Pork, a historic staple of Alabama's agriculture and diet, was displaced by poultry. In the 1950 agricultural census, Alabama farmers reported selling just over 5 million chickens. By 2012, the total was more than a billion. A major new agricultural industry had emerged in less than sixty years.

Another big loss for Alabama's economy during these years was the closure of major military bases—Brookley Field at Mobile (1969), Craig Field at Selma (1977), and Fort McClellan at Anniston (1999). Fortunately for the state, Fort Rucker, Maxwell Air Force Base, and Redstone Arsenal continued. In 1956, the missile group that had been posted to Redstone six years earlier expanded to become the Army

Ballistic Missile Agency (ABMA). After the Russians launched two Sputnik satellites in late 1957, federal officials turned to ABMA for America's first satellite. The Huntsville team successfully launched Explorer 1 on January 31, 1958.

Later that year, Congress passed a bill submitted by President Dwight Eisenhower creating the National Aeronautics and Space Administration (NASA). On July 1, 1960, almost 5,000 civilian employees of ABMA and 1,840 acres of land at Redstone were transferred to NASA and became part of the George C. Marshall Space Flight Center. At a joint session of Congress less than a year later—and just five days after the attack on the Freedom Riders in Montgomery—President Kennedy called for the United States to "commit itself to achieving the goal, before this decade is out, of landing a man on the moon and returning him safely to the earth."

Through the early and mid-1960s, Marshall and Huntsville throbbed with the energy of thousands of engineers working on rocketry and other related programs to achieve the goal Kennedy had set for the nation. On July 20, 1969, their labors were rewarded as they watched astronaut Neil Armstrong take his first step onto the surface of the moon. Alabamians had played a substantial part in making that giant step possible.

Apollo 11 mission officials celebrate in the Launch Control Center following the successful Apollo 11 liftoff on July 16, 1969. Wernher von Braun is wearing the binoculars.

Even as Armstrong began his return to earth, however, the rocket program at Huntsville was being scaled back. Escalating demands of the Vietnam War and new commitments to President Johnson's War on Poverty pulled money away from NASA. Significant work did continue as the Marshall Center turned its attention to Skylab and the Space Shuttle, but the level of commitment to those efforts was far below that of the moon landing.

As NASA jobs disappeared, many of the bright engineers in Huntsville began looking for new opportunities. Through their initiative, Huntsville became a center not only for defense and space research, but also for computer development, geographic information systems, telecommunications, aeronautics, and even genetics.

When IBM decided to create and sell personal computers, it turned to a Huntsville company, SCI (Space Craft Incorporated), to make the first large group of test models. After the models proved satisfactory, IBM contracted with SCI to begin manufacturing its PCs. The first units went on sale in the late summer of 1981, and SCI expanded to produce millions more of the first PCs for IBM and for other companies as well.

More recently, the HudsonAlpha Institute for Biotechnology in Huntsville has become an international center of genetics research. The Institute also serves as a host facility and incubator for new companies developing commercial applications based on DNA research.

Rocket production continues in Alabama at the United Launch Alliance at Decatur. Its great plant, which stands on land that for generations before grew cotton, now makes rockets for government and private-sector use. Rockets made at Decatur launched many of the satellites for America's orbital communications and research systems. An Atlas V rocket made by the United Launch Alliance sent the New Horizons mission to Pluto.

Technology-oriented businesses also grew in Alabama's university towns. Tuscaloosa and Auburn both became centers of prosperity in a state where much of the economy was shrinking. Medical services and research at the University of Alabama at Birmingham helped salvage economic hope and pride in a city where traditional industries had been ravaged.

Some other economic developments during these years helped the state partially offset its losses. The discovery of natural gas in Mobile Bay in 1978 led to the sale of drilling rights and to new investments in oil and gas production. One achievement of Governor Forrest "Fob"

One of the first generation of PCs, made in Huntsville for IBM by SCI.

James's administration was setting up a trust fund into which revenue from drilling-rights sales and royalties was deposited.

The trust fund's earnings were designated to support the state's beleaguered General Fund, with a portion allocated for counties and cities. Later constitutional amendments made several adjustments in the fund structure and its uses, including setting aside a portion to promote economic development. A 1992 amendment allocated up to $15 million a year from the natural gas revenues for the "Forever Wild" program, to buy and protect unique land and water properties in the state.

Alabama's places of natural beauty, along with its rich history, helped spur a major increase in tourism during these years. The beaches of Baldwin and Mobile counties and the shores of Mobile Bay became attractions to hundreds of thousands of visitors, and to new residents as well.

In 1993, Mercedes-Benz announced it would build a new automobile assembly plant near Tuscaloosa. Governor James E. "Jim" Folsom Jr. led the push to win Mercedes, and that success helped Alabama secure two more major auto assembly plants. Honda built a new facility at Lincoln, near Anniston, where its first vehicles rolled off

Below: Roberts Beach Cottages, Gulf Shores, Alabama, in the late 1940s. The reverse of the card states that the cottages were directly on the beach and were air-conditioned. Their phone number was 342. Bottom: A recent shoreline view at Orange Beach.

ROBERTS BEACH COTTAGES, Gulf Shores, Alabama

the line in 2001. The next year, Hyundai broke ground for a plant at Montgomery that became a major employer in central Alabama.

As these auto assembly plants ramped up production, supplier plants sprang up around them, extending the impact of this new industry in Alabama. A huge ThyssenKrupp steel plant near Mobile added further to the state's industrial growth, followed by Airbus's announcement that it would construct an airplane assembly plant at Mobile's old Brookley Air Field.

For a few years in the 1990s and early 2000s, Alabama became a national banking center. Through a period of consolidation that began in the 1980s, several Alabama banks emerged as major players in the Southeast, adding a substantial boost to Birmingham's economy. Some of these banks, however, were bought by banks outside of Alabama, and two others merged. Alabama's standing as a national banking center waned even more quickly than it had waxed.

Despite significant areas of success, the loss of tens of thousands of manufacturing jobs in the late 1900s and early 2000s retarded the state's growth. Alabama's relative economic stagnation was reflected in its lagging population growth. Between 1950 and 2010, Georgia's population grew by 181 percent, South Carolina's by 118 percent, Tennessee's by 93 percent, and Florida's by a whopping 578 percent. Alabama's grew at 56 percent, exceeding only Mississippi's rate of 38 percent. The slow population growth also cost Alabama two seats in Congress, where the state's number of representatives decreased from nine to seven during this time.

Mercedes-Benz assembly line at Vance in Tuscaloosa County in May 2010. The facility continued to grow from the mid-1990s, and by 2015, Mercedes Benz produced five different lines of vehicles there.

PERHAPS the most important factor in Alabama's economy from the New Deal into the early 2000s was the steady flow of federal money into the state. For decades, Alabama received substantially more federal funds each year than it sent to Washington in taxes—often in excess of $1.50 for every dollar (and some studies calculate a much higher return). States like Delaware and Illinois, which on average received less than fifty cents back for each tax dollar, helped to prop up Alabama's economy.

Some of this federal money came directly, through programs such as Social Security, veterans' benefits, federal pensions, Medicare, and military expenditures. Other federal money came through programs created by the federal government but managed by the state, such as food stamps, welfare, Medicaid, and unemployment assistance. Federal funds also helped sustain some of the core functions of state government, such as education, highway construction, public health, environmental management, and public safety.

Benjamin Russell Hospital for Children. With this recently completed, state-of-the-art facility, the Children's Hospital serves young patients from across Alabama.

Along with federal money, however, came various degrees of oversight. Federal oversight agencies sometimes challenged the adequacy of the state's matching contributions and its performance in meeting federal standards, leading to irritation and political maneuvering on both sides. Several major state agencies, such as those managing prisons,

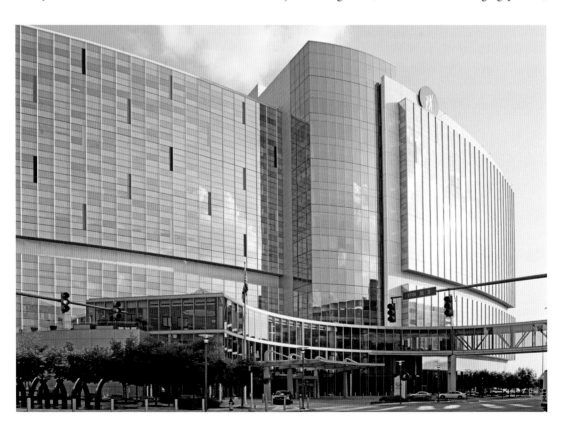

mental health programs, and youth services, were sued in federal court for failing to meet basic levels of humane care. Alabama almost always lost these cases, and the state agencies then came under monitors who were assigned by the courts to oversee mandated improvements.

In many ways, inadequate state support for social services reflected the long-standing hostility of many Alabamians toward government itself, and especially toward the federal government. The natural disinclination to pay taxes was reinforced by widespread suspicions about both the administrators and the beneficiaries who might be unfairly exploiting the programs.

Despite popular antipathy toward the federal government, federal money assisted hundreds of thousands of Alabamians and was a vital source of support for the state's overall economy. And Alabama's members of Congress continued to strive to bring more home. Yet, through this time, the taxes Alabamians imposed on themselves remained low, barely enough to provide the minimal match that the federal programs required. The tax burden per person in Alabama has been rated in most studies as the lowest in the United States.

A LARGER WORLD OF CHANGE

WHILE Alabamians struggled through decades of racial readjustment and an economy in stress, other great social and technological changes also swept through the state. Though the innovations were largely beneficial, almost all were disruptive to traditional ways of life.

One change people happily embraced was air conditioning. In 1955, air conditioning was generally limited to commercial buildings such as movie theaters and department stores where cool air attracted customers. In most homes, people adjusted windows and fans during the summer months to keep hot air out and let cool air in, according to the time of day. In the evenings, adults moved to their porches while their houses cooled, and children played outside. People in towns walking along sidewalks could see, hear, and usually speak with their neighbors. By the early 2000s, most Alabama homes were air conditioned and closed during the summer, with the residents inside, often watching television.

Air conditioning also made cars more comfortable and traveling easier. Many people who moved to or visited Alabama would not have done so without air conditioning. The relatively mild winters and air-conditioned summers made Alabama a destination for some northerners relocating to escape long, hard winters. They could play golf

Pilot in front of his helicopter at Fort Rucker. Rucker is the U.S. Army's primary training base for aviation and a major employer in southeast Alabama.

The Shoals course, on the Tennessee River in northwest Alabama. The Shoals is one of eleven sites with twenty-six beautiful courses developed by Retirement Systems of Alabama as part of its Robert Trent Jones Golf Trail. This course uses the Tennessee River as its backdrop, with the other courses also located in beautiful natural settings.

year-around, and a string of elegant public courses developed by the Retirement Systems of Alabama added to the state's allure.

A particularly dazzling set of changes came in media and telecommunications. In 1955, many of the Alabamians who had telephones spoke first with an operator who would ask: "Number, please?" Long-distance calls were so expensive that they were only used for special occasions. A half century later, most Alabamians carried cellular phones and portable computers that were many times more powerful than mainframe computers of the 1950s. With these devices, they kept in almost continuous contact with their extended world—friends, family, and business associates. They could constantly monitor news, sports, weather, and a virtually unlimited array of personal interests.

In the mid-1950s, only a small percentage of families had television sets. The little black-and-white screens were often flaked with "snow" because of poor signal reception. Viewers could watch as many as three networks, but most people still relied on their radios. By the 2010s, virtually every home had at least one television set that showed large, high-definition color images and was fed by fiber optic cables or satellites. Program options were in the hundreds.

Changes in the role and status of women were another major part of this era of change. Despite the opportunities that had opened during World War II, most Alabama women who worked in the early 1950s held traditional women's jobs. They were secretaries, nurses, cooks, domestic workers, telephone operators, teachers, and textile workers.

Alabama was actually ahead of many states at the time in the number of women elected to statewide office. But, like all women in the state, these female officials could not serve on juries. A decision by Judge Frank Johnson in 1966 (*White v. Crook*), about jury discrimination in Lowndes County, required Alabama counties to add not only black men to juror roles, but black and white women as well.

The first oral birth control pill was approved by the U.S. Food and Drug Administration in 1960, and "the pill" was in general use by the middle of the decade. Having more control over when they had children gave women a new ability to manage their lives and their careers. Women also enjoyed more educational opportunities, especially increased access to professional schools. By 2010, they occupied prominent roles in virtually all professions in Alabama, and they made as much money as the men in many families. Women's growing financial and legal equality also brought changes in family life, as couples had to work out new ways of handling their joint responsibilities.

Other norms of social behavior changed as well. In the 1950s, most Alabamians regarded divorce as a scandal, as was having a child outside of marriage. By 2010, divorce was common, and many families were headed by single women. More couples also lived together without being married, and more women gave birth outside wedlock.

Agnes Baggett, October 1964. Baggett served as Alabama's secretary of state from 1951 to 1955, 1963 to 1967, and 1975 to 1979. She was state treasurer from 1959 to 1963 and from 1967 to 1975, and served as state auditor from 1955 to 1959.

Medicine and health care in the early 1950s seem almost primitive by today's standards. Penicillin, the first major antibiotic, had only been in use since World War II. Many doctors still made house calls and carried most of what they needed in a handbag. Malaria had finally been controlled in Alabama by 1950, but other contagious diseases, such as polio, were major threats to life and health.

By the early 2000s, healthcare options included whole catalogs of new medications, society-wide immunizations, sophisticated imaging systems, rooms of diagnostic and testing devices, arthroscopic and robotic surgery, large research hospitals, rehabilitation centers, and increasingly narrow areas of physician specialization. The life expectancy of Alabamians, like that of their countrymen across the nation, had increased to the point that the fastest growing segment of the population was the elderly. Retirement communities and large nursing homes had hardly existed three generations earlier.

The diets of Alabamians in the early 1950s still depended heavily on what was in season or could be easily preserved. Bananas were shipped in, but fresh tomatoes, berries, and other fruits and vegetables out of season were either unavailable or very expensive. In many stores, butchers still carved off slices of meat on demand from carcasses hanging behind their counters. Most Alabamians had never seen a pizza, Chinese food, or a burrito. By the early 2000s, grocery stores—usually big chains—carried foods from all over the globe, and constantly stocked varieties of fresh food that would have astonished shoppers sixty years earlier. Fast-food chains and a wide range of restaurants offered new worlds of dining options that were a regular part of life for many people.

In the 1950s, mainline Protestant denominations generally overshadowed other expressions of religious life in the state, and they heavily influenced Alabama's social and political life. Regular church attendance was the norm, and most businesses closed on Sundays. Alcohol was still not legal in many parts of Alabama. Schoolteachers began every day with the Pledge of Allegiance and a prayer.

By the early 2000s, federal court rulings had raised walls of separation between church and state, ending formal prayers in school classrooms. Mainline Protestant denominations were losing members to new nondenominational megachurches and to growing evangelical denominations. Increasing numbers of Alabamians reported no church affiliation at all, while growing numbers of non-Christians, such as Buddhists and Muslims, were opening new worship centers. Sundays had become another day for work or shopping for many Alabamians, and alcohol was readily available across most of the state, even on Sundays.

In the 1950s, most Alabamians were classified in the census as either white or black. Foreign-born residents made up only one half of one percent of the population. By 2010, that number had grown seven-fold to three-and-a-half percent. Although this percentage was still small by comparison with many states, it was large enough to begin altering the old sense of Alabama society as being composed only of black and white people. In some communities, Hispanics made up a significant portion of the population, while growing numbers of

Highlands Bar and Grill in Birmingham. Chef Frank Stitt opened this award-winning restaurant in 1982. His example and his coaching of other chefs have helped make Birmingham a travel destination for people who enjoy fine dining.

people of Asian ancestry lived in all the state's larger towns. Some of them were leaders in new manufacturing facilities in the state, as well as in medicine, science, and technology.

POLITICS OF DISCONTENT

As a whole, changes during the last half of the twentieth century brought new comforts, conveniences, liberties, and amusements. But many Alabamians saw their relative economic status diminished as their segment of the economy faltered.

Hispanic businesses in Collinsville, Alabama. The business on the left mentions El Salvador, Guatemala, and Honduras on its signs.

Almost everyone faced new pressures to adjust and compete. And many people were aggrieved to see values and traditions they cherished being cast aside.

Most white Alabamians during the 1950s and 1960s felt that the civil rights movement was an attack against their "way of life." As their level of anger rose in the 1950s, new political voices emerged, both stoking that anger and drawing support from it. The hostility resembled previous upsurges of discontent which seem to be a recurring feature of Alabama political life—from the anti-aristocracy campaign of William Long in the 1820s, to the anti-abolitionists of the 1850s, the Populists of the 1890s, and the second Klan of the 1920s.

Through the 1960s, most successful politicians in Alabama played to this discontent. Their primary targets were "outside agitators" and the federal government, as they roused their audiences with bold calls for defiance. One reason the civil rights movement enjoyed such success in Alabama was that the state's politicians became such excellent foils for protest leaders to target. From Bull Connor in Birmingham to George Wallace in Montgomery and James Clark in Selma, Alabama politicians helped create high drama that turned local confrontations into media spectacles. Civil rights leaders learned to provoke Alabama politicians into excesses that were captured on film and then played back to national television audiences.

George Wallace excelled at the politics of discontent, though he was far more adroit than most of the others in playing the media. Through the 1950s, Wallace had actually been something of a progressive in state politics, leading the legislature in promoting economic development and even serving on the board of trustees of Tuskegee Institute. But after his failed 1958 campaign for governor—the only one he lost—he saw the passion that segregationist defiance could

Governor George Wallace initiated a number of programs that followed the old populist traditions of Alabama politics, such as highway improvement projects.

rouse. By his 1962 campaign, he had fully pivoted to that issue, and he overwhelmed his opponents.

Wallace also appealed to the old populist constituency with occasional attacks against big businesses, such as the Alabama Power Company. He pressed several reform initiatives, including free textbooks for students, increased highway construction, and an expanded junior college system. His popularity helped him secure the election of his wife Lurleen to succeed him as governor in 1966 and his own reelections in 1970, 1974, and 1982.

Wallace also ran for president of the United States four different times. After drawing substantial support from outside the South in 1964 and 1968, he seemed to be emerging as a serious national contender in 1972 when he was severely wounded in an attempted assassination. One of the more poignant stories in recent political history is that of Wallace's efforts in the latter part of his life to make amends to black Alabamians. Wheelchair-bound and in constant pain, he visited black churches and met with black leaders, seeking reconciliation. In 1982, he won election as governor for his last time with support from thousands of forgiving African American voters.

Wallace's personal dominance slowed the development of the Republican Party in Alabama. As early as the 1950s, some business leaders such as Winton Blount began efforts to rebuild the party in the state. In 1964, Alabama voted Republican in a national election for the first time since Reconstruction, but this 1964 vote was largely against President Lyndon Johnson, whose activist administration had just pushed through the Civil Rights Act.

Inside Alabama, state constitutional offices, the legislature, the courts, and local governments all remained solidly in Democratic hands. As new black voters entered state political life through the late 1960s and 1970s, most of them also became Democrats. With the exception of one term won by Vietnam War hero Jeremiah Denton in the early 1980s, Alabama's U.S. senators were all Democrats until the mid-1990s.

Although Democrats controlled the legislature by large majorities, they were divided into factions. A coalition supported by schoolteachers, African Americans, labor unions, and trial lawyers was the more liberal faction. Legislators affiliated with manufacturing, commerce, agriculture, and forestry were the conservatives. Each side was generally able to block the major initiatives of the other, and the work of the legislature tended to lurch along in small steps. Essential bills were passed in late-session compromises marked by heavy deal making. Large, long-term issues, such as education, criminal justice, adequate financing, and state social services, were either neglected or subjected to patchwork modifications.

The election in 1986 of Alabama's first Republican governor since Reconstruction was the by-product of a clash between the two Democratic factions. The conservative candidate, Charles Graddick, won the Democratic primary runoff election by a narrow margin. But the Party's leadership, controlled by the liberal faction, accused him of improperly soliciting and benefitting from Republican crossover votes. Under Democratic Party rules, a person who voted in another party's primary was not eligible to participate in the Democratic runoff. The rule had never been enforced, but the party had enjoyed such preeminence that its enforcement had never been needed. In 1986, the Democratic Party's Executive Committee concluded that ineligible crossover votes had made the difference in Graddick's victory, and it awarded the nomination to Bill Baxley.

Governor George Wallace visiting an African American church. After the 1972 assassination attempt, Wallace lived in almost constant pain and had to use a wheelchair. The date of this visit and the name of the church were not recorded on the photograph.

Angered by this ruling, many conservative Democrats bolted in the general election to vote for the relatively unknown Republican nominee, Guy Hunt. But even after Hunt's election, the process of party realignment proceeded slowly. After Governor Hunt was convicted of an ethics violation in 1993 and removed from office, he was succeeded by the Democratic lieutenant governor, Jim Folsom Jr. Folsom was defeated the next year by a former Democrat who had turned Republican, Fob James, who was himself defeated after one term by another Democrat, Don Siegelman. Bob Riley, a Republican, defeated Governor Siegelman in 2002, but then struggled for the next eight years against a legislature that was still overwhelmingly Democratic.

Gambling was a major ongoing issue. During the 1980s, several Alabama counties passed local amendments to the state constitution to permit dog racing or charitable bingo, or both, within the county. As

Members of Alabama's legislative leadership in 2011, from left to right: Senator Arthur Orr, President Pro Tempore of the Senate Del Marsh, Senator Trip Pittman, Speaker of the House Mike Hubbard, Representative Micky Hammon, Senator James Thomas "Jabo" Waggoner, Lieutenant Governor Kay Ivey, and Representative Jay Love.

new facilities began offering "electronic bingo" on devices that closely resembled slot machines, gambling increased dramatically, with millions of dollars wagered every day.

Don Siegelman ran for governor in 1998 calling for a state lottery to support college scholarships for Alabama students. After his victory, he won legislative passage of a resolution to amend the state constitution to permit the lottery. In the statewide campaign for ratification, however, opponents warned against the lottery's potential for corruption. Alabama voters rejected the lottery amendment despite having just elected its author to be their governor.

In the last part of his administration, Governor Riley led an effort to shut down gambling facilities he regarded as illegal. After an acrimonious struggle, the only surviving casinos in 2011 were those on land owned by the Poarch Creek Indians, whose operations were beyond state control, plus one at a dog track in Greene County.

THE ELECTIONS OF 2010

THE state elections of 2010 were another landmark in Alabama's political history. In a spectacular reversal of control, Republicans won complete dominance in the legislature, as well as all constitutional offices and appellate court judgeships. Their legislative majority was so large that they could easily sweep aside objections and resistance efforts by the Democratic minority.

In many ways, the 2010 elections resembled those of 1874. They both marked a major political reversal, from a more liberal to a more conservative regime. And the alignments of interest groups were similar, though the party labels had flipped. In 1874, the Democratic Party had united business interests and yeoman farmers to defeat the incumbent Republican Party, composed mostly of African Americans and more liberal whites. In 2010, the Republican Party united business interests and social conservatives to defeat the incumbent Democratic Party, composed mostly of African Americans and more liberal whites.

The new conservative leadership of 2010 also resembled that of 1874 in that it was not entirely an easy and natural alliance. Business-oriented legislators and social conservatives joined in common cause against a more liberal regime they both opposed, and they shared a number of common values, such as a commitment to limited government and low taxes. But they also struggled over differing approaches to many other important issues, such as efforts to improve education, abortion regulation, immigration policy, special accommodations to business, and the kinds of services that government should provide.

Many of the issues Alabama leaders faced in 2010 bore an almost eerie resemblance to those of 1874: economic development challenges, budget deficits, widespread poverty, a struggling education system, anemic social services, and a problematic criminal justice system. In addition, there were tough new questions of how best to move Alabama forward in a highly competitive global economy dominated by complex new technologies.

The greatest difference between the 1874 and the 2010 elections was that, by 2010, most Alabamians had come to accept the idea that all citizens are entitled to equal rights. And African Americans continued to be part of the political process, controlling many county and municipal governments as well as a substantial numbers of legislative seats.

Looking back from 2010, Alabamians had come through a social revolution of a magnitude that is rare in human history without great violence. Although there had been bitter conflict and even a number of deaths, Alabamians appeared to have emerged from the ordeal of desegregation with a remarkable degree of good will remaining.

The adjustment process was, of course, still in progress in 2010. Old barriers from the past—not just racial, but social, sectional, and economic—still hampered coordinated efforts to address the state's problems. But the historic racial divisions that had created two different and unequal worlds were no longer unbridgeable. Alabamians were regularly working together in new ways, and they enjoyed a stronger and healthier social foundation from which they could build for the future. How well they will succeed in that building process seems likely to be the major theme of the next chapter in the state's history.

Governor Robert Bentley of Tuscaloosa, elected governor in 2010 as part of the sweeping Republican victory in the November state elections.

AFTERWORD

Aspiring astronauts experience a simulated space walk at Space Camp, which offers a variety of programs for children and adults at the U.S. Space and Rocket Center in Huntsville.

IT APPEARS TO ME THAT ALABAMA has probably already entered a new period of its history, at least in terms of the framing concepts used in this book. The fierceness of global economic competition and the dizzying pace at which technological innovations appear help mark the beginnings of this new era.

These great change agents pose formidable challenges for Alabama's future. We can see from the past that history is not always a story of progress. Every society encounters challenges and setbacks, some of which can cause long-term damage. We have suffered major setbacks of our own in Alabama. And if we fail to meet adequately the challenges of this new era, another period of corrosive stagnation is a real possibility.

Readers have probably sensed my sympathies with people in the past who have worked to build and improve Alabama. I have tried to respect the views of those who have opposed new initiatives, whether their reasons were fear of governmental intrusion, suspicion about the sponsors' motives, or other concerns. But I do not think societies can grow and prosper by ignoring problems and trusting in chance to resolve them. To me, the challenges we face today call for higher levels of adaptability, innovation, and cooperation than we have usually achieved in the past.

This book has focused on Alabama as a whole, trying to track the broad story of the state's development. But the place where most of us can have a real impact is in our own communities. Much of what has been achieved in rebuilding and revitalizing Alabama has been at the local level. Many communities have launched their own efforts to strengthen their schools, renew downtowns, nur-ture the arts, improve social services, promote economic development, build civic pride, create attractive public spaces, and offer activities where people come together and enjoy themselves. Local pockets of excellence across the state are one reason for optimism about our future.

As a state, perhaps the most important single lesson we can learn from our past is that we should not only accept, but celebrate, the remarkable social changes of the last sixty years. Our old racial divisions were not only wrong and unfair, they also were constant barriers to progress. They required enormous expenditures of energy, by both black and white Alabamians, that were unproductive of any larger good. For white Alabamians, racial

discrimination also flagrantly violated basic principles we said we believed in, such as "liberty and justice for all," as well as generally recognized moral ideals, such as kindness and compassion toward others.

Virtually every country in the world is now struggling to harmonize the interests of people of diverse backgrounds. One of America's strengths as a nation has been our ability to do this for more than two centuries. For us in Alabama, embracing our differences rather than turning them into sources of conflict seems to me to be a basic requirement for our future success. Many of the great achievements of human civilization have grown out of the synergies that develop when people of different backgrounds learn to work together.

Despite how far we have come in Alabama, probably the greatest hurdle we face today is the accumulated divisions from our past that still tend to pit us against each other—whether they are racial, social, cultural, economic, or sectional. It would be unrealistic to think that long-standing divisions will not continue, at least to some degree. But perhaps our recent, hard-won achievements in working through some of them can help us find ways to work through others in the future. Although the progress we made was sometimes against our wishes, maybe we can learn from what we experienced.

History looks to the past for understanding, but its real importance is for the present and the future. A deeper understanding of history can help us to see and overcome barriers from the past that divide us, and it can help us make better informed decisions in dealing with new issues we face. My highest hope for this book is that it will contribute, at least in some degree, to an improved understanding of history in Alabama, and thereby to a more successful and happy future for our state.

NOTES ON SOURCES

A S NOTED IN MY INTRODUCTION and acknowledgments, this book reflects the ideas and insights of a large number of historian colleagues whose books and articles I have read, whom I have heard make presentations, and with whom I have talked over the course of a fairly long career. Research notes and files we assembled for the exhibits at the Alabama Department of Archives and History have been another major resource.

There is one other general source I need to credit, the online *Encyclopedia of Alabama*. The site is loaded with great biographical sketches, period overviews, and many articles about a variety of specific subjects. Some days I used it multiple times for quick reference information, for leads to other sources, and as a convenient sounding board for ideas I was trying to think through. We are lucky to have this wonderful resource in Alabama, and I want to commend Wayne Flynt, Jeff Jakeman, Steve Murray, and their colleagues for all they have done to make it a reality.

In the rest of this section, I will list some of the books I have relied on directly and that also should be easy for interested readers to acquire if they want to pursue any of the topics further. The major general history is *Alabama: The History of a Deep South State*, by Leah Rawls Atkins, Wayne Flynt, William Warren Rogers, and Robert David Ward, which I consulted throughout my writing. Another very useful and informative general work is *Alabama Governors*, edited by Margaret E. Armbrester and Samuel L. Webb. I have also depended on a collection of articles and lectures by J. Mills Thornton due to be published in 2016, entitled *Archipelagos of My South: Essays in the Molding of a Region, 1835 to 1965*. Yet another core book on Alabama history, at least through the 1901 constitution, is Malcolm Cook McMillan's *Constitutional Development in Alabama, 1798 to 1901: A Study in Politics, the Negro and Sectionalism*.

For very early Alabama Indian history, I drew heavily on *The First Alabamians* exhibit at the Alabama Department of Archives and History, for which Craig Sheldon was our scholar consultant. Useful books include John H. Blitz's short book *Moundville*, Emma Lila Fundaburk's *Sun Circles and Human Hands: The Southeastern Indians Art and Industries*, and two of Charles Hudson's works, *The Southeastern Indians* and *Knights of Spain, Warriors of the Sun: Hernando de Soto and the South's Ancient Chiefdoms*.

For Indian history starting after sustained European contact, see Kathryn E. Holland Braund's important work *Deerskins and Duffels: The Creek Indian Trade with Anglo-America, 1685–1815*. Albert James Pickett's *History of Alabama and Incidentally of Georgia and Mississippi, from the Earliest Period* was first published in 1851, but it is a classic work and still a terrific book to read. Herbert James Lewis's book *Clearing the Thickets* is an informative and interesting recent book covering Alabama history from colonization to the Civil War.

Henry deLeon Southerland and Jerry Elijah Brown's *The Federal Road through Georgia, the Creek Nation, and Alabama, 1806–1836*, is an interesting and very readable account of this key passageway through the Creek heartland. Claudio Saunt's *Black, White, and Indian: Race and the Unmaking of an American Family* tells the remarkable story of the Grierson/Grayson family. Gregory A. Waselkov's *A Conquering Spirit: Fort Mims and the Redstick War of 1813–1814* is the definitive work on the key battle,

William Bartram's *Travels through North & South Carolina, Georgia, East & West Florida, the Cherokee Country, the Extensive Territories of the Muscogulges, or Creek Confederacy, and the Country of the Chactaws* (Philadelphia, 1791) includes some of the earliest descriptions of what would become Alabama. Historical markers commemorating Bartram's travels can be found across Alabama.

but it also offers great insight into conditions in the Creek Nation leading up to the war. Wyley Donald Ward's *Original Land Sales and Grants in Covington County, Alabama* provides valuable information about the early sale of public land in Alabama.

For the antebellum period, the seminal work is J. Mills Thornton's *Power and Politics in a Slave Society, Alabama 1800–1860*. Thomas P. Abernethy's *The Formative Period in Alabama, 1815–1828* and John T. Ellisor's *The Second Creek War: Interethnic Conflict and Collusion on a Collapsing Frontier* were also helpful sources. John W. Quist's *Restless Visionaries:*

The Social Roots of Antebellum Reform in Alabama and Michigan examines the story of social change. Harvey H. Jackson's *Rivers of History: Life on the Coosa, Tallapoosa, Cahaba, and Alabama* tells about the emergence of steamboats, and much more. Eric H. Walther's *William Lowndes Yancey and the Coming of the Civil War* helps explain events leading up to the Civil War through the life of that pivotal figure. An excellent general work of American history that helped me in setting the larger framework for this period is Daniel Walker Howe's *What Hath God Wrought: The Transformation of America, 1815–1848*. Edward E. Baptist's *The Half Has Never Been Told: Slavery and the Making of American Capitalism* is an extraordinary book on the institution of slavery and its impact on the development of the United States.

Two more books by Malcolm C. McMillan are excellent sources on the Civil War in Alabama: *The Alabama Confederate Reader* and *The Disintegration* of a Confederate State: Three Governors and Alabama's Wartime Home Front, 1861–1865. Jack Friend's West Wind, Flood Tide: The Battle of Mobile Bay tells the story of probably the most important battle fought in Alabama during the war.

For the Reconstruction period, Michael W. Fitzgerald's The Union League Movement in the Deep South: Politics and Agricultural Change during Reconstruction and Splendid Failure: Postwar Reconstruction in the American South are excellent resources. Richard Bailey's Neither Carpetbaggers Nor Scalawags: Black Officeholders during the Reconstruction of Alabama 1867–1878 helps bring to life previously neglected stories of Alabama's first group of African American legislators. It is an important resource, as is Sarah Woolfolk Wiggins's work on white Republicans, The Scalawag in Alabama Politics, 1865–1881. Loren Schweninger's James T. Rapier and Reconstruction is another useful book for the period. A recent work by G. Ward Hubbs offers a unique and compelling view of Reconstruction through the lives of four men of radically different backgrounds: Searching for Freedom after the Civil War: Klansman, Carpetbagger, Scalawag, and Freedman.

The years from Reconstruction to the start of World War I include a variety of interesting but more specialized works. They include Leah Rawls Atkins's The Valley and the Hills: An Illustrated History of Birmingham & Jefferson County; James R. Bennett's Tannehill and the Growth of the Alabama Iron Industry and Iron and Steel: A Guide to the Birmingham Area Industrial Heritage Sites (with Karen R. Utz); Douglas A. Blackmon's Slavery by Another Name: The Re-Enslavement of Black Americans from the Civil War to World War II; Wayne Cline's Alabama Railroads; Mary Ellen Curtin's Black Prisoners and Their World, Alabama, 1865–1900; James Sanders Day's Diamonds in the Rough: A History of Alabama's Cahaba Coal Field; Walker Evans and James Agee's Let Us Now Praise Famous Men; Johnston Allen Going's Bourbon Democracy in Alabama, 1874–1890; Mark D. Hersey's My Work Is That of

Conservation: An Environmental Biography of George Washington Carver; William Warren Rogers's The One-Gallused Rebellion: Agrarianism in Alabama, 1865–1896; Theodore Rosengarten's All God's Dangers: The Life of Nate Shaw; Mary Martha Thomas's The New Woman in Alabama: Social Reforms and Suffrage, 1890–1920; Samuel L. Webb's Two-Party Politics in a One-Party South: Alabama's Hill County, 1874–1920, and Gavin Wright's Old South, New South: Revolutions in the Southern Economy since the Civil War.

From World War I to the early 1950s, see Leah Rawls Atkins's Developed for the Service of Alabama: The Centennial History of the Alabama Power Company, 1906–2006; Allen Cronenberg's Forth to the Mighty Conflict: Alabama and World War II; Nimrod T. Frazer's Send the Alabamians: World War I Fighters in the Rainbow Division; Glenn Feldman's Politics, Society, and the Klan in Alabama, 1915–1949; Virginia Van Der Veer Hamilton's Hugo Black: The Alabama Years; Evans C. Johnson's Oscar W. Underwood: A Political Biography; Robin D. G. Kelley's Hammer and Hoe: Alabama Communists during the Great Depression; and Martin Olliff's The Great War in the Heart of Dixie: Alabama during World War I. David M. Kennedy's Freedom from Fear: The American People in Depression and War, 1929–1945 was an important general work of American history for me.

For all of the twentieth century, see Wayne Flynt's impressive work Alabama in the Twentieth Century. The two books on the civil rights movement that I used most heavily were Gene Roberts and Hank Klibanoff's The Race Beat: The Press, the Civil Rights Struggle, and the Awakening of a Nation and J. Mills Thornton's great work Dividing Lines: Municipal Politics and the Struggle for Civil Rights in Montgomery, Birmingham, and Selma. Dan T. Carter's The Politics of Rage: George Wallace, the Origins of the New Conservatism, and the Transformation of American Politics is also an important and very readable introduction to the period and an overview of the life of one of its key figures.

INDEX

ILLUSTRATION CREDITS